The Virtual Prison

The last twenty-five years have seen dramatic rises in the prison populations of most industrialized nations. Unable to keep up with increased numbers of convicted offenders, governments and criminal justice systems have been seeking new ways to control and punish offenders. One sanction adopted in Canada and some parts of Europe and the USA is community custody, which attempts to recreate the punitive nature of prison but without incarceration. This book analyses the effectiveness of this approach and explores its implications for offenders and society as a whole. It demonstrates that if properly conceived and administered, community custody can reduce the number of prison admissions and at the same time promote multiple goals of sentencing. When appropriately constructed, community custody is a sanction which holds offenders accountable for their conduct but which permits them to change their lives in ways that would be impossible if they were in prison.

JULIAN V. ROBERTS has been working in the area of sentencing and public opinion for over twenty years. He is editor of the *Canadian Journal of Criminology and Criminal Justice* and has written and co-edited ten books including *Public Opinion, Crime, and Criminal Justice* (1997); *Making Sense of Sentencing* (1999); and *Criminal Justice in Canada* (2003).

Cambridge Studies in Criminology

Edited by
Alfred Blumstein, *H. John Heinz School of Public Policy and Management, Carnegie Mellon University*
David P. Farrington, *Institute of Criminology, University of Cambridge*

The Cambridge Studies in Criminology series aims to publish the highest quality research on criminology and criminal justice topics. Typical volumes report major quantitative, qualitative, and ethnographic research, or make a substantial theoretical contribution. There is a particular emphasis on research monographs, but edited collections may also be published if they make an unusually distinctive offering to the literature. All relevant areas of criminology and criminal justice are included; for example, the causes of offending, juvenile justice, the development of offenders, measurement and analysis of crime, victimization research, policing, crime prevention, sentencing, imprisonment, probation, and parole. The series is global in outlook, with an emphasis on work that is comparative or holds significant implications for theory or policy.

Other books in the series

The Virtual Prison
Community Custody and the Evolution of Imprisonment

Julian V. Roberts

CAMBRIDGE
UNIVERSITY PRESS

PUBLISHED BY THE PRESS SYNDICATE OF THE UNIVERSITY OF CAMBRIDGE
The Pitt Building, Trumpington Street, Cambridge, United Kingdom

CAMBRIDGE UNIVERSITY PRESS
The Edinburgh Building, Cambridge, CB2 2RU, UK
40 West 20th Street, New York, NY 10011–4211, USA
477 Williamstown Road, Port Melbourne, VIC 3207, Australia
Ruiz de Alarcón 13, 28014 Madrid, Spain
Dock House, The Waterfront, Cape Town 8001, South Africa

http://www.cambridge.org

First published 2004

Printed in the United Kingdom at the University Press, Cambridge

Typeface New Baskerville 10/13 pt.   *System* LATEX 2$_\varepsilon$ [TB]

A catalogue record for this book is available from the British Library

Library of Congress cataloguing in publication data
Roberts, Julian V.
The virtual prison: community custody and the evolution of imprisonment /
Julian V. Roberts.
     p.   cm. – (Cambridge studies in criminology)
Includes bibliographical references and index.
ISBN 0 521 82959 3 (hardback) – ISBN 0 521 53644 8 (paperback)
1. Community-based corrections.   2. Community-based corrections – Canada.
3. Home detention – Canada.   I. Title.   II. Cambridge studies in criminology
(Cambridge University Press)
HV9279.R63   2004
365′.6 – dc22   2004049733

ISBN 0 521 82959 3 hardback
ISBN 0 521 53644 8 paperback

Contents

Figures and tables

Figures

Tables

Foreword

The dominance of imprisonment in many Western penal systems is well known. Some governments have tried to bring about reductions in the use of imprisonment by introducing alternative sanctions, but successes in this endeavour have been relatively rare. Criminologists have analysed the causes of the frequent failures of efforts to reduce reliance on imprisonment, and are ready to raise doubts about the prospects of new initiatives of this kind. This study, however, is different. It discusses an alternative form of sentence that was designed to reduce reliance on imprisonment and appears to have done so, and this gives Julian Roberts the opportunity to explore the conditions for success and methods of avoiding the route to failure.

The measure that is the focus of this study does not have a single name internationally, even though variations of it have been tried in several different jurisdictions. In Canada it is called a conditional sentence of imprisonment, whereas in other jurisdictions it is referred to as home detention, home confinement, or some other term. What it involves, usually, is a sentence placing an offender under curfew in his or her home for certain hours of the day and/or at weekends. In certain cases 'absolute house arrest' is a condition, and the offender is confined at home at all times except for a very limited number of court-authorized absences. The sanction is enforced by random checks by probation officers, or through the use of electronic monitoring. In all cases, judges have the power to commit the offender to prison in the event that conditions of the sentence are breached without reasonable excuse. The home becomes the prison, at least during the hours of confinement. This experience is clearly not the same as being sent to prison, since it is not a form of social exclusion, does not expose the offenders to the close company of other prisoners, and lacks some of the other pains of imprisonment. On the other hand it is certainly restrictive, preventing much normal socialization and inevitably imposing strain on social relationships and creating hardships for the offender's family or spouse.

In what terms can it be said that the introduction of community custody in Canada has been a success? The use of conventional prison sentences has declined since 1996, when the new measure became available. Criminologists would look immediately for signs that community custody is being used in cases where imprisonment itself would not have been imposed prior to 1996, but there appears to be evidence of only a small 'net-widening' effect of this kind, dwarfed by the overall decline in custody. Moreover, the proportion of orders that have been completed without breach is high; this will dampen fears that community custody might become a 'back-door' route into prison for non-compliant offenders. Other jurisdictions with these kinds of sentence report similarly positive results.

In practice, of course, this means that sentencers have 'played ball'. Measures of this kind cannot succeed if they are either infrequently used by the courts or not used in the intended way. The prospects of success would also be reduced if there were public and media opposition. But Julian Roberts, a world leader in the assessment of public opinion on crime and sentencing, is able to show how public support for such measures can be mobilized – by giving publicity to the details of what the orders involve and the restrictions they impose, thereby confronting the misapprehensions that often drive opposition.

The book concludes with a set of well-argued propositions about the requirements for introducing a successful measure of this kind, emphasizing the importance of presenting it as a form of custodial sentence, and dealing with some of the obvious difficulties such as the reactions of victims to having offenders living close by. This study does not duck the many issues of principle raised by new measures of this kind, such as whether they are humane, whether the effects on third parties are likely to be disproportionately destructive, and so on. It represents a well-rounded and searching examination of the claims of community custody to have broken away from the trend of failure of alternatives to the prison, an examination all the more pertinent to English readers in view of the introduction of the new suspended sentence and kindred measures under the Criminal Justice Act 2003. The book may be said to chart a journey by Julian Roberts from sceptic to supporter, from agnostic to advocate of community custody when it is appropriately constructed and imposed, and others will surely be persuaded to join him. It is a privilege to be able to commend this volume to policy-makers and criminologists alike.

Andrew Ashworth
Vinerian Professor of English Law,
University of Oxford

Preface

In 1996, community custody came to Canada, when Parliament created a new community based form of custody called the conditional sentence of imprisonment. Since then I have been grappling with understanding this sanction in light of similar developments in other jurisdictions. It struck me that one way to understand the nature and potential of this sanction was to write a book about the topic. Whether I have achieved this understanding, the reader alone will decide.

Some readers may find the central thesis – that community custody with house arrest should be more widely used – inherently conservative; an attempt to promote punishment, and to recreate the conditions of imprisonment in the last refuge from state power: our homes. To these readers I would add (if they are still reading) that community custody should only ever be used as a substitute for secure detention, and that community custody permits offenders to influence their lives and the sentences they are serving. This can only but benefit these individuals, their families and the communities to which they belong.

I would like to thank the following for funding assistance with respect to the research reported here: the Social Sciences and Humanities Research Council of Canada; the Department of Justice, Canada and the University of Ottawa. As well, I am grateful to Tom Finlay and the library of the Centre of Criminology at the University of Toronto, and Noella Morvan and the library of the Ministry of the Solicitor General in Ottawa for bibliographic assistance.

Tappio Lappi-Seppala and Sherri Matta provided materials relevant to the research described in this volume. I am indebted to the following individuals who provided comments on earlier versions of some or all of the chapters published here: Jean-Paul Brodeur, Michelle Grossman, Voula Marinos, Ron Melchers, Kent Roach, Ivan Zinger. In particular I am grateful to two members of the judiciary, Judge David Cole, and Judge Gilles Renaud, both from the Ontario Court of Justice, for taking the time from their onerous judicial duties to read this manuscript. I would like to acknowledge Sarah Caro, Susan Beer and Alison Powell from the Cambridge University Press, as well as David Farrington from the Institute of Criminology at the University of Cambridge, for helping to bring this volume to press.

I must thank the following colleagues – indeed friends – in Canada for their insight into the subject of sentencing over the years, and whose work has undoubtedly guided my thinking: Anthony Doob, Patrick Healy, Allan Manson, David Daubney, Judge William Vancise, and Mary Campbell. My thanks, too, to Ray Davies and the late John Dowland, whose work has provided much needed diversion during the course of this project.

Julian V. Roberts
Ottawa

ONE

Introduction to the concept of community custody

Imprisonment is when a man is by public authority deprived of liberty.
(Hobbes, 1651/1957, p. 206)

The contention

Prisons have failed to achieve their goals, and so, in large measure, have most of their alternatives. The failure of our prisons to reform or reintegrate offenders has been apparent since John Howard toured Europe's prisons in the eighteenth century (see Howard, 1929; Lilly and Ball, 1987; Selke, 1993). More recently, research has made it increasingly clear that prison does not deter offenders any more effectively than most community punishments (e.g. Doob and Webster, 2003; von Hirsch, Bottoms, Burney, and Wikstrom, 1999). A significant body of research has now accumulated to demonstrate the negative effects of prison, beginning with the seminal work by Sykes on the pains of imprisonment (1958). Perhaps the best that can be said of prison is that prisoners emerge no worse than when they were admitted (Zamble and Porporino, 1988), and that is not saying very much. Although prison has failed to rehabilitate, its destructive force remains undiminished.

Yet the prison continues to dominate the penal landscape, and to maintain its status as an iconic legal punishment around the world. Indeed, when asked to 'sentence' an offender many people's first reaction involves custody. This is particularly true for the more serious offences. Support for custody is not restricted to Western nations, as revealed by the responses to the International Crime Victimization Survey (see Mayhew and van Kesteren, 2002). When asked to impose a sentence in a case of burglary, approximately a quarter of respondents in Western nations favoured incarcerating the offender. The proportion favouring incarceration was significantly higher in Africa and Asia, where 69 per cent and 60 per cent of respondents chose this sentencing option respectively (Mayhew and van Kesteren, 2002). The widespread support for custody reflects in large measure the punitive power of imprisonment: *to the public, nothing appears to punish like prison.*[1]

David Garland has observed that the prison has become a 'massive and seemingly indispensable pillar of contemporary social order' (2001a, p. 14). At the same time, there has been growing recognition by scholars, courts, and even some legislatures that imprisonment – in its traditional institutional form – carries few if any benefits for the offender, and many costs. The pains of imprisonment are not restricted to the prisoner, they are shared with his or her family and community as well. While the prison's position in the penal landscape has become more entrenched, and its limitations as a penal tool more apparent, the search for plausible and effective alternative sanctions has intensified.

Alternative sentences have failed in a different respect; they have yet to achieve significant reductions in prison populations, the purpose for which they were conceived and developed. Nellis (2002) and others (e.g. van Kalmthout, 2002) have described the limited success of community penalties, and the lowered expectations associated with these sanctions at the advent of the millennium. These sanctions have not been used often enough in most jurisdictions to reduce the use of incarceration as a sanction. One reason is that they appear to lack the denunciatory power and the punitiveness of imprisonment. The advantages of community penalties – their ability to promote rehabilitative or restorative goals, their relatively low costs – do not appear to overcome the limited ability of community punishment to denounce criminal conduct, or to adequately hold offenders accountable.

What is needed is a sanction that offers some of the penal 'bite' of imprisonment – so that it really is a potential alternative – but which nevertheless spares the offender (and his or her intimates) many of the 'pains of imprisonment'. Hence the search in recent years for 'intermediate sanctions', those lying between prison and probation (see Morris and Tonry, 1990). But intermediate sanctions have to date failed seriously to encroach on the custodial caseload – as evidenced by the stable or rising prison populations, even in the face of declining crime rates.

A new sanction also needs to promote a fresh vision of imprisonment and indeed of legal punishment. Properly constructed and administered, community custody, or community imprisonment offers such a solution. Although this disposition has been around for many years in some jurisdictions (see Lilly and Ball, 1987, for a history of house arrest, the potential of community custody has yet to be fully realized. Considerable progress has been made in some countries, and that experience is reviewed in this book.

While a number of countries created community custody sanctions in the 1990s, the statistical evidence pertaining to the use of custody (reviewed in chapter 2), reveals that little has changed: with a few exceptions, these regimes have failed so far to reduce prison populations. The reasons for this failure will be explored over the course of this volume, but they include the following: the community custody sanctions have not been sufficiently used; there has been considerable judicial and community resistance to the concept; the statutory platforms have permitted 'widening of the net' to occur.

The evolution of community punishments

Community-based sentences have proliferated in recent decades; most jurisdictions now provide judges with a wide array of alternatives to imprisonment at the adult and juvenile levels. Yet community sanctions have not displaced the use of prison as a sanction, except for the least serious offences. Alternatives to imprisonment must generate public and professional confidence; they must constitute credible replacements (see discussion in Davies, 1993). This credibility has proven hard to come by. When imposed for serious crimes of violence, community sanctions continue to attract public opposition as a result of critical media stories and adverse commentary from politicians. Judges, too, are often sceptical of these sentencing options, particularly regarding the extent to which offenders in the community are adequately supervised. Lacking confidence in the administration of the sentence, many judges curb their use of these sanctions.[2] This has certainly been the experience in Canada, where judges have restricted their use of the certain community-based sentences when they have lacked confidence that supervision is adequate (see also Zvekic, 1994 for similar experiences in other jurisdictions).

One consequence of these problems with alternative sanctions is that politicians continue to promote imprisonment as the most appropriate response to more serious forms of offending – witness the proliferation of mandatory sentences of imprisonment created in the USA, Canada, Australia, and England and Wales during the 1990s (see Roberts, Stalans, Indermaur, and Hough, 2003). Judges continue to impose imprisonment as a primary sanction, and this has resulted in stable or rising custody rates in many jurisdictions such as England and Wales (Hough, Jacobson, and Millie, 2003).

The search for alternative sanctions has led to the adoption of a wide array of penal measures, including curfews, electronic monitoring, and other innovations. Community penalties received fresh impetus with the evolution of technology by which to ensure the offender's presence at home. However, the alternatives devised to date are 'partial sanctions' imposed to achieve a limited goal – often compliance with other court ordered conditions such as mandatory treatment or abstinence. They do not represent a transformation in the way that we think about imprisonment, but simply offer alternative means by which to hold offenders accountable without requiring their detention. This severely limits their ability to replace prison as a punishment.

Community custody and the Sword of Damocles

This volume explores a form of imprisonment that is served in the community. Such a sanction exists in many nations and goes under different names: community custody; community control; a suspended sentence of imprisonment; conditional sentence of imprisonment; home detention. The common element is that the offender is serving a sentence of custody in the community, with the threat of institutional confinement hanging over his head, should he or she fail to comply with a set of conditions. The presence of the threat explains the many literary references in the literature to the legend of the 'Sword of Damocles'. Damocles was a courtier forced to remain motionless while sitting under a sharp sword that was hanging by a horsehair. One careless movement would result in rather unpleasant consequences for the man. He was obliged to endure this punishment by his ruler, to illustrate what it was like to live under constant threat of death (the ruler, a tyrant, was singularly unpopular, and the object of numerous assassination attempts).[3]

Since the landmark volume by Ball, Huff, and Lilly on house arrest was published in 1988, much has changed. Community custody regimes have proliferated and become more diverse. They are used instead of pre-trial detention, as a stand-alone sentencing option and also as a form of early release from prison. Despite much progress, many problems remain, not the least of which is the image of the sanction. Members of the public and crime victims often believe that offenders confined to their homes do little more than stay at home and out of trouble – what law-abiding members of society do all time. Not surprisingly, offenders see matters differently.

Clearly some rapprochement between these two perspectives is necessary, if the sanction is to attract widespread public support.

Distinguishing community custody from other sentences

A community custody sentence shares some characteristics with other dispositions, but is nevertheless conceptually distinct. The stringent conditions imposed, along with the presence of the offender in the community brings to mind enhanced probation sentences. These were introduced to address traditional probation's lack of credibility, but the basic philosophy of probation remains unchanged and as Clear (1997) notes, most ISPs in the USA are not designed to divert offenders from prison, whereas that is one of the central goals of community custody. The closest other sanction is a suspended sentence in which the offender is obliged to follow certain conditions for a specific period of time.[4]

The differences between the two sanctions are nevertheless apparent. Suspended sentences are inchoate sanctions: a term of community supervision is imposed, with the threat of imposition of a harsher sentence in the event of non-compliance. A suspended sentence (accompanied by a period of probation) is an indeterminate punishment, the precise nature of which (within statutory limits) is determined (and imposed) in the event that the offender breaches the terms of probation. The indeterminacy of the sentence to be imposed undermines its efficacy as a sanction; the offender has little or no idea what to expect. Indeed, courts in Canada have been discouraged from identifying in advance the sanction that will be imposed in the event of non-compliance.[5]

The two sanctions are applicable to quite different offender profiles. A suspended sentence was conceived for low risk offenders, convicted of crimes of relatively low seriousness, or serious crimes committed in very exceptional circumstances.[6] These offenders usually need nothing more than the threat of imprisonment to return to a law-abiding life; indeed many will have been deterred by the process of conviction alone.

Offenders serving terms of community custody, however, are drawn from a much wider spectrum of crime seriousness and criminal history. Whether community custody is appropriate for offenders convicted of the most serious crimes short of murder is very contentious; in most Western jurisdictions the use of this sentence in such cases is likely to provoke widespread public opposition and negative media coverage. This explains in part why some criminal justice systems exclude certain offences from consideration for this kind of sanction. However, as will be discussed later in this volume, punishments that appear unacceptable today may become unremarkable within a few years.

The sentence of community custody therefore is conceptually distinct from a suspended sentence. The distinction confers a clear advantage upon this form of imprisonment, as the sanction is therefore applicable to a wider range of cases. Most members of the public (and many criminal justice professionals) regard a suspended sentence as a warning, rather than a sentence *per se*: desist from criminal behaviour, and no sanction will ensue; violate the conditions of the probationary period, and the sentence of imprisonment will be executed. A person on whom a suspended fine was imposed would not be perceived by the public to have been punished, if, after six months the threat of the fine was lifted, leaving the individual with nothing to pay. Suspended sentences, then, are quite limited in their scope of application, and offer little promise in terms of reducing admissions to custody.

Community custody sentences are also to be distinguished from conditional sentences. Under these dispositions, if the offender obeys those conditions, a more severe (yet unknown) punishment is waived. For example, according to the Swedish Penal Code, a conditional sentence may be imposed if a more severe sanction is not needed 'to restrain him from further criminality' (chapter 27, s. 1). The offender is placed on probation for two years, during which time he or she 'shall lead an orderly and law-abiding life, avoid harmful company, and seek to support himself according to his ability' (chapter 27, s. 4). In the event of non-compliance, a number of measures may be invoked, including extending the probationary period and imposing another sanction. In the present penal climate, such a sanction will have only a limited applicability as a substitute for imprisonment; to use the Swedish term, the 'penal value' of the sanction is simply too low. Indeed, the statute appears to recognize this because a conditional sentence may not be given if the gravity of the crime is high.

Sometimes the threatened sentence is made explicit, as when a six-month term of custody is imposed and immediately suspended. In other sentencing regimes, the offender is put on probation and warned that non-compliance will lead to a return to the court at which point some other sanction will be imposed and executed. Community custody is different in the critical respect that the offender is deemed to be serving a term of imprisonment, albeit while remaining in the community. A harsher fate awaits the non-compliant offender, but it consists of a change in the location in which the sentence of custody is served: the offender can be transferred from the community to a correctional facility. Offenders who fail to comply with their community custody conditions therefore will enter prison; it is the same journey that prisoners released on parole make – only in the reverse direction.

Finally, community custody needs to be distinguished from a group of sanctions in which the offender is obliged to perform a number of tasks, and is subject to a number of restrictions on his or her liberty, but is not confined to home by means of house arrest or a curfew. For example, in Poland the 1969 Penal Code created a sanction of 'limited liberty'. This can be imposed for a period of up to two years. A number of conditions apply: among these the offender has to perform community service, make payments out of his or her salary, and is restricted from working in particular occupations (Stando-Kawecka, 2002). Absent the element of confinement (albeit in the community), this sanction cannot be considered a sentence of imprisonment.

Historical use of house arrest

In many jurisdictions, community custody often includes house arrest as a condition. Indeed, some people consider the two to be interchangeable, although they are not. House arrest has been used down the centuries for other purposes, principally to isolate an individual who posed a threat to the ruler or government. For example, England's King Richard II was confined in this way in Pontefract castle in 1399. The purpose of his confinement was that he 'should be deprived of all commerce with any of his friends or partisans' (Hume, 1834, p. 39). Five centuries later, house arrest is still employed by authoritarian governments to isolate (and hence neutralize) dissidents from other like-minded individuals. Imprisonment would not achieve the same degree of isolation, and inevitably generates protests from Western industrialized democracies.

Historically, house arrest has been unprincipled in scope and duration;[7] it is indeterminate, lasting until the individual dissident recants, or until the regime topples. Community custody, on the other hand, is a penal sanction imposed consistent with specific legal requirements. It is accordingly determinate in length, and principled in nature. Moreover, it is imposed because the individual has offended, not on account of the threat that he allegedly poses to the government. Finally, community custody is inclusive; the purpose is to retain the individuals' links with society and with their social milieu, albeit under certain restrictions, rather than to isolate them.

Exclusionary and inclusive penal sanctions

'A universal feature of imprisonment is the way it snatches its participants from everyday life and places them in an abnormal environment,
divorced from their routines, and exposed to quite different pressures and
imperatives . . . Constructive human reactions and behaviour become more
difficult' (Stern, 1998, p. 107). This quote from Vivien Stern captures well
the asocial world of prison, to which community custody is a clear alternative. The rise of the prison was a consequence of a movement towards
exclusionary penal policies that replaced very punitive, indeed brutal, cor-
poral punishments (such as branding) but which kept the offender in the
community.

Community custody represents a return to more *inclusive*, communitarian
responses to offending: the message to offenders is that they are punished
by, but not excluded from, their community. This punishment requires the
offender to fulfil certain social obligations common to all members, while
simultaneously denying them some, but by no means all of the privileges that
membership in the community confers. Prison creates spacial separation
between offenders and victims, and between offenders and the communities
to which they belong (Stern, 1998). This feature of prison goes back to the
period in which it was first use to detain offenders as a punishment. As
Bellamy (1973) observes, prisoners in the late middle ages were hidden
from society at large. A less destructive kind of separation is also possible by
means of carefully constructed sentences of community confinement.

More than this however, community custody attempts to achieve a transformation both in the way that we punish offenders, and the way in which
we conceive of imprisonment. In this sense, it represents another step in the
evolution of imprisonment, and one that carries as yet unrealized potential
to achieve safe and principled reductions in prison populations. It is not the
first transformation in the concept of imprisonment, but the latest in a series
of evolutionary steps. A person living during the nineteenth century would
have found the concept of weekend (or intermittent) custody a novelty: in
those days offenders went to prison, and did not emerge until the sentence
had been served.

Today, many jurisdictions permit judges to sentence offenders to weekend
or periodic terms of imprisonment. It is not just the schedule of imprisonment that has evolved, but the manner in which time is served. Members
of the public living earlier in the twentieth century would also have been
shocked to learn that many prisoners are allowed to vote, and that some
prisons now have trailers in which prisoners may receive conjugal visits, and

have the benefits of many recreational facilities. The public would have had difficulty in seeing such programs as appropriate to prison because of the bright line that existed in popular imagination between prison and community life.

Community custody strips imprisonment of many of the elements that have caused it to be so destructive: the removal from family and friends, the disruption of professional life, the enforced intimacy with strangers, the loss of employment and its accompanying social status, and the many stigmatizing consequences of penal sequestration. At the same time, if properly conceived, imposed, and administered, community custody sentences can achieve some of the goals of custody (such as denunciation and deterrence) by replicating many of the features of detention: restricted movement, the denial of certain privileges, and the existence of institutional surveillance. These are punitive features of community custody, but this sanction can also include conditions designed to promote the offender's rehabilitation and reintegration into society, as well as restorative goals. If the conditions of community custody are appropriately crafted and enforced, they can help promote desistance from further offending by weakening criminogenic relationships, and strengthening pro-social links. Thus community custody is a sanction that is sufficiently punitive to constitute an acceptable substitute for imprisonment, sufficiently flexible (in duration and with respect to the conditions imposed) to assure proportionality in sentencing, and capable of advancing sentencing objectives that are well beyond the power of prison to promote.

This emerging form of custody also carries considerable dangers, however, which will be explored in this book. In many respects, conditional imprisonment constitutes a penal paradox: the offender is sentenced to imprisonment, yet returns to his home to serve the sentence. Some members of the public will view such a sentence as another *sleight of hand* by the sentencing process. The court imposes one sentence (a term of custody) but the offender serves another (community detention). In a similar way, some people object when a court imposes a life sentence of imprisonment and the offender serves 'only' ten years, or when the court imposes a nine-year sentence and the offender is back in the community after eighteen months.[8] This has created pressure on legislatures to create 'truth in sentencing' legislation.

The 'top of the head'[9] reaction of most members of the public in Western nations to parole is negative, at least in the context of violent offenders. Part of this reaction is merely punitive; people see little benefit in mitigating the punishment imposed on such offenders. But from the perspective of a layperson, an offender granted release on parole a year or so into a nine-year sentence has at least served some time inside prison; a community custody offender begins and ends (assuming compliance with conditions) the sentence without going near a correctional facility.[10] Community custody carries the potential therefore, to exacerbate the already significant problem of low levels of public confidence in the courts. Recent polls conducted in Britain, Canada and elsewhere have demonstrated that the sentencing process attracts lower performance ratings than any other component of the criminal justice system (see Hough and Roberts, 2004a, for a review).[11]

Victims, and victims' advocates often approach community custody with considerable scepticism. Many victims come to court with little knowledge of sentencing trends, and expectations that most offenders convicted of a crime of violence spend significant periods in custody. Matters can become much worse for victims when they are allowed, indeed encouraged, to submit their views to the judge about the impact of the crime. Victim impact statement forms sometimes include ambiguous directions that allow the victim to address any other issue that they believe is important for the court to consider.[12] It may come as an unpleasant surprise to the victim when the court rejects the victim's (or prosecutor's) plea to impose a lengthy prison term and instead imposes a term of community custody, permitting the offender to resume living at home. Under the existing adversarial justice system, victims' views should not be determinative of the sentence that should be imposed. If they were, the concepts of state punishment and public wrong would be irreparably harmed. Nevertheless, any sanction that carries the potential to increase the suffering of victims will require careful handling by courts.

Offenders too, might have reasons to be wary of community custody. While being allowed to serve their terms of imprisonment at home rather than in detention must be of benefit to them, there are also dangers. Terms of community custody are often longer than the sentences of imprisonment that they replace. If an offender is ordered to serve a twelve-month community custody sentence instead of, say, six months 'inside' (and subject to parole release), he or she may risk a longer period of detention, if conditions are breached after four months and the court orders him or her to serve the remaining eight months in a correctional institution. The technological devices used to monitor compliance with house arrest can be intrusive and potentially demeaning.

Third-party interests have to be considered. Community confinement carries important consequences for the partner and family members who share the offender's residence. His or her continued presence in the house may affect their lives in a negative fashion, and they may feel drawn into the role of community custody 'officers'. If the offender breaks curfew, or violates some court-imposed condition, must they alert the criminal justice professional responsible for supervising the individual? To what extent are these co-residents obliged to participate in the enforcement of the community custody conditions? Community custody thus places the co-residents of the offender in an invidious position.

Finally, the community may have reason to be wary of the widespread use of community custody. Persons convicted of criminal offences are not randomly distributed across a city or town; they live in specific high crime neighbourhoods. If a high proportion of these offenders are sentenced to serve terms of custody at home, areas of a city are likely to contain a disproportionate number of 'individual' prisons, and this will have important, as yet unexplored consequences for these neighbourhoods. These areas will become characterized by high incarceration rates as well as high crime rates.

This book thus explores the concept of a sanction which goes under many names, but which I shall call *community custody*: sentences of imprisonment that are served in locations other than a correctional facility (usually the offender's home). Home detention is a primary component of all community custody sanctions, and has critics as well as advocates. Mirko Bagaric, for example, describes the home detention sentence in the Australian state of Victoria as 'undesirable' and at best an unnecessary reform (2002; see also Muncie, 1990). Critics argue that home confinement cannot advance the objectives of sentencing and has the potential to create great disparities in sentencing, as the conditions of confinement are to a degree defined by the nature of the offender's lifestyle. Simply put, some people have much more pleasant homes in which to live than others. It is also argued that the sanction favours offenders with stable home environments. How cogent are these (and other) critiques? The goal of the volume is to explore the way in which community custody can contribute to advancing the objectives of sentencing while simultaneously reducing the number of people sent to prison.

If the single aim of community custody were to reduce the number of prison admissions, there would still be an interesting story to tell about the experience in different jurisdictions. However, there is much more at stake; community custody pursues more ambitious goals. It aims to pursue multiple penal objectives as well as changing public and professional conceptions of imprisonment. Couched in these terms, community custody aims to have effects on the judiciary who impose sentence, on other criminal justice professionals such as prosecutors who in most (but not all) common law jurisdictions have an important impact on sentencing decisions, and on offenders who experience the sanctions imposed by the courts. And, ultimately, an important goal is to transform community views of the way in which we punish offenders convicted of the more serious crimes, those that currently result in the incarceration of the offender. For this reason, the issue of public opinion will be explored in some depth throughout this volume.

Community custody has the potential to assimilate increasing numbers of cases bound for prison, assuming that the level of societal comfort with this form of imprisonment increases. Whether it does may well depend on changing current conceptions of punishment. It is possible that offences which today routinely attract terms of custody will tomorrow attract a term of community custody without provoking public concern. Many strategies have been adopted to reduce the use of incarceration, but at the end of the day, as Kuhn (2003) notes in his review of European attempts to change sentencing practices, ultimately, changes in prison populations occur because of a change in attitudes.

The emergence of community custody: why now?

As noted, community custody, in some form or other, has been around for many years now. Considerable scholarly interest arose in the USA during the 1980s (see Lilly and Ball, 1987; Ball and Lilly, 1988; Ball, Huff and Lilly, 1988; Chicknavorian, 1990), only to subsequently recede. Developments have accelerated during the past decade when a number of other jurisdictions have introduced or amended community custody provisions. A community custody sanction was introduced in South Africa in 1991, and over the next decade a number of other countries introduced similar sanctions. Although they will not be reviewed in this book, pilot electronic monitoring schemes have recently been launched in most continental European countries, including Italy, France, Belgium and Germany. Other countries such as Sweden have adopted home curfew orders that can, at the discretion of correctional authorities, replace sentences of custody of up to three months in duration.

All penal innovations are a product of their time, and this one is no exception. In order for a new sanction, or a new form of imprisonment to proliferate, it has to be consistent with some important penal philosophy. Intermittent detention for example was used occasionally as a sanction in the seventeenth century, but periodic detention only became a more widespread sanction in the latter half of the twentieth century.[13] How are we to explain the current resurgence of interest in community custody? The sanction has recently assumed more importance as a consequence of six developments: (i) increased interest in restorative justice around the world; (ii) the growth of reintegrative shaming as a way of addressing offending; (iii) the pressure to contain or reduce rising prison populations; (iv) the rapid evolution of electronic surveillance technologies; (v) increased interest in what might be termed multidimensional sanctions that simultaneously promote multiple sentencing goals, and (vi) a growing public acceptance of community based sanctions.

Restorative justice

Restorative programs, policies and legislation now permeate all stages of the criminal process from pre-charge diversion to conditional release from prison (e.g. Braithwaite, 1999; Johnstone, 2002; von Hirsch, Roberts, Bottoms, Roach and Schiff, 2003; Weitekamp and Kerner, 2003). Whatever its promise and problems – and there has been much discussion of both – the attractions of restorative aims are undeniable.

Restorative justice claims many advantages for crime victims, and almost as many for offenders. It is an inclusive form of justice; the goals of restoration include restoring relationships between victims and offenders, and between the offender and the community against which he or she has offended. Imprisonment is anathema to the concepts of restorative justice. The prison is exclusionary, punitive and divisive, creating populations of victims and offenders that share an agonistic relationship. Community custody, in contrast, is inclusive, and promotes social relationships. By maintaining the offender in the community it also advances a view that communities contain people who have offended, not victims and offenders. It is no coincidence, for example, in Canada that the community custody sanction was introduced at the same time that Parliament codified a number of restorative objectives in sentencing[14] (Roberts and Roach, 2003). Roach (2000, p. 255) refers to the 'mainstreaming of restorative justice' that has occurred in Canada and elsewhere, and this development has given an important impetus to sanctions such as community custody that are able to promote restorative goals in sentencing.

Reintegrative shaming

'If visible shaming plus reintegration are the real stuff of crime control, then contemporary imprisonment would seem a terribly misguided institution' (Braithwaite, 1989, p. 179).

The literature on special deterrence has demonstrated that shame in the eyes of the offender's family and friends is a more important deterrent than the fear of legal punishment (see Braithwaite, 1989). Ahmed, Harris, Braithwaite and Braithwaite (2001) for example found that the disapproval of others held in high regard by the offender creates a much stronger sense of guilt regarding the offence than formal punishment. Placing an individual in prison is less likely to provoke this kind of emotion. But shame must have a reintegrative character. Prison is the quintessential penalty in terms of stigmatizing shame. Prisoners are shamed through their exclusion from the community, and the nature of the environment in which they are detained. In contrast, community custody contains a shaming component – the offender is serving his sentence in the presence of his family or spouse – but the experience is also characterized by its communitarian nature.[15]

Rising prison populations and the fiscal crisis in corrections

The search for and application of alternatives to custody has long been driven by fiscal considerations (see Vass, 1990). The evolution of home confinement in particular owes much to the prison overcrowding that has occurred in many jurisdictions (Renzema, 1992). The Home Detention Curfew scheme introduced in England and Wales in 1999 is an example of this pressure. Mair (2001) observes that this was introduced as a direct result of the dramatic increase in the number of prisoners in England and Wales. Most prisoners serving between three and four years became eligible for release on home detention up to sixty days early as a result of this legislation. The need to constrain public spending has intensified in recent years. The rising costs of imprisonment, and the increasing sophistication of surveillance technologies have impelled a number of jurisdictions to release prisoners to home detention schemes, and allow judges to sentence offenders directly to such programs. The attraction of a sanction that would divert offenders from entering prison is clear.

The evolution of electronic surveillance technologies

The growing interest in risk management throughout the criminal justice system has also played a role in managing offenders at home through more intensive forms of electronic monitoring. New surveillance technologies have opened the door to managing risk in the community. House arrest accompanied by electronic monitoring has emerged as a highly visible feature of what Lilly (1990) referred to as the 'new age of surveillance' (p. 230). Indeed, as Cullen, Wright and Applegate (1996) note, the proliferation of home incarceration would have been inconceivable without the concomitant development of a means of ensuring offender compliance. The most recent developments include the arrival of global positioning systems (GPS) which permit the state to monitor the movements of offenders beyond the confines of their residences. These technologies have increased the appeal of community sanctions by addressing public concerns about the risk posed by offenders to the community.

The search for multidimensional sanctions

Another explanation for the rise in community custody as a sanction involves the increase of interest in what may be termed 'polyvalent' or multidimensional sanctions that simultaneously attempt to promote multiple sentencing goals. Dispositions that fulfil only one of the many sentencing objectives are becoming less popular. This explains in part the transformation of probation from a purely rehabilitative disposition, to one that seeks to impose restrictions that constitute a punishment. In a similar way, correctional regimes over the past few decades have striven to rehabilitate offenders as well as punish or incapacitate. Most judges (and members of the public) expect a sentence to do more than simply punish or rehabilitate the offender. When people are asked to identify the most important sentencing purpose, or to rate the importance of a list of sentencing objectives, all principal purposes are assigned high ratings; people expect the system to punish, to rehabilitate, and to deter (Roberts and Stalans, 1997). By promoting more than a single penal aim, community custody offers far more to the criminal justice system, and is likely to prove popular with members of the public.

Growing public support for community-based sentences and disenchantment with prison

The final explanation for the rise of interest in community custody and other more humane forms of imprisonment (such as weekend detention) concerns the growing public acceptance of alternative sanctions. Community based sanctions do not naturally spring to the mind of many people when asked to consider sentencing offenders; indeed, as will be seen many people have trouble identifying the alternative sanctions available to sentencing courts. Nor do many people support the use of community sanctions for offenders convicted of the most serious crimes of violence. However, the public in many Western nations has become more supportive of these alternatives for a wide range of offenders. In part this springs from a growing public disenchantment with prison. The traditional public view of imprisonment was that it was an experience that served to discourage offending:

three quarters of the polled public in 1982 agreed that prison serves as a deterrent (Mande and Butler, 1982). A generation later, although the public still strongly supports the use of imprisonment for violent offenders, it is for reasons of punishment and incapacitation.

Thus, in 2000, a nationwide survey conducted in Britain found that a significant majority of the public disagreed with the statement that 'prison works' (MORI, 2000). One major reason why people have lost faith in prison is that it is perceived to be ineffective in helping prisoners reform themselves. The same MORI poll found that respondents were far more likely to agree than disagree with the statement that 'most people come out of prison worse than they went in'. In fact, only 14 per cent disagreed with the statement (MORI, 2000). Americans share this view of prisons. A poll conducted in Florida asked respondents to rate the prison system on a number of critical functions. While approximately two-thirds of the sample thought that the state correctional system did a good job in preventing escapes, only 14 per cent rated the system as doing a good job in rehabilitating criminals (Florida Department of Corrections, 1997).

Another reason for this public disenchantment is that prison is no longer regarded as an effective way of reducing crime. A recent British poll asked respondents to identify ways of reducing crime, and putting more offenders in prison was endorsed by only 8 per cent of the sample (Rethinking Crime and Punishment, 2002).[16] The consequence of this loss of faith in imprisonment is that significant proportions of the public support the use of alternatives even for people currently in prison. A survey of the British public asked respondents whether they supported or opposed 'measures to reduce the prison population by electronically tagging offenders and making them serve their sentence outside of the prison'. Over half the sample supported such measures (*Observer*, 2003). Since most people see prisoners as constituting serious offenders, this is a striking finding.

The public also expect the sentencing process to provide victims with some tangible benefit. Indeed, a number of public opinion studies have demonstrated that the public in many jurisdictions are willing to waive incarceration of the offender, if, in so doing, the victim has received compensation (e.g. Pranis and Umbreit, 1992; Galaway, 1984 and discussion in Roberts and Stalans, 2004). A sanction that simply punishes (or only rehabilitates) is unlikely to attract much support, except for a small number of offenders convicted of the most serious crimes; for these offenders, most people see no adequate substitute for secure detention.

Of all the sanctions developed in recent years, community custody carries the greatest potential to advance multiple sentencing goals. An offender confined to his residence except for court-authorized absences and who is subject to stringent conditions is undoubtedly undergoing a punishment. At the same time, conditions such as mandatory treatment or employment training and non-association and prohibition orders will promote his adherence to a law-abiding lifestyle. And by permitting the offender to remain in the community, the sanction allows, and the court should order, the offender to make compensation to the victim of the crime. The challenge to courts is to ensure that the right balance is established, through the judicious combination of conditions. A community custody order that serves only to punish offers little advantage over conventional custody; one that promotes rehabilitation without regard to other sentencing goals will also offer little to the sentencing process.

A generation ago, Fattah (1982) observed that 'Public opposition to alternatives to incarceration is a major obstacle in the way of making wide use of those alternatives' (p. 383). As will be seen in chapter 7, the nature of public reaction to sentences remains an important consideration for judges who impose alternatives and legislatures that create them. Nevertheless, public attitudes have evolved considerably, and community custody can capitalize on the growing disenchantment with prison accompanied by the renewed interest in alternatives to imprisonment.

Purpose and plan of the book

This book reflects an examination of community custody regimes around the world. It is not about house arrest alone – although I shall later argue that home confinement should be a mandatory condition of community custody – but about a broader, and more complex sanction that makes onerous requirements of offenders yet offers them far more control over their lives than is possible in prison. Particular attention is paid in this volume to the experience in Canada since 1996. In that year, a sentence of community custody was created with the explicit goal of reducing the volume of admissions to custody (see Roberts, 1997; Roberts and Cole, 1999). Seven years later, the results of that penal experiment have become clear. Unlike the experience elsewhere (for example in Florida), the introduction of the community custody sanction in Canada has reduced the number of admissions to prison.

The findings from Canada are summarized in the present volume; they carry important lessons for other jurisdictions such as England and Wales, where the Criminal Justice Act 2003 created a community custody sentence, called a suspended sentence of imprisonment. As well, this book draws upon empirical research upon home detention schemes in several jurisdictions such as New Zealand and Florida, interviews with crime victims, victims' rights advocates; focus groups with offenders serving terms of imprisonment in the community as well as their partners and families; interviews with and surveys of criminal justice professionals such as judges, prosecutors and probation officers.

The purpose is to understand the nature, potential and limits of this sentencing option, both in terms of its ability to reduce the use of imprisonment, and promote multiple sentencing goals. The judicious use of community custody can divert significant numbers of offenders from prison, and back to their homes, where they may retain the dignity to discharge their sentences, and where possible and appropriate, make reparation to the victims against whom they have offended. However, community custody sentences also carry clear dangers.

Improperly conceived, imposed and administered, community custody may lower public confidence in the administration of justice, inflict additional suffering upon victims of crime and undermine the principles of proportionality and equity on which the sentencing process is founded. Much depends upon the ambit of the sanction. Applying the sanction indiscriminately will result in these adverse effects; constructing a term of community custody with a very narrow range will prove to be ineffective in reducing the use of imprisonment as a sanction. The volume is not about electronic monitoring, or the technology of assuring that the offender is in fact complying with house arrest. This research is covered elsewhere (e.g. Ball, Huff and Lilly, 1988; Whitfield, 2001; 1997).

The central propositions advanced in this book are the following:

- community custody offers a plausible and progressive alternative to institutional imprisonment, one that has greater range of application than other community-based sanctions such as intensive supervision programs;
- although forms of community custody have been part of the penal landscape for some years now, the potential of the sanction has yet to be fully realized;
- properly constructed and implemented, community custody can effect a significant reduction in the number of offenders admitted to custody;
- if improperly constructed, community custody regimes will further undermine public confidence in sentencing;
- if the sanction carries appropriate conditions, and offenders are adequately supervised, community custody can promote the principal

objectives of sentencing more effectively than imprisonment and apply to a broader range of offenders than other community-based penalties;

- over time, the use of community rather than institutional custody can substantially lower correctional expenditures by changing the ratio of offenders in prison rather than the community;
- if employed widely enough, community custody will eventually transform societal conceptions of imprisonment away from the current exclusive emphasis on institutionalization.

Overview of contents

This book explores the issue of community custody in the following way. Chapter 2 summarizes recent trends with respect to the use of imprisonment as a sanction in Western nations. As will be seen, custody continues to be used frequently as a sanction – even for some crimes of low seriousness. The result is that prison populations in many countries have failed to decline in recent years. This is the intractable criminal justice problem for which community custody is a solution. Chapter 3 explores the concept of community custody in greater detail, and discusses its relation to the objectives of sentencing. This chapter attempts to clarify the differences between community and institutional custody; although they are both forms of imprisonment, the former carries greater potential as a sanction.

Chapter 4 describes the community custody dispositions that exist in a number of jurisdictions. Particular attention is focused on one of the most recent community custody regimes, the conditional sentence of imprisonment created in Canada in 1996. This is followed in chapter 5 by an exploration of the experiences and perceptions of offenders and the people who share many of the court-ordered restrictions on liberty, as a result of living in the same residence as the offender. The picture of community custody that emerges from the accounts of offenders is at odds with the popular image of offenders enjoying life in the comfort of their homes. Few members of the public stop to consider the impact of curfews and house arrest on the family of the offender.

Chapter 6 provides a discussion of the most important research question concerning community custody: does it reduce the number of admissions to prison, or result in 'net widening'? Although far from universal, the experience in several countries has demonstrated that community custody can reduce the number of admissions to prison with only a minimal degree of widening of the net.

Since the reaction of the community is critical to the success of any sanction, and in particular terms of imprisonment served at home, chapter 7 examines public opinion regarding the concept of community custody. Without public support, or at least acceptance, a sanction such as community custody will never take over a significant proportion of offenders sentenced to prison. As will be seen, public scepticism about community custody changes into acceptance if the conditions of the sanction are made salient to people. There will still be important limits on the extent to which the public will accept this form of imprisonment when it is imposed in serious personal injury offences. However, there is evidence that public attitudes are evolving in the direction of increased tolerance for the use of community punishments. The concluding chapter (8) is prescriptive in nature; it suggests ways in which community custody should be implemented, drawing upon the accumulated experience in a number of jurisdictions.

The goal of the book is to attempt to maximize the utility of this particular form of imprisonment. Although the advantages of the sanction have been recognized for years now (e.g. Ball and Lilly, 1985), to date its potential has not been accomplished. Over a decade ago, Baumer and Mendelsohn (1992) predicted that 'the primary target for home confinement will continue to be "low risk" offenders who are not thought to be a threat to public safety. In this sense, home confinement may be an acceptable sentencing alternative, but its application as an alternative to secure custody appears to be limited' (p. 65). There is reason now to believe that matters have changed; home custody regimes have proliferated beyond the USA and now apply to a significantly wider range of offender, including higher risk cases.

This book is about custody: *community custody*. The assumption is that real inroads into the admissions to prison will only be achieved when our perceptions of imprisonment undergo transformation. I also assume that for all its weaknesses as a sanction, and for all the dangers it carries with respect to the dignity of offenders and the lives of their families, community custody is preferable in almost all cases to confinement in even the most modern prison cell.

Electronic monitoring – the most intrusive component of community custody regimes – was introduced in the USA in 1984. Since then, some scholars have predicted the most dire consequences, usually involving the proliferation of penal control throughout society. Thankfully, these dystopian predictions have yet to come to pass.[17] This book will attempt to show that even though community custody has been imperfectly conceived and implemented in different jurisdictions, the overall experience has been positive, to the benefit of offenders and the societies in which they live.

It is trite to observe that conceptions of punishment have evolved; to the ancient jurists, imprisoning an individual as a legal punishment was inconceivable; execution was an appropriate response to the most serious crimes. Capital punishment is today regarded by parliamentarians in most jurisdictions as an unconscionable exercise of state power. Even in countries in which the death penalty attracts wide support, members of the public are deeply divided and favour restricting the sanction to the offence of murder. If the tools of punishment evolve, so too may conceptions of imprisonment, from a penalty involving confinement in a correctional facility, to one that includes different forms, including community-based detention, which is the subject of this book.

TWO

The way we punish now

Despite the proliferation of alternatives to incarceration over the past two decades, and the decline in reported crime in many Western nations during the 1990s – which might have relieved some of the pressure on politicians and sentencers to 'do something about crime' – custody continues to be widely used as a sanction. In fact, over the past decade, there has been little change in the proportionate use of prison as a sanction in many countries. This chapter reviews trends with respect to the use of imprisonment over the past decade. No attempt is made to summarize statistics from all jurisdictions, but rather to highlight common trends. These data document the problem to which community custody is a response. They reveal the resilience of the prison as a penal sanction and the relative failure of alternatives to displace imprisonment as a punishment even for less serious categories of offending. The analysis then focuses on the sentences of imprisonment that are most likely to be replaced by a community custody sanction. As well, the chapter summarizes findings from the International Crime Victimization Survey; these data demonstrate that there is considerable variability in the extent of public acceptance of alternatives to custody. This variation is important because it places the rates of custody in some context, and suggests that a high use of incarceration is not an immutable reality. The chapter concludes by discussing a specific impediment to the greater use of alternative sanctions, including community custody: judicial perceptions that these alternatives are not as effective (as imprisonment) with respect to achieving the traditional goals of sentencing.

Trends in the use of custody as a sanction

The use of imprisonment as a sanction has not declined over the past decade; in many jurisdictions it has even increased. This point can be made by examining a number of measures: historical trends in the number of people in prison; the proportionate use of custody now and in recent years, and sentence length statistics.

Trends in prison populations, 1990–2000

The 1990s was a decade in which imprisonment rates might have been expected to decline. The number of alternative sanctions proliferated during this period, offering judges more (and more plausible) alternatives to custody as a sanction. In addition, a number of developments augured well for the development and expansion of non-custodial sentencing options, including codification of directions to judges to only use incarceration when all other sanctions are inappropriate.[1]

Moreover, crime rates declined throughout the decade in many Western nations, thereby easing pressure on politicians to pass harsher sentencing laws, and judges to resort more often to the use of custody. For example, in 2000, Canada recorded a decline in crime rates for the ninth consecutive year (Logan, 2001). One of the most visible indicators of violent crime in the United States – the homicide rate – revealed a significant decline; the number of homicides across the country declined by 32 per cent from 1991 to 1999 (Bureau of Justice Statistics, 2000).[2] In England and Wales, crime recorded by the police dropped by 11 per cent over the decade 1991–2001 (Barclay and Tavares, 2003, Table A). Similar declines were observed in other countries as well. The average decrease across the European Union was 26 per cent (Barclay and Tavares, 2003, Table A). With a declining crime rate, the number of convictions recorded, and number of offenders sentenced to prison should decline. Despite these developments, the declines in prison populations never materialized.

Most researchers use the number of prisoners per adult population as an index of the use of imprisonment as a sanction, although these statistics are frequently confounded by the presence of prisoners on remand. Table 2.1 summarizes recent prison population trends across a number of jurisdictions. As can be seen, many Western nations experienced significant increases in their prison populations during the 1990s.[3] The increase in the volume of prisoners has been most marked in the USA, where the number of prisoners reached 2,078,570 by mid-2003 (US Department

Table 2.1. *Prison population trends, selected Western nations, 1990–2000.*

Jurisdiction	% increase in prison population, 1990–2000
Netherlands	101
United States	68
Germany	56
Australia	52
England and Wales	44
Portugal	39
Ireland	37
Spain	37
New Zealand	37
Belgium	30
Canada	19
Norway	17

Source: Barclay and Tavares (2002).

of Justice, 2004) – a manifestation of mass imprisonment by any standard (Garland, 2001b). But other countries, with less punitive criminal justice systems have also experienced record or near record numbers of prisoners.

Prison populations increased in most Australian jurisdictions over the past decade (Brown and Wilkie, 2002). In 1989, Australian prisons contained 12,965 prisoners; by 1998 this figure had risen to 19,906, an increase of 54 per cent (Carcach and Grant, 1999). The prison population in England and Wales reached 72,853 in April 2003, up 3 per cent from the previous year, 25 per cent over the number five years earlier and 75 per cent higher than a generation earlier (Hollis and Cross, 2003; Home Office, 1999). The volume of admissions to custody in Florida declined somewhat at the beginning of the 1990s, but as the decade wore on, increased again. Thus the number of admissions in 2001 was 18 per cent higher than in 1995–6 (Florida Corrections Commission, 2003). Since the end of the 1990s, the growth of prison populations has slowed in several countries (see Barclay and Tavares, 2002); nevertheless, the fact remains that imprisonment continues to occupy its central position in the criminal justice response to crime in most countries, as the following statistics reveal.

Table 2.2. *Proportionate use of custody for adult offenders, selected jurisdictions.*

Jurisdiction (source)	Year	% of dispositions involving immediate custody
Canada (Thomas, 2002)	2001	35
New Zealand (Spier, 2002)	2000	28*
England and Wales (Secretary of State, 2002a)	2001	7
Finland (Lappi-Sappala, 2002)	2000	13
New South Wales (New South Wales Bureau Justice Statistics)	2001	7**
United States (state courts, felony convictions) (U.S. Department of Justice, 2003)	2000	61

Notes: * includes periodic (i.e. intermittent) detention; ** local courts only.

Proportionate use of custody as a sanction across jurisdictions and over time

The difficulty with prison populations as a measure of incarceration is that they vary according to the number of convictions recorded, and this figure reflects changes in the volume of crime. A 'purer' measure of the use of custody (than the size of prison populations) as a sanction is the proportion of convictions resulting in a term of custody. Table 2.2 presents data pertaining to the proportionate use of imprisonment in a number of Western jurisdictions. Several conclusions may be drawn from this table. First, while prison is not imposed in the majority of cases in any jurisdiction,[4] it nevertheless accounts for significant proportions of sentences imposed, and hence large numbers of individual offenders.

Second, there is considerable variation across jurisdictions in the use of custody as a sanction, a finding consistent with recent research comparing sentencing patterns for a single offence (see Freiberg, 2002).[5] Some of this variation in custodial rates can be accounted for by variability in the seriousness of offences, the presence of firearms or the existence of mandatory sentencing laws for a small number of offences. However, these explanations can account for only part of the story. More likely, different custody rates reflect variation in the acceptability of imprisonment as a sanction. Countries appear to have evolved a rough tariff with respect to imprisonment.

The data regarding the proportionate use of custody reveal trends consistent with the prison population statistics.[6] For example, the proportionate use of custody has been stable, in the face of rising (and falling) crime statistics, legislative interventions (such as the introduction of mandatory minimum terms of custody), and other influences. In Canada for example, 30 per cent of convictions in 1991/92 involved custody (Turner, 1993). In 1997, at the onset of the new community custody regime, 33 per cent of convictions involved a term of custody (Brookbank and Kingsley, 1999).

New Zealand, another jurisdiction that is included in this survey, also shows a stable proportionate use of custody. In 1992, 28 per cent of convictions involved custody or periodic detention. A decade later, this percentage was unchanged (Spier, 2002). The use of continuous (i.e. non-periodic custody) increased slightly over the period 1992–2002 (Spier, 2002). The proportion of community-based sentences actually declined; these dispositions represented 36 per cent of all convictions in 1992, and only 30 per cent a decade later (Spier, 2002). Spier concluded that these trends could not be accounted for by an increase in the seriousness of cases being sentenced by the court (see Spier, 2002, Table 2.5; see also Brown and Young, 2000). Sentence length statistics also reveal an increase in the use of custody in New Zealand: in 1992, the average custodial sentence length was 22 months; this rose over the decade and was 26.4 months in the most recent year for which data are available (2001; see Spier, 2002). As was the case in Canada, this increase took place during a period in which the offence rate was declining.[7]

Examination of trends over a seven-year period (1996–2002) in New South Wales reveals a slight increase in the proportion of cases involving immediate custody in local courts, and a more significant increase in the proportionate use of custody in superior courts (New South Wales Bureau of Crime Statistics and Research, 2002). The number of inmates admitted to prison increased over the previous six years (1990 to 1995), particularly for prisoners sentenced to shorter terms of custody (Thompson, 1996). Similar trends are observed in other jurisdictions, even when the custody rate is relatively low. For example, in New South Wales, most cases are sentenced in the local courts which have a low proportionate use of custody (7 per cent of cases in 2002 were sent to prison).[8]

In England and Wales, the 1990s witnessed an increase in the proportionate use of custody. Across all offences, 7 per cent of convictions in 2002 resulted in the imposition of immediate custody. Custody accounted for 25 per cent of indictable cases in 1999. Comparisons between sentencing patterns in 1989 and 1999 are shown in Table 2.3. Overall, the use of custody

Table 2.3. *Changes in use of custody, England and Wales, 1989–1999.*

Offence category	% cases receiving immediate custody, 1989	% immediate receiving custody, 1999	Percentage change, 1989–1999
Violence	18	34	+16
Sexual offences	35	66	+31
Burglary	37	58	+21
Theft and handling	11	21	+10
Fraud and forgery	14	21	+7
Drug offences	16	19	+3
Motoring (indictable)	9	20	+11
All indictable offences	17	25	+8

Source: Home Office (2001).

increased; a term of custody was imposed on only 17 per cent of cases in 1989. In 1999, there were 24,000 more custodial sentences than in 1989 (Home Office, 2001). For some specific offence categories the increase was even more striking, as can be seen in Table 2.3. Moreover, government projections indicate that the sentencing reforms introduced in the Criminal Justice Act 2003 will increase the prison population still further. Home Office minister Lord Falconer acknowledged that the sentencing provisions would 'modestly increase' the prison population.[9] Academics too, seem pessimistic about the impact of the Act's new sentencing options on the prison population. Thus Newburn (2003) writes that 'Both the "custody plus" and "custody minus" sentences . . . have the potential to lead to further increases in custodial sentencing' (p. 49). Roberts and Smith (2003) also express apprehension that the new Act will increase the use of custody.

Sentence length statistics

In light of the theoretical and practical problems arising from the application of community custody to the most serious forms of offending (that would give rise to the longer terms of custody), the profile of offender most likely to be targeted by a community custody regime involves those individuals sentenced to relatively brief periods of imprisonment. Table 2.4 summarizes such sentence length statistics for a number of Western nations. As can be seen, with the exception of Portugal, in all other nations, over half the sentences of custody were under twelve months in length. Indeed

Table 2.4. *Sentence length statistics, nine Western jurisdictions.*

Jurisdiction	% of custodial sentences under six months	% of custodial sentences between six months and twelve months	Cumulative per cent of sentences less than twelve months
Denmark	91	6	97
Canada	85	92	95
Sweden	64	17	81
France	61	23	84
Scotland	57	18	75
England and Wales	39	21	60
Northern Ireland	30	33	63
Germany	23	34	57
Portugal	11	24	35

Source: European Sourcebook of Crime and Justice Statistics; Canadian Centre for Justice Statistics.

in many countries, the majority of sentences of imprisonment were under six months, reduced by parole to even shorter periods.

In addition, the periods of custody to which most offenders are sentenced are very brief; sentencing statistics show that the median prison term imposed in Canada was thirty days, while the median time actually served in custody was twenty-one days (Roberts and Reed, 1999). Similar trends can be seen in other jurisdictions. In England and Wales, almost half the defendants sentenced to custody for an indictable offence in 1999 were sentenced to less than six months (Home Office, 2001). Offenders sentenced for short periods are being committed to custody purely for punishment. Incarceration for such brief periods cannot promote the rehabilitation of the offender, or any restorative sentencing objective. Individuals sentenced to thirty days in prison are being punished in the only way that judges believe can adequately reflect the seriousness of the case. These cases offer considerable opportunities for the use of a community custody sanction. If home detention is properly conceived and administered, the punitive element of the custodial sanction can be captured, while still leaving scope in the sanction for other sentencing goals.

The increase in admissions to custody is not uniformly distributed across all sentence length categories. The relatively dramatic increase in prison admissions in England and Wales is found in sentences of less than twelve months (Hough et al., 2003). The cases receiving sentences of custody in this range are the ones that are most likely to be sentenced to community custody. A general finding in the literature on imprisonment is that reductions in the custodial populations can best be achieved by reducing the number of admissions, rather than the average length of sentence at admission. Most recently, for example, Kommer's (2003) analyses of sentencing statistics in Europe led him to conclude that the dramatic increases in prison populations are principally attributable to an increase in the number of prison sentences. Short prison sentences therefore hold the key to reducing prison populations.

Use of custody as a sanction for less serious cases

The next table (2.5) provides more information on the specific offences most likely to be targeted by a home confinement sentence for one jurisdiction. This table presents the proportion of cases resulting in a term of custody, for a number of common offences or offence categories in one country (Canada). As can be seen, a number of crimes of relatively low seriousness nevertheless have quite high incarceration rates. For example, approximately half the convictions for theft resulted in the imprisonment of the offender. Taken together, these offences and offence categories account for over 40,000 admissions to custody within a single year.

Neither the gravity of the offences nor the dangerousness of the offender can justify imprisonment in these cases; accordingly the explanation must lie elsewhere. One possibility is that these offenders have substantial criminal records. Unfortunately, sentencing statistics in Canada do not include information on the offender's criminal history. Still, the most plausible explanation for these trends is that these offenders are recidivists, with multiple previous convictions. Earlier 'one-off' studies of sentencing trends in Canada and other countries have demonstrated that the probability of incarceration rises in direct proportion to the number of previous convictions (see Roberts, 1997).

Another explanation for the use of custody in such cases is that these offenders have previously been sentenced to alternative sanctions such as probation. They have been caught up in the natural 'escalation' of the courts, judges having imposed prison after several community sanctions have 'failed'. Research involving sentencers in several jurisdictions has documented the existence of this judicial logic. One sentencer in research reported by Hough et al. (2003) noted that 'when community penalties have been tried and failed, then prison becomes inevitable' (p. 31). Doob (2001)

Table 2.5. *Use of custody as a sanction, selected offences in Canada, 2001/2.*

Offence or offence category	% of cases sentenced to prison	Median sentence length (in days)	Number of cases
Breach of probation order	51	30	9,663
Possession of stolen property	49	60	4,708
Traffic offences	46	42	3,423
Other property offences	38	90	493
Theft	37	30	9,921
Uttering threats	37	45	3,863
Fraud	33	60	4,035
Possession illegal weapons	29	54	1,034
Prostitution	25	8	273
Public mischief	20	30	1,456
Disturbing the peace	13	10	240
Possession of drugs	12	10	1,374
Total			40,483

Source: Adult Criminal Court Survey, Canadian Centre for Justice Statistics.

reports a similar finding from a survey of judges in Canada. An alternative sanction that carries some of the characteristics of imprisonment might well serve to interrupt, or slow, the inevitable escalation from a community sanction to a term of custody. In short, many offenders are committed to prison to reflect their previous offending, or their previous sentencing.

There is another reason why short sentences constitute the most fertile ground for home confinement sentences. As the sentence length increases, the plausibility of the argument that community custody can be considered the equivalent of institutional custody diminishes. For example, two years in one's home – however stringent the conditions imposed – cannot match the penal equivalent of two years in prison, even if part of the latter is served in the community on parole. However, replacing three weeks in prison with a community custody sentence is likely to prove far more acceptable to the public and the judiciary alike. And, if the 21-day prison term is replaced by two months of community custody (or some period longer than the prison term), it is hard to see many people considering the latter to be a lenient substitute for the former. In short, penal equivalence between community custody and institutional custody is easily achieved for short sentences, much more difficult for very long ones.

Impediments to the proliferation of alternatives to institutional custody: attitudes towards the use of custody and alternative sanctions

The question of why prison populations have risen (or not fallen) is beyond the scope of this volume, and has been addressed by many other scholars. A number of authors have attempted to explain why alternative or intermediate sanctions have failed to fulfil their promise to replace terms of custody (e.g. Bishop, 1988; Lappi-Seppala, 2002). Some of these are sentence-specific, having to do with limitations on particular dispositions, such as a fine (e.g. Morris and Tonry, 1990, pp. 15–17). Other explanations are more general, and apply to most alternative sanctions. Of the general impediments, a lack of interchangeability has been identified by several authors. For example, Morris and Tonry (1990) stress the importance of this concept when they note that 'A comprehensive integrated sentencing system must include a system of interchangeable punishments, particularly covering the middle range of severity of crime' (p. 77).

A related issue common to many alternative sanctions is one of image as much as substance. These sanctions lack the standing of imprisonment in the eyes of the public and many criminal justice professionals. One of the reasons then for the stable prison statistics is the inability of alternative sanctions to offer a credible alternative in the eyes of the judiciary and the community. It is this lack of credibility that in large measure drives the political timidity with respect to the use of alternative sanctions (see Willis, 1986).

The Council of Europe's study on non-custodial sanctions in Europe concluded that 'a major constraint on the use of non-custodial alternatives was the level of public tolerance' (Bishop, 1988). While there appears to have been some growth in the acceptance of these sanctions by the public since then (see Roberts, 2002b), alternatives to custody still suffer an image problem. An indication of the visibility and profile of the community penalties in general can be gleaned from responses to the 1998 British Crime Survey. Respondents were asked to identify sanctions other than imprisonment, a question that few could answer with more than one response. Only one-third of the sample identified a sanction as well established as probation, while a mere 7 per cent came up with tagging as a response (see Hough and

Roberts, 1998). This lack of awareness on the part of the public is indicative of the low profile of community penalties. (Public reaction to community custody is addressed in greater detail in chapter 7 of this volume.)

Another important impediment to the wider use of alternatives emerges from research with judges. Several studies have revealed a considerable degree of scepticism on the part of judges with respect to the alternatives to custody. Van Kalmthout (2002) identifies 'A lack of belief in the punitive character of community sanctions' (p. 590) as one explanation for judicial reluctance to use alternatives in the place of prison. In some countries, judicial discretion at sentencing has been removed or highly circumscribed for certain crimes, as a result of mandatory sentencing legislation. Mandatory sentencing provisions were introduced in many Western nations in the 1990s. Yet these laws affect a relatively small percentage of the total caseload sentenced by criminal courts. Mandatory sentences of imprisonment cannot alone account for the continued use of custody as a sanction. The critical decision-maker is the judge, particularly in countries in which formal sentencing guidelines do not exist.

Many common law jurisdictions have codified the sentencing principle of restraint, namely that offenders should be imprisoned only if no other sanction is capable of achieving the statutory objectives of sentencing.[10] Even without such direction from the legislature, judges are unlikely to send offenders to prison without having established that only this sanction is adequate. That said, few studies have explored the nature of judicial reaction to imprisonment. Recent interviews with sentencers in England and Wales make it clear that judges and magistrates take the 'sanction of last resort' principle seriously (or at least report that they do so; see Hough et al., 2003). Why then, do sentencers in Britain, Canada and elsewhere see custody as necessary for so many offenders?

A number of considerations emerge from the recent research by Hough et al. in England and Wales (2003), and earlier work elsewhere. A central theme concerns the unique character of custody as a sanction and its power to send a message to the offender and society that simply cannot be conveyed by a community sentence. For serious crimes of violence, this made custody unavoidable from the perspective of the sentencer. The sentencers participating in this research attributed the rise in the prison population in England and Wales to an increase in the seriousness of cases appearing before the courts (Hough et al., (2003) pp. 30–1).[11]

A survey of judges in Canada revealed that the most important consideration with respect to the imposition of a term of custody was the seriousness of the offence (Doob, 2001). As the seriousness of the crime increases, the perceived utility of a community penalty appears to decline. Judges in other jurisdictions share this perspective. Haverkamp (2003) reports the results of surveys of judges in Germany and Sweden regarding home confinement with electronic monitoring. She found strong support for this sentencing option, but only for short prison sentences, and principally for less serious, low-risk offenders. Walters (2002) found a similar degree of reluctance on the part of magistrates in England and Wales to impose curfew orders; there was a general lack of confidence in the value and effectiveness of the sanction. This explains why it was generally ordered in less serious cases. Why do sentencers see home confinement/curfew sanctions as inappropriate for the more serious cases? In all probability, it is because community penalties are not perceived to be as effective as prison in advancing the objectives of sentencing for serious cases.

Judicial attitudes to imprisonment can be approached in another way. Rather than ask judges why they would impose a term of custody, a survey conducted in Canada asked members of the judiciary about their perceptions of the relative effectiveness of community custody versus imprisonment (Roberts, Doob and Marinos, 2000). Respondents were asked about the effectiveness of the two sanctions in terms of achieving the principal sentencing objectives of denunciation, deterrence, proportionality and rehabilitation.[12] The results support the conclusion emerging from the British sentencers: community custody fails, in the eyes of judiciary, to match the effectiveness of imprisonment with respect to certain key sentencing objectives. Table 2.6 summarizes these findings regarding the objectives of sentencing. As can be seen, community custody (called a conditional sentence of imprisonment in Canada) was generally seen as being the equal of imprisonment in terms of achieving the rehabilitation of the offender, but not the denunciation of the crime.

Thus almost three-quarters of the sample responded that community custody could be as effective as prison for rehabilitation, but only approximately a third of the judges held this view with respect to denunciation or deterrence. This finding underscores an important weakness associated with many community sentences: they fail to carry the impact of custody.[13] It must be recalled that the sanction in question here (the conditional sentence of imprisonment) is the most punitive sanction in Canada other than imprisonment itself. The other alternative sanctions would undoubtedly have fared far worse in comparison to custody with respect to these sentencing objectives. In a later chapter, I shall review data from the public which suggest that judges may under-estimate the denunciatory and deterrent power of community custody; for the present it is sufficient to note that judicial belief

Table 2.6. *Judicial perceptions of the effectiveness of community custody compared to prison**.

	% Proportionality	% Denunciation	% Deterrence	% Rehabilitation
Always/usually as effective as prison	51	35	35	72
Sometimes as effective as prison	34	33	41	24
Almost never/ never as effective as prison	15	32	24	4
	100	100	100	100

Source: Roberts, Doob and Marinos (2000).

Note: * Question wording: 'Can a [community custody sentence] be as effective as imprisonment in achieving (proportionality)?'

in the effectiveness of even this rigorous alternative to custody is a cause of the continued dominance of imprisonment as a sanction. Indeed, judicial reluctance to impose these sanctions has been a significant impediment to the wider implementation of intermediate punishments (Moore, 1997).

Interviews with judges and magistrates in England and Wales conducted by the Home Office Sentencing Review (2001) suggest that the judiciary in this country hold similar attitudes towards community penalties. Alternatives to imprisonment were regarded as a purely rehabilitative sentencing option. In the words of the Review's report, community penalties were not regarded 'as suitable where punishment was the aim' (p. 120). This perspective creates a cleavage between sanctions that prevents alternatives from cutting into the caseload of offenders bound for prison. Finally, judges are not the only criminal justice professionals to see important limitations on house arrest as a sanction. Sigler and Lamb (1996) asked a sample of criminal justice system employees[14] to rank the effectiveness of a number of punishments, including jail and intermediate punishments such as shock probation, house arrest and community service. Jail was perceived as being the most effective sanction at achieving community safety and deterrence.

Public attitudes to the use of custody as a sanction

The sentencing statistics reveal considerable variability across jurisdictions with respect to the proportionate use of custody and the average length

Table 2.7. *Percentage of ICVS respondents choosing custody as sanction, selected Western nations.*

Jurisdiction	% of sample endorsing prison
United States	56
Northern Ireland	54
Scotland	52
England and Wales	52
Canada	45
Netherlands	37
Australia	37
Sweden	31
New Zealand	26
Portugal	26
Belgium	21
Denmark	20
Finland	19

Source: International Crime Victimization Survey.

of custodial sentences. These differences reflect variation in the penal culture of different countries, a point that can also be made by examining the sentencing preferences of the public. These findings derive from the International Crime Victimization Survey (ICVS). Members of the public across a wide diversity of nations were asked to sentence a 21-year-old male offender convicted of burglary. They were permitted to use one of only three sanctions: prison, community service or a fine.

Respondents were only given a brief description of the case – little more than a phrase. The consequence is that support for custody is stronger than it would be had the respondents been provided with a more detailed description of the case. However, even accepting this limitation, the support for custody in many countries is high. In addition, with the same fact scenario presented to all respondents, differences in the 'incarceration rate' must be accounted for by different levels of public acceptability of particular sanctions, in this case custody. Table 2.7 shows the proportion of respondents who favoured incarcerating the offender described in the scenario.

As can be seen the public response to the same fact situation varies considerably. And, since there are only three penalties available to respondents, where support for custody is strong, there is consequentially less support for fines or community service (see Kury, Obergfell-Fuchs, Smartt and Wurger, 2002, Figure 2). This table suggests that the relatively high use of custody as a sanction does not reflect universal public support. The level of public tolerance exercises an important constraint upon the use of alternative sanctions (Bishop, 1988). The influence can be seen in the reluctance of legislators to create new alternatives, or to expand the ambit of existing alternatives and judicial reluctance to impose these sanctions for fear of provoking public opposition. The ICVS data suggest that in many countries there is 'room to move' with respect to public acceptance of alternative sanctions. The challenge to progressive legislators is to consider how this transformation in public attitudes might best be achieved. As well, the variable public response to the use of alternative punishments suggests that the range of applicability of this sanction will differ: the public in some countries will be more willing to countenance the use of community custody for crimes of violence.

Conclusion

Several conclusions may be drawn from this summary of recent sentencing trends. First, despite the proliferation of alternatives to imprisonment or the declining crime rates in many Western nations during the 1990s, there is little evidence that prison populations are declining, or that the use of custody (relative to other sanctions) is waning. If anything, prison populations in many countries have increased in size in recent years. As Mathieson (2000) notes, 'the general tendency is very clear . . . the prison as an instrument of punishment has escalated further in importance and solidified its position' (p. 173). Fully a generation ago, Stanley and Baginsky declared that: 'The English prison system is in a crisis. This is now an accepted fact' (1984, p. 7). Since then, matters have worsened still further.

An important cause of this problem has been the inability of alternative sanctions to assume some of the prison-bound case load. In 1990, Antony Vass wrote of the failure of sentencing alternatives to 'challenge the prison and check its rising population' (p. 164).[15] Little progress appears to have been made since that time. More recent reviews of the impact of community sanctions in general have reached equally gloomy conclusions (e.g. van Kalmthout, 2002, p. 600; Albrecht and van Kalmthout, 2002, p. 10; Tonry, 1996, p. 120; Faugeron, 1996, p. 122). Similar conclusions have been reached with respect to house arrest/home confinement regimes. Thus in a recent discussion of alternatives in the United States, Michael Tonry (2002) concurs with Baumer and Mendelson (1992) and concludes that 'house arrest will continue primarily to be used for low risk offenders and will play little role as a custody alternative' (p. 559).

Second, imprisonment continues to be used for offences of relatively low seriousness, such as fraud. Offenders convicted of these crimes are committed to custody for quite brief periods of incarceration, principally because they have significant criminal records, or a history of having received alternative sentences in the past. Such cases represent prime targets for a sentence of community custody. Third, one of the explanations for the slow progress with respect to the use of alternative sanctions concerns resistance on the part of the judiciary. Many judges do not see these sanctions as capable of replacing imprisonment. Increasing judicial confidence in the use of alternatives to imprisonment therefore constitutes a priority for any sentencing system hoping to reduce the use of custody as a sanction. Fourth, there is considerable variability in public acceptance of alternatives to imprisonment. The public in certain countries are far more accepting of community sanctions, and appear to countenance the use of these sanctions for a wide range of cases. This means that there is probably considerable scope for the public in some jurisdictions to accept a community custody sanction, as long as it is appropriately constructed, implemented and explained. The next chapter explores the nature of community custody in more detail, and identifies its potential as a replacement for imprisonment in an institution.

THREE

Conceptualizing community custody

I have been studying how I may compare
This prison where I live unto the world:
And for because the world is populous
And here is not a creature but myself,
I cannot do it . . .[1]

The nature of community custody requires careful elucidation. Although community custody regimes vary widely, they share many common elements, and all differ in important ways from terms of imprisonment in a penal institution. This chapter compares and contrasts community custody and institutional imprisonment. Imprisonment is *exclusionary*, destructive and anathema to the sentencing objectives such as restoration and rehabilitation. In contrast, community custody is an *inclusive* sanction; although carrying a punitive element, it also encourages rehabilitation and restoration. Community custody is also an active disposition; offenders are encouraged to use their time, rather than simply pass it in a prison cell. Indeed, through the use of specific conditions, many community custody orders compel this kind of active participation in the sentence. The 'virtual prison' therefore has the potential to offer much more than its institutional counterpart. Comparisons between the two sanctions must also address the following question: to what extent can community confinement promote the traditional goals of sentencing? The response to this question must perforce be comparative rather than absolute in nature. For example, how much more (or less) effective than prison, or the alternative punishments, is community custody? In this chapter I therefore examine the relationship between community custody and some of the traditional purposes of sentencing.

The evolution of legal punishment and the concept of imprisonment

A number of excellent discussions of the evolution of punishment and imprisonment exist (e.g. Pratt 1992) from which some points will be extracted for their relevance to the issue of community custody. The prison originated as a means to detain people awaiting trial, or execution, not as a legal sanction. For example, although houses of detention were a familiar feature of life in ancient Rome,[2] and Roman law prescribed a number of punishments, imprisonment was not one of them (Kirkpatrick, 1880). Although prisons were built in Saxon times, it was not until later, in the Middle Ages, that imprisonment was used both to punish offenders and to encourage compliance with other penalties. For example, an individual would be imprisoned, and required to pay a fine. Once the fine was paid, the prisoner was freed (Bellamy, 1973). Prison was not intended during this period for the correction of offenders – another illustration of the evolution of imprisonment over the ages.

Once imprisonment began to be imposed as a punishment, the necessity for prisons became more apparent, leading to the construction of penal institutions to accommodate prisoners for long periods of time. From Tudor times, prisoners began to be detained for longer periods, often years. As Pratt (1992) notes, punishment was increasingly likely to comprise the deprivation of time – and the restriction of freedom – rather than the direct infliction of pain (such as branding). Yet this form of punishment took place in circumscribed locations to which the public would have only very limited access. Prisoners were sequestered from society. Therein lies the origin of the concept of penal sequestration; prisoners were not part of society but inhabitants of a world apart.

Through the use of institutions that were sealed from the world (except for the limited access of visitors and staff), the history of the prison has contributed to the stigma attached to prisoners, who acquired a status, or rather anti-status, that has persisted to this day.[3] The effect can be seen in public reaction to offenders punished outside the prison; people who have discharged their sentences in the community meet with a very different reaction from society than offenders released from prison. The opposition to the creation of halfway houses from potential host communities (the 'Not in my backyard' syndrome) is a consequence of the negative views that many people hold towards prisoners. And the often intense hostility to parole in some countries springs in part from a public perception that prisoners are dangerous, and likely to commit further offences.[4]

Definitions of imprisonment

We have come to conceive of imprisonment as an institutional phenomenon, but this is a relatively recent conception. The origin of the word prison also sheds light on the original meaning of the word, namely to restrict movement, but not necessarily to confine within a penal institution.[5] In his classic work, Blackstone described imprisonment in the following terms: 'every confinement of the person is an imprisonment, whether it be in a common prison, or in a private house'.[6] The quote from *Leviathan* by Hobbes with which this book began makes the point clearly, and is worth quoting in full here: '*Imprisonment*, is when a man is by public authority deprived of liberty . . . Under this word imprisonment, I comprehend all restraint of motion caused by an external obstacle' (p. 206). This conception of imprisonment persisted into the next century, when Samuel Johnson compiled the first dictionary of the English language. Dr Johnson defines the verb 'to imprison' in the following way: 'to shut up, confine, keep from liberty' (Johnson, 1979, reprint). Contemporary dictionaries preserve the restraint-based definition of imprisonment. The *Oxford English Dictionary* defines the verb 'to imprison' in the following way: 'to confine in a prison or other place' and 'to keep in close confinement' (*Oxford English Dictionary*, 1933/61).[7] The concept of restraint is as important as institutionalization to these definitions.[8] The French verb 'emprisonner' carried a similar connotation, being defined as 'retenir quelq'un *comme* dans un prison', and 'fait d'être privé de liberté' (*Dictionnaire Historique de la langue Française*, 1992, emphasis added). This general, rather than institutional, definition still exists, although it has clearly been lost to popular conceptions of imprisonment involving institutions.

Beattie (1986) notes that imprisonment became more popular than other sanctions because it allowed 'fine gradations of punishment to be assigned to each offence and offender' (p. 608). It represented another stage in the evolution of legal punishment. Community custody also permits these gradations (to reflect the relative seriousness of offences and culpability of offenders), but it also carries another advantage that will be explored later in this chapter, namely its ability to advance multiple sentencing objectives. For the present, I simply propose that this characteristic of community custody confers an advantage over its institutional counterpart, and therefore represents another stage in the evolution of legal punishments.

Home detention schemes exist at several stages of the criminal justice systems of Western nations. They have been available in various forms for over thirty years now,[9] with the French concept of 'contrôle judiciaire' constituting perhaps the earliest incarnation (see Ball and Lilly, 1985, for information about the origins of home detention). House arrest is employed at several stages of the criminal process. Accused persons released on bail can be subject to such restrictions. More frequently, prisoners are released to serve the last part of their sentences of imprisonment at home, subject to the home confinement requirements. None of these applications represents an attempt to change the paradigm of legal punishment. Subjecting accused persons or parolees to home confinement conditions is simply a way of ensuring some other objective: attendance at trial, or compliance with the conditions of another sentence (imprisonment). In contrast, community custody is an autonomous sanction designed to replace custody; it represents a way of achieving the retributive and restorative objectives of sentencing without confining the offender within an institution.

The argument advanced in this book is that if it is properly conceived and administered, community custody can appropriate the role of the prison for much larger numbers of offenders than is currently the case. By transforming the concept of imprisonment into one which has many forms, including a community-based version, community custody can result in offenders being spared the pains of institutional custody. This represents another stage in the evolution of imprisonment, which may one day consist almost entirely of prisoners serving time at home, with a very small number of individuals detained in prison – those who represent an immediate and compelling threat to the safety of others. Such a development will be seen by many as progressive; another step along the road to the dismantling of the prison system.

On the other hand, community custody may be seen by others as quite the opposite: the 'prisonization' of yet another community-based sanction. Originally conceived to be purely rehabilitative in nature, sanctions such as probation have now acquired a punitive element in many countries. Some alternative sanctions such as ISP (Intensive Supervision Probation) can be highly punitive, and are perceived as such by offenders. Research on offender perceptions (to be reviewed in chapter 5) reveals that many offenders would prefer to go to prison than receive one of the tougher alternative sanctions. This tendency to invest rehabilitation-oriented sanctions with a punitive element has been decried by some penologists.

With respect to community custody, such critics might argue that rather than changing the nature of imprisonment, the prison is instead changing the character of its alternatives. According to this view, the prison is metastasizing and society is becoming more like prison, rather than custody becoming more like the community. Indeed, the once distinct domains of prison and its alternatives are now territories with ever-shifting boundaries. Some offenders serving prison sentences live at home, on parole (subject to minimal supervision), while some offenders serving alternative sentences either live under much tighter constraints or languish in prison as a result of non-compliance with their conditions (see Van Zyl Smit, 1994, for discussion of the overlap between custodial and non-custodial sanctions). The originally clear line between community and custody has become much less distinct.[10]

The concept of custody-at-home also may be rejected by those who believe that it represents the proliferation of the prison. Rather than restricting the carceral milieu to a relatively small number of prisons, imprisonment now may affect thousands of homes in communities throughout the country. This objection echoes some of the opposition to Closed Circuit Television (CCTV); some regard the omnipresent surveillance cameras as an unwelcome intrusion into public and private spaces, with a consequent loss of privacy for vast numbers of people in many social contexts. Perhaps, but this is why it is so important to understand the reaction of offenders to this form of custody, and also to recall that community custody is a form of imprisonment, a replacement for institutionalization, not a sanction to be imposed on offenders who might otherwise be placed on probation or ordered to pay a fine.

To the extent that community custody resembles imprisonment, it carries great potential to reduce the number of people committed to custody. As the simulacrum of prison, it can assume the role of imprisonment for a wide range of offenders. This gives it a clear edge over the other alternative sanctions that fall short of imprisonment in terms of severity. A more effective way of reducing the volume of offenders admitted to prison would be to create 'non-imprisonable' offences; to identify a list of crimes for which courts would lack the power to imprison. This strategy would have to go further and prevent courts from imprisoning offenders who defaulted on the conditions of their community penalties. A proposal of this kind was made by Vass (1990, p. 178), among others. But in most countries such an approach is not yet politically acceptable. Legislatures would vigorously oppose creating a schedule of non-imprisonable offences, and judges would reject any move to deprive them of the back-up sanction of custody. How, they will argue, can a compensation order or community service be enforced, if not through the threat of imprisonment in the event of non-compliance? The next best solution appears to be community custody.

Community custody and the pains of imprisonment

In 1958, Sykes identified five primary characteristics of life that are denied prisoners: liberty; heterosexual relations; goods and services; personal autonomy, and personal security. Community custody restores these deprivations, albeit in a limited fashion. Offenders confined to their homes have their liberty curtailed, and their autonomy restricted but are spared the other pains of imprisonment. The critical question confronting community custody regimes is whether sparing the offender these costs associated with imprisonment undermines the ability of this form of custody to serve as a replacement for 'the real thing'.

Community custody and home confinement regimes

A later chapter reviews community custody regimes in a number of jurisdictions. For the present, it is worth summarizing the salient differences between custody at home and imprisonment in a correctional facility. Community custody confers a high degree of autonomy upon offenders (relative to imprisonment at least), and permits – indeed, should encourage, individuals to use this relative or restricted freedom to make reparation to victims and the community. As well, the conditions imposed on offenders serving prison terms in the community should enhance their rehabilitative prospects, by requiring attendance for treatment or therapy, abstention (where appropriate) and other rehabilitative steps. Prisoners in most Western prisons are encouraged to follow educational and professional training in prison, but the range of courses and programs offered is far more restricted than in open society. Simply put, the prison is the least conducive environment for self-improvement.

Of course there are, and need to be, important common elements between community custody and the prison. If they were totally distinct, they would not be as interchangeable. Community custody prisoners are subject to important restrictions, principally regarding their freedom of movement. Community custody regimes usually involve strict curfews, often enforced by electronic monitoring. In addition, although this is not always the case, community custody regimes should include incentives for the prisoner. Most Western correctional systems employ some form of discretionary conditional release mechanism by which offenders may earn the right to spend the last portion of their sentences of imprisonment in the community. The severity (but not the duration) of the sentence is mitigated thereby. Community custody prisoners cannot earn parole – they are already serving a form of parole in the community – but they should be able to earn, through

Table 3.1. *Critical differences between institutional and community custody.*

Institutional custody	Community custody
Exclusive in nature; prisoners are outside society	Inclusive; offenders remain part of community
Excludes family and partners: family members visit the offender only according to rigid institutional timetables	Family-oriented: family members and partners are instrumental in administering the sentence
Stresses and often ruptures social and marital relations	Preserves social and marital relations
Interrupts employment	Permits continued employment
Emphasizes punishment, and allows no possibility for reparation or other restorative gestures towards the victim or the community	Stresses punishment *and* restoration: reparation and community service are integral elements of the sanction
Prison is essentially a passive experience; prisoners are expected to adhere to institutional rules and timetables, responding to the institution's dictates	Community custody represents a more active experience; prisoners are able to pursue their own activities, albeit within the limits of the conditions imposed (e.g. curfew)
Prison strips prisoners of personal dignity, subjecting them to public degradation	Community custody permits the offender to undergo legal punishment while retaining personal dignity
Prison deprives people of privacy; it is public experience, shared with other prisoners	Community custody prisoners retain a high degree of privacy
Prisons are collective in nature; prisoners sometimes double and triple bunked	Community custody is individual in nature; the sentence is served in the absence of other prisoners
Imprisonment offers few incentives and limited opportunities for self-improvement	Offers many opportunities for offender to improve life skills
Custody is hostile to therapy, or contains impediments to the therapeutic process	Conducive to therapy and permits offenders to have a wider range of social contacts
Exposes prisoners to the health and safety risks of assaults of various kinds	Reduces the probability of victimization, by reducing risk factors
Prison is very visible: prisons and prisoners are readily identifiable buildings and people	Invisible: offenders serving custody at home can do so in most cases without even their neighbours being aware of the court order

compliance with conditions over a protracted period of time, some reduction in the severity of their conditions. This issue will be explored more thoroughly in the final chapter of this book. For the present, Table 3.1 summarizes the important differences between the two forms of custody.[11] This table summarizes benefits for the offender, although there are clear advantages for the community and the correctional system as well.

The correctional system benefits in some obvious ways, such as cost savings. Even the most expensive electronic monitoring programs cost less than secure custody. In addition, a significantly higher proportion of the costs of administering a community custody order are consumed by salaries, rather than infrastructure which is less adaptable to changing correctional needs. Widespread use of community custody as a sanction is likely to change the nature as well as the size of the prison population, which is going to become increasingly homogeneous. This makes it easier to program services; a major challenge to correctional authorities at present is coping with a very diverse offender population in terms of their risks and needs.

Community imprisonment

The destructive impact of prison derives in large measure from its isolation, from the fact that it sunders the links between the offender and the family and community to which he belongs. Contemporary correctional regimes attempt to mitigate the negative effects of imprisonment by increasing the accessibility of prisoners to their partners and families. Important though such visits are, they create additional stress for both prisoners and their partners. Kemp (1981) reports findings from a rare research project involving prisoners' wives. With respect to prison visits she found that 'the majority [of partners] had often felt frustrated, tense and unable to discuss intimate matters with their husbands during visits (whether contact or no-contact)'. The consequence of restricted access of this kind is often conflict and ultimately separation.

Active and passive sentences
A central feature of a prisoner's life is its passive nature. Prisoners react to institutional rules and requirements, take far fewer decisions and generally have much less control over their lives than people in open society. Despite the use of an active verb, the phrase 'doing time' often refers to the passive passage of time;[12] many prisoners who are doing time, are actually doing very little with their time (Wright, 1982).[13] This has been characteristic of the prison for centuries. Writing of prisons in the late middle ages, Bellamy

notes that: 'For most prisoners the period in gaol must have been a time of infinite boredom' (1973, p. 174). John Howard found matters unchanged in the eighteenth century: 'The prisoners have neither tools, nor materials of any kind: but spend their time in sloth . . .' (1929 (reprint) p. 1).

Interviews with prisoners and ex-prisoners as well as prisoners' memoirs confirm that prison life has changed little in this respect. One describes prison in the following terms: 'Prison did many things to me as it did to my fellow prisoners. It caused physical discomfort . . . humiliation, and degradation. But the greatest injury it inflicted on us all was psychological, for by exerting complete external control over our life, and thus making us totally dependent on the prison for all our needs, it forced us to regress into our childhood' (Turner, 1964, pp. 7–8).[14]

Prisoners spend their time being shaped by the institution (Duguid, 2000). This is particularly true in correctional facilities in which inmates have few resources, as a result of 'get tough' policies that have resulted in a high degree of penal austerity. The prospect of early release on parole may encourage a degree of active participation in programs. However, a number of jurisdictions have abolished parole and some correctional systems incorporate release mechanisms in which prisoners are entitled to spend part of the sentence in the community without having to take any active steps towards self-improvement.[15] Prisoners are managed, supervised and regulated.[16] The very term 'corrections' connotes this unidirectional exchange: it refers to people who are corrected, not those who correct themselves.

In contrast, a properly constructed community custody order transfers much of this 'sentence management' into the hands of the offender. He or she must actively comply with court ordered conditions such as following treatment. Indeed, the presence of a house arrest condition requires the offender to contemplate the organization of his or her life with greater care than the average person; court authorized absences cover a limited amount of time, and offenders must be prudent to ensure that they have returned home by the specified hour. As will be seen in a later chapter (5), this pressure creates considerable stress upon community custody offenders, but also carries benefits.

As Sykes (1958) pointed out, prisoners are subject to confinement in two ways; they are confined within a specific institution, and once in prison their freedom of action is further limited. Sykes describes this in the following way: 'the inmate suffers from what we have called a loss of autonomy in that he is subjected to a vast body of rules and commands which are designed to control his behaviour in minute detail' (1958, p. 73).[17] Although community custody prisoners are also confined to a specific location (except for court-authorized absences, the equivalent of temporary passes from prison), they have far more freedom of movement within their own homes. This less restrictive lifestyle should empower prisoners to assume more control over their lives (and the lives of others such as children, for whom they are responsible).

Related to the active nature of community custody is the notion of flexibility and what Ball and Lilly (1986) refer to as the virtue of 'reversibility'. Once the basic common elements have been established (to confer some definition and predictability upon the sanction), community custody orders are crafted to respond to the specific needs of individual offenders. Conditions are devised to address particular issues in offenders' lives. In contrast, imprisonment casts all prisoners in the same general mould. Individualization is minimal, and two offenders with very different needs will be treated similarly. As well, if community custody regimes permit periodic reviews of the order, courts can review the offender's progress and gauge whether the individual, non-statutory conditions imposed from the outset are still necessary and useful.

Private versus public imprisonment

Prisons are visible public institutions, and much of the stigma that attaches to prisoners derives from the very public nature of penal sequestration. The experience of imprisonment is public; indeed one of the defining characteristics of the prison is the highly restricted privacy permitted inmates. Being confined to one's residence is a private experience, limited to the offender and the people with whom he shares the residence.[18] A sanction that permits punishment in so private a fashion is clearly superior to the public debasement accompanied by admission to custody. It represents a further step in the evolution of prison policy, and is inconsistent with the trend towards humiliating and public sanctions (see O'Malley, 2004; Pratt, 2000).

Is community custody the equivalent of institutional detention?

If there are (or should be) so many differences between the two forms of imprisonment (institutional and community-based), is it plausible to classify community custody as a term of imprisonment? A common theme in the sentencing alternatives literature, and particularly with respect to home confinement, is that being confined to one's residence is not a particularly onerous experience. Some criminal justice professionals hold this view. Malcom Davies cites a correctional official in California who described home

confinement as 'sitting around watching TV, and getting someone pregnant' (Davies, 1993, p. 17). Probation officers charged with supervising
community custody offenders in Canada have expressed the view that
community custody has little impact on the life of the offender (Roberts,
Maloney and Vallis, 2003). Criminal justice professionals in Canada sometimes express the view encapsulated by one probation officer who described
the community custody sanction as 'probation by another name'.

As well, some appellate courts have rejected the notion that community
custody can ever match the status of a sanction that carries the same impact
as prison. For example, in Canada, the Alberta Court of Appeal described the
Canadian community custody sentence in the following terms: 'It is not his
prison. What is staying in the comfort of one's own home, sleeping in one's
own bed, remaining with one's family, phoning, watching TV, listening to
the radio or stereo, and reading whenever one wants? In essence it is carrying
on with one's life, except possibly for working. We cannot equate that with
actual custody . . . The citizens of this country would never equate house
arrest with prison' (*R. v. Brady*, pp. 522–3[19]). The New South Wales Court
of Criminal Appeal made the same point with respect to home detention:
'Any suggestion that such inconvenient limitations upon unfettered liberty
equate in any way at all to being locked up full-time in a prison cell . . .
should not be accepted' (*R. v. Jurisic*, p. 295).

Interviews with offenders and families around the world support a rather
different perspective on the issue. If properly constructed, this sanction can
approach the punitiveness of a jail term, even if some community custody
orders may fall short of the penal equivalence of custody. Moreover, what this
sanction loses in mere punitiveness it gains in other ways relating to reparation and restoration. For most offences, the most critical and sceptical con-
stituency regarding community custody – the public – is more interested in
reparation than punishment. In a later chapter (7), I shall provide evidence
that the public will accept community custody as an acceptable substitute
sanction, if the sentence carries significant restrictions on the offender's
liberty, and if these restrictions – and the consequences of violating them –
are properly constructed and explained to the public.

However, there seems little question that for the vast majority of people, home is a more congenial location than prison in which to pass time.
Most scholars agree on this point (e.g. Clear, 1997[20]). This is one reason
why statutory regimes that require judges to match prison time to community custody time make little sense; the sanctions are not, in Morris and
Tonry's (1990) sense, isomorphically interchangeable. Community custody
sentences should be longer than the term of custody which might otherwise

be imposed. The matching procedure, according to which a court imposes six months' custody and then allows the offender to serve exactly six months at home, was abandoned in Canada shortly after the community custody regime was introduced. This move followed a guideline judgement from the Supreme Court that allowed judges to impose a longer conditional sentence than the term of imprisonment which would have been served in a correctional institution (*R. v. Proulx*).

The more desirable nature of community custody is also apparent from responses of prisoners themselves. A number of studies have been conducted with offenders serving community custody sentences (including one for this volume). This literature will be reviewed in a later chapter of this volume, but for the present it is simply necessary to note that a clear message from that literature is that people prefer community custody to spending time in prison. This finding emerges whenever offenders are asked about the two sanctions.[21] Research conducted by the Home Office found that the mere prospect of being released from prison to home detention (HDC) affected prisoners' behaviour while they were still in custody (see Dodgson et al., 2001). However, this preference is not based solely on the perception that community custody is easier; it also offers more opportunities than prison.

Community custody should not therefore be described to the public as the exact equivalent of imprisonment. The lack of direct equivalence in terms of penal value has been recognized around the world, and there are several ways of demonstrating this. The fact that imprisonment serves as a 'back-up' sanction in the event of non-compliance demonstrates that it is a more severe sanction. If the sanctions were equivalent, one could hardly serve as a back-up for the other – it would be tantamount to imposing a fine on a person in an attempt to compel them to pay a previously imposed fine. In addition, some statutory frameworks carry a condition that community custody cannot be imposed on an offender convicted of an offence carrying a mandatory term of imprisonment.[22] If community custody were the direct equivalent of custody, such a condition would be unnecessary. The fact that prison is, almost always, a more onerous sanction than a community custody sentence *of the same length* does not mean that the latter sanction is not a form of imprisonment. Nor does it mean that serving a sentence of custody at home is an easy sanction.

What's in a name?
Community custody sanctions carry different labels around the world, including: 'home incarceration', 'home detention', 'house arrest', 'home

confinement', 'conditional sentence of imprisonment', 'domiciliary detention', 'community control', 'correctional supervision' and many other
terms. The name applied to the sentence is worthy of some consideration,
as it will play a role in shaping public and professional reaction. There are
two general directions that can be taken, each with its advantages and drawbacks. The name could invoke a more intensive form of probation, such as
intensive supervision probation. This term captures the fact that the sanction is more rigorous than conventional probation, and also that it is served
in the community.

On the other hand, this terminology may associate community custody
too closely with probation, thereby undermining (on a symbolic level), its
carceral nature and by implication its ability to replace imprisonment. Calling the sanction 'home detention' or 'home confinement' makes the nature
abundantly clear (if all offenders subject to the sanction are in fact restricted
to their residence), yet fails to capture the more general nature of the disposition. In several countries, house arrest is merely one of many conditions
that may be imposed on the offender, and it may not even be the most
frequently imposed.[23] The term used in South Africa – 'correctional supervision' – fails to clarify exactly what the sanction entails.

The more radical route is to use a name that conveys to the world a sense
of what community custody is supposed to be, namely a term of imprisonment. This approach was adopted by legislators in Canada when they named
the sanction a conditional *sentence of imprisonment* (rather than simply a conditional sentence).[24] Using such terminology may help to crystallize in the
minds of offenders, victims and criminal justice professionals the notion of
community custody. The deficiency of this strategy is that as long as conventional conceptions of imprisonment predominate, such a label will be seen
as a paradox; the offender is ordered to serve a sentence of imprisonment,
yet is free to live at home. Indeed, the conditional sentencing regime has
come under much criticism from the public and media for this very reason.
Adding the word 'conditional' simply creates more confusion and fails to
change the fact that the sanction is still seen by many as a legal fiction.

To some degree, this understandable reaction reveals the close link in the
public mind between custody and institutionalized imprisonment. For most
people, a sentence of custody must involve committal to a secure institution.
Open custody, or minimum security facilities often attract negative media
commentary, or are decried by populist politicians because they are 'not
really prison'.[25] Popular conceptions of imprisonment have yet to embrace
the idea that custody can mean custody at home. It is this way of thinking
that community custody is conceived to transform. In order to be acceptable

to the public, community custody must be portrayed as another stage in the evolution of imprisonment.

As noted, the earliest use of imprisonment was to ensure the presence of the accused at trial, or to detain an individual (temporarily) deemed to be dangerous. The concept of periods of detention, calibrated in length to reflect the seriousness of the offence or the culpability of the offender would have been quite foreign to the ancient world. In Elizabethan England detention was used to isolate the individual, and no thought was given to creating an environment in which other objectives might be pursued. When imprisonment first began to be used on a widespread scale as a punishment, it did not include time off for good behaviour, or the possibility of discretionary release on parole, but those forms of relief eventually became part of the administration of prison sentences around the world.

Today, flat-time sentencing, in which prisoners serve every day of the sentence imposed in court, is relatively rare, being restricted to certain American states. Over the past fifty years, many jurisdictions have also witnessed the introduction of weekend or periodic custody as a sanction, with the prisoner signing in at 5 pm on Friday evening and out again on Sunday night.[26] This version of imprisonment would have seemed very radical to the Victorians, but is routinely accepted, and indeed supported by the public around the world,[27] as it permits the offender to discharge his or her sentence while continuing to work and support a family.

Community custody can easily be mistaken by critics for something far more punitive. The purpose of home detention is not to replace a 300-bed facility with 300 personal prisons. Rather, it is to replace the concept of communal, penal sequestration with individual penal confinement, in a way that allows the offender to retain a considerable degree of personal autonomy and to assume some responsibility for his life choices.

Community custody and the purposes of sentencing

Despite the volume of publications on home confinement, very few have explored the relationship between community custody and the objectives of sentencing.[28] Sanctions are conceived to promote the purposes of sentencing. As with all other sentences, community custody must 'be evaluated primarily by its capacity to promote the objectives of a well-developed sentencing system' (Bagaric, 2002, p. 435). Many Western jurisdictions, including New Zealand and Canada, have codified these objectives. In the USA, the guideline systems of many states and the federal sentencing guidelines[29] identify a number of purposes that sentencing is designed to achieve.

Although the mix of purposes varies from country to country, a number are common to most jurisdictions, including deterrence, incapacitation, rehabilitation and retribution. More recently, restorative goals or considerations have been added to the list in a number of countries (see Braithwaite, 1999; Roberts and Roach, 2003; Walgrave, 2002).

Some dispositions – like institutional custody – are relatively limited in the number of objectives that they promote. Imprisonment can punish and incapacitate (for a limited period of time), but does little to rehabilitate the prisoner, restore him or her to the community or reconcile victims with offenders. Indeed, the prison usually impedes progress towards these restorative objectives by depriving the offender of the opportunity (and means) to make amends, or reform his life. Community custody on the other hand, has far more potential in this regard (see Rackmill, 1994).[30] Appropriately constructed, community custody can deter as effectively as prison, and yet also contribute to rehabilitative and restorative goals.

Little needs to be said about the effectiveness of prison and community custody with respect to two utilitarian sentencing objectives. Community custody is clearly a more effective way of promoting rehabilitation than custody. Aside from the lack of adequate opportunities and rehabilitation programs in prison, the environment is hardly conducive to life improvement. Through the conditions imposed, community custody can encourage offenders to assume life changes that would have been difficult if not inconceivable in prison. To date, much of the interest in home confinement – particularly when accompanied by electronic monitoring – has been from the perspective of toughening an intermediate sanction. Yet the concept has great potential to engineer changes in offenders' lives through more humane interventions than mere threats and surveillance. This reality is not reflected in the evaluation literature on community custody, where most studies explore issues relating to re-offending. The few studies that have explored the issue have found positive results. For example, in an early study involving home confinement offenders in California, Rubin (1990) found that these individuals had reduced their drug and alcohol use, and that these reductions carried over into life after the sentence had ended.[31]

If community custody carries a clear edge in terms of rehabilitation, the same cannot be said with respect to incapacitation. The incapacitation achieved by home confinement rests to a large degree on the offender's desire to comply with conditions in order to avoid committal to secure custody. Incapacitation cannot be assured with respect to offenders in their homes, without the most intrusive surveillance techniques. For this reason, offenders who pose a serious risk should not be candidates for a term of community custody. Most statutory regimes have an exclusion to this effect. However, only a small number of offenders need to be excluded on these grounds.

Community custody and offender compliance

Before examining the question of whether community custody can deter offenders, it is worth addressing a related issue: compliance. All sanctions encourage or attempt to enforce compliance. In a recent work, Bottoms (2001) has conceptualized compliance as comprising several forms: instrumental, normative, constraint-based, and compliance-based on routine activities. Instrumental or prudential compliance involves the use of incentives and disincentives. Generally speaking, prison emphasizes the latter far more than the former. Strong disincentives exist to elicit prisoners' compliance with institutional rules. One of the few incentives involves the possibility of early release in those jurisdictions in which parole exists. Community custody also confronts the offender with a powerful disincentive: non-compliance will result in arrest and confinement in a prison cell. But there should also be strong incentives built into the regime. Continued compliance with conditions such as curfews, community service and the like should result in relaxation of these conditions.

Constraint-based compliance involves the imposition of physical requirements or restrictions on the individual offender. Constraint-based compliance is obviously easier to achieve when the offender is in prison. However, house arrest, accompanied by electronic monitoring, can approach the level of control present in an institution, at least with respect to ensuring compliance with a requirement to remain in a specific location (the home). Bottoms (2001) identifies 'a central political problem for community penalties . . . by their nature, they inevitably find it more difficult to deliver constraint based physical restrictions on an individual than does the prison' (pp. 92–3). In comparison to other community-based penalties, community custody has a clear advantage in this respect. Compliance based on habit or routine is another of the central advantages of community custody. Prison disrupts daily routines, and creates new and artificial ones that carry few positive benefits. In contrast, community custody permits and encourages the offender to preserve positive routines such as work and family business, by identifying these as court-authorized exceptions to home confinement. As well, community custody creates salutary new routines – for example when the court orders the house-bound offender to comply with treatment programs and regimes.

Finally, normative compliance in Bottoms' typology takes several forms, one of which is highly relevant to a sanction that keeps the offender in the community. Much of the power of normative compliance derives from the preservation of 'key social relationships that link the compliant individual to other individuals or social groups' (2001, p. 91). This returns us to the very essence of community custody: the offender is kept in a social milieu which promotes pro-social conduct. If the community custody sanction is properly conceived by the court and administered by community corrections officers, the prospects for normative compliance are enhanced immeasurably. From the perspective of achieving compliance, then, community custody offers significantly more than either imprisonment or the other alternatives.

Deterrence

In theory, community custody can offer the same degree of deterrence as its institutional counterpart. Being restricted to one's home and prevented from participating in a wide range of social activities is a punishment that most people would want to avoid. In practice, however, much will depend upon the nature of conditions imposed, and the manner in which offenders serving time at home are supervised. If the conditions are not particularly stringent, offenders will regard the sanction as little more intrusive than probation, and will be tempted to violate conditions with impunity. Some community custody sentences imposed in Canada have carried an 11 pm to 7 am curfew. This is so close to the routine daily life of many people that it hardly represents a penal restriction or a punishment. As well, the courts' reaction to breaches will be critical (see below). An indulgent response to breaches of conditions will encourage more breaches and undermine still further the deterrent power of the sanction.

Critics of community penalties sometimes argue that they fail to provide adequate general or individual deterrence, because although the offender's liberty is structured, it is not restricted to any great degree. The public, too, are likely to be sceptical of the deterrent function of community penalties (including community custody), as the popular view of deterrence assumes a clear relationship between the severity of a sanction, and its deterrent power. Indeed, this has been one of repeated criticisms of the sanction in popular discourse. This may explain why a recent poll in the USA found that the sample was almost equally divided on the question of whether house arrest constituted an effective form of protection against crime (University of Arkansas, 1998).

How can the state ensure that the offender will be deterred by the prospect of being confined to his home? To the extent that criminal sanctions deter offenders, can the threat of confinement at home (with conditions) inhibit further offending to the same extent as imprisonment? The answer is probably that it depends upon a variety of factors.

Critics of community custody would probably argue that the decreased level of correctional control over offenders serving this sanction is likely to result in higher rates of re-offending. As well, absent a restriction on imposing a community custody sentence on someone who has already served such a disposition, offenders may well feel less inclined to refrain from further offending. However, this line of reasoning overlooks the significant body of research that shows that the severity of any punishment has only a limited impact on the probability of re-offending (see von Hirsch et al., 1999, and Doob and Webster, 2004, for reviews). Put another way, when background variables (such as criminal record) are controlled for, the recidivism rate is approximately the same for offenders released from prison for less severe sanctions, such as probation. Langan's (1998) finding is typical: the recidivism rate of probationers was not significantly different from the rate associated with prisoners. Other researchers, such as Petersilia and Turner (1998) report that prisoners released from custody had a higher recidivism rate than probationers. Nevertheless, the apprehension about higher re-offending of community-based offenders needs addressing, if only because many members of the public believe that offenders serving sentences in the community represent a threat.

The literature on electronic monitoring in the USA provides some insight into the relationship between community custody and re-offending. Of interest is the recidivism rate of offenders serving sentences at home relative to the re-offending rates of offenders committed to prison. In making such comparisons, it is of course necessary to control for 'pre-treatment' or a priori risk of re-offending: community sentence offenders typically represent a lower risk for re-offending. Indeed, to an important degree that is why they are serving their sentences in the community rather than prison. The early research on this issue failed or was unable to control for relevant background variables (see Rogers and Jolin, 1989), but a review of these studies concluded that 'electronically monitored offenders have generally fared neither better nor worse than similar offenders sentenced to more restrictive sanctions' (Rogers and Jolin, 1989, p. 141).

There is little likelihood of community custody offering the same degree of deterrent value as institutional custody if offenders perceive it as being little different from an enhanced form of probation. An early lesson of the research literature is that deterrence is a subjective phenomenon; offender perceptions are therefore critical. As will be seen in a later chapter, offenders' reactions towards community custody sanctions vary, depending upon the nature and intrusiveness of the conditions attached to the order. The experience in Canada and New South Wales sustains the view that if community custody includes house arrest, and other conditions that offenders experience as being punitive, they regard the sanction as very different from probation. Although they may prefer community custody to imprisonment, the former sanction is clearly something that they wish to avoid in the future. In order to maximize the deterrent value of community custody, the constraints upon the offender have to be real, and the threat of committal to prison must be realistic.

Research into offender reactions to community custody also speaks to the issue of individual deterrence. In order for a sentence to serve as a deterrent, offenders must be aware that violations of conditions will be detected and punished. But few jurisdictions employ the kind of monitoring equipment that can detect violations of some conditions. How, for example, can a probation officer know whether an offender granted three hours away from home for the purposes of food shopping is in fact in designated rather than prohibited locations? Probation officers in Canada have expressed considerable scepticism about compliance with court-authorized absences from home (Roberts et al., 2003).

Most of the offenders interviewed for the pilot programme evaluation of home detention in New Zealand 'thought it would be easy to break the rules without being caught' (Church and Dunstan, 1997, p. 6). As one New Zealand home detainee expressed it: 'The home detention officer gives me permission to go [to a specific destination] ... I might just detour down to the pub and have a couple of drinks and I'll be back in time' (cited in (Church and Dunstan, 1997, p. 6).[32] Similarly, an offender in Canada said that 'I've got three hours on Saturday for [for shopping]. How do they know where I might be going?' (Roberts et al., 2003). Under such conditions, deterrence will be hard to achieve, suggesting that home confinement should be restricted to lower-risk individuals who need few deterrents to comply with conditions.

At the end of the day, the deterrent power of the sanction will depend upon the effective administration of the sanction, and this will reflect the correctional resources devoted to the supervision of community custody offenders. When the community custody regime was created in Canada, no new resources were devoted to supervising offenders placed on the sanction. These individuals are supervised by probation officers, working as conditional sentence supervisors. Provincial correctional authorities undertook some re-assignment of caseloads: community custody cases receive more intensive supervision than the other population (probationers), but caseloads are still far too high for effective supervision in that country.

In addition, a guideline judgment from the Supreme Court in 2000 directed trial judges to make the regime tougher, by imposing house arrest in most cases. In fact, the number and intrusiveness of conditions imposed increased significantly as a consequence of this decision, and also because judges were using the sentence for a broader range of cases, including higher risk individuals who need more structure in their daily lives (see Roberts 2002a). Courts generally impose more (and more restrictive) conditions on the higher risk cases and this means that more is expected of the supervising officers. As a result, one of the themes emerging from interviews with community custody cases in Canada was that a significant minority of offenders felt confident that they could violate conditions without detection. Lack of correctional resources, therefore, can undermine the deterrent power of the sanction.

Finally, one last element of community custody speaks to the issue of deterrence. Bottoms (2001) drawing upon research by Sherman (1992) notes that 'deterrence works best for those persons who have strong ties of attachment to familial or social groups or institutions, in a context where those groups or institutions clearly disapprove normatively of the behaviour at which the deterrent sanction is aimed' (p. 104). This is one of the explanations for the relative failure of the prison to deter. The individuals to whom the prisoner is attached, and who are likely to disapprove of the conduct giving rise to his status are the very people from whom he has been separated. While correctional officers, too, will disapprove of the conduct, their power to amplify a message of deterrence is undermined by the agonistic relationship and the power imbalance, that they share with prisoners. Instead of these people, an offender committed to custody will associate with other prisoners, who, due to the prison environment and their pre-existing values, are less likely to disapprove of criminal conduct.

Offenders serving terms of community custody, however, are kept, by order of the court, among the people closest to them: family members and partners. Moreover, the fact that the conditions of the order create hardships for these other individuals is likely to sensitize offenders still further to the consequences of their offending, and thereby contribute to any deterrent effect. This is particularly true when the offender is a relatively young person, living at home with his or her parents. Interviews with young adults in this situation in Canada revealed a keen awareness among the offenders both of their parents' disapproval of their conduct, and of the impact of the sentence upon members of the family.[33] Finally, those interviews also revealed that family members' awareness that their loved one had been spared the experience of custody brought the family closer together. The affection of parents and their simultaneous disapproval of the offending behaviour was clearly exercising a powerful influence on the offender. This was likely to serve as a stronger deterrent than the legal threat of committal to custody in the event of breaching of conditions.

Response to breach of conditions

The thorny question of how the state should respond to breach of a community custody order will be explored in a later chapter. This is a crucial aspect of any community custody regime. However, it is clearly relevant to the question of deterrence. The three elements of a penalty that deter are certainty, severity and celerity. Breaches of conditions that pass unpunished, or, worse, undetected, will encourage recalcitrance among offenders, and lead to the perception that this sanction is a form of enhanced probation. As well, there is the argument that breaches of prison conditions are punished expeditiously; prisoners caught AWOL are returned to custody. If community custody is a form of imprisonment, the response to breach must be more rigorous than that which applies to breach of other community penalties.

The consequence is that community custody regime should permit a rapid breach hearing, at which the offender has the opportunity to explain the breach. Absent a justification, there should be a presumption that he will enter custody, and for the balance of the order. Anything less severe than this can only undermine the deterrent power of the sanction in the eyes of the offender and the community. This policy also sets community custody clearly apart from the breach arrangements for many community penalties. For example, the Criminal Justice and Court Services Act creates a presumption of custody upon the second breach of a community order. Breaching a community custody order is a more serious act that requires a more rigorous response from the court. The offender serving a term of community custody is deemed to be serving a sentence of imprisonment, and this conception cannot be sustained if substantive breaches are treated in the same manner as breaches of community penalties.

Communicative theories of sentencing

Communicative theories are central to the current debate about sentencing. Consider first the censure-based account of sentencing advanced by von Hirsch (e.g. 1993), according to which the sanction should express censure of the offender, and impose punishments according to the central guiding principle of proportionality. Community custody may offer great potential in terms of restorative objectives (see below), but it creates some important difficulties for proportional sentencing. The principle of proportionality is now codified in many countries such as Canada and New Zealand.[34] According to this perspective, sanctions should be arrayed in a manner commensurate with the seriousness of the offence. This requires a hierarchy of both crimes and punishments. Creating a hierarchy of severity is relatively straightforward for many sanctions such as fines and imprisonment. However, the inherently protean character of community custody makes it hard to locate the sanction on a scale of severity, since so much depends upon the number and nature of conditions imposed as well as the likely penalty to be imposed in the event that these conditions are breached (see Wasik, 1994).[35] Yet it is not impossible to fix the sanction on a scale of severity. This issue will be discussed further in the final chapter.

Community custody also helps to promote an important sentencing principle related to proportionality based theories: restraint with respect to the use of custody. This principle is codified in many jurisdictions, and requires judges to impose custody only when no other form of punishment will achieve the goals of sentencing. Transposed to the level of sentence administration, the principle of restraint requires that prisoners be detained at the least restrictive level consistent with correctional goals. Community custody is the least restrictive form of imprisonment and therefore offers courts a way of adhering to the principle of restraint.

What of the other communicative theories? Antony Duff is one of several theorists who regard the sentencing process as an exercise in communication.[36] According to Duff, 'criminal punishment should be conceived of as a communicative enterprise that aims to communicate to offenders the censure they deserve for their crimes, and thus to bring them to repent their crimes, to reform themselves, and to reconcile themselves with those they have wronged' (2001, p. 129). To expect all such outcomes from a single sanction may be somewhat optimistic, and few offenders who have served community custody sentences will actually complete the arduous journey from repentance through reformation to reconciliation. Nevertheless, the potential to achieve some or all of these benefits resides more with community custody than many other sanctions, especially imprisonment. The concept of community is central to Duff's position: 'Punishment as thus conceived is consistent with, indeed expressive of, the defining values of a liberal political community. It addresses offenders, not as outlaws who have forfeited their standing as citizens, but as full members of the normative political community; it is inclusionary rather than exclusionary . . .'

(pp. 129–30). And of course, community custody is a communitarian form of imprisonment; the offender is constrained but not rejected.

Imprisonment is a punishment that is anathema to a communitarian sentencing perspective. The prison excludes and degrades, and offers no forum in which the offender may pursue avenues leading to repentance, reformation or reconciliation. How does community custody fit into this scheme? Community custody offers a penal response that carries a very different communication from imprisonment. The message to offenders who are imprisoned is one of exclusion: they are being excluded from, and denied almost all the fruits of, membership in the society to which they once belonged. Offenders detained in their own homes receive a quite different message, one that emphasizes the links with the society against which they have offended. Their freedom is significantly curtailed. Privileges accorded others, and taken for granted by free members of society, are withdrawn from community custody offenders. The extent to which these privileges is withdrawn reflects the seriousness of the offender's criminal conduct. But the essential link between a community and one of its members is preserved.

The reach of most community custody regimes fails to include the most serious forms of offending. This too is consistent with Duff's penitential theory of punishment, according to which imprisonment becomes an appropriate response to these most serious offenders because they have broken the bonds tying them to their community (Duff, 2001, pp. 150–1).

Restorative justice
Restorative justice has made rapid inroads into the criminal justice systems of most Western nations (Braithwaite, 1999; Johnstone, 2002; von Hirsch et al., 2003; Walgrave, 2002). Most restorative justice initiatives involve diverting suspects and accused persons away from traditional processing by the courts. However, restorative principles have also been applied to the sentencing process (see discussion in Young and Hoyle, 2003).

At first glance, the restorative elements of a community custody sanction may not be apparent. After all, restorative justice attempts to replace a punitive paradigm with one that privileges restoration. Some restorative justice advocates would withhold the label 'restorative' from any sanction that claims to be a form of imprisonment. As well, some restorative justice advocates see little role for proportionality in restorative sentencing (e.g. Braithwaite, 1999).[37] Certainly, a community custody order is not a 'pure' restorative sanction in any sense of the word. Were it such, it would be unable to assume anything other than a small proportion of the custodial caseload.

Community custody is more consistent with a view of restorative justice that incorporates some retributive element (e.g. Daly, 2003; Duff, 2002;[38] see discussion in Young and Hoyle, 2003; Johnstone, 2002, pp. 107–9). The hitherto sharp distinction between restorative and retributive justice is far less apparent today, and the community custody sanction is consistent with this amalgamation of the two perspectives.

Despite its punitive character, community custody generates important opportunities for the kinds of transformations pursued by restorative justice. One important objective of restorative justice is to encourage offenders to assume responsibility for their offending, and to express regret. Conferences involving victims and offenders attempt to evoke feelings of remorse and shame in the offender (Daly, 2003[39]). Community custody offenders are confronted on a daily basis, with people aware of their offending, and on whom that offending has had an impact. This may well promote acceptance of responsibility, and if not an expression of apology to the victim, at least it may increase a sense of remorse. And, the offender's continued presence in the community will enhance the likelihood that compensation to the crime victim is ordered or offered.

The hybrid sanction

By promoting some restorative and punitive objectives, community custody can be considered a hybrid sanction, one that incorporates elements of punishment and restoration.

This distinguishes it from 'purer' dispositions such as probation, which is aimed at rehabilitating the offender, and prison which is primarily punitive (in order to denounce and deter), and can offer the offender little in terms of rehabilitation. Imprisonment offers almost nothing with respect to restorative justice;[40] indeed, the prison represents the antithesis of restoration, as it isolates the offender, breaking links with the community and the victim. It also deprives offenders of the means by which to make reparative gestures; apologies will pass unheeded in a prison cell, and more practical steps to repair the damage will be prevented by the prisoner's inability to generate income.

This perspective on the Canadian sanction was endorsed by the Canadian Supreme Court in a leading judgment (*R.* v. *Proulx*). In that decision, the Court examined the sanction in light of the codified objectives of sentencing. These include the usual utilitarian goals of deterrence, denunciation and rehabilitation. However, in addition, Parliament added the following restorative objectives to section 718 of the *Criminal Code*:

(d) to provide reparations for harm done to victims or to the community
and
(e) to promote a sense of responsibility in offenders, and acknowledgement
of the harm done to victims and to the community.

In *Proulx*, the Court noted that the restorative objective would be
achieved by the imposition of a community custody sanction that would
promote these objectives. However, the Court also recognized that these
restorative considerations were not the only purposes of sentencing
and must be balanced, in the construction of the community sentence order, with the punitive objectives of sentencing, and the codified
fundamental principle of proportionality.

Although there are some dangers associated with this concatenation of
restorative and retributive perspectives in sentencing (see Roberts and
Roach, 2003), the Court's direction regarding community custody points
the way to an accommodation between these perspectives. Like any com-
promise, this one carries dangers for both sides. Nevertheless, by keeping
the offender in the community, the sanction permits the kinds of initiatives
associated with restorative justice. At the same time, the imposition of rigorous conditions such as house arrest helps to ensure that the sanction carries
the penal equivalence of a custodial term, which is important to establish
public and judicial confidence in the sanction. Finally, by modulating the
number and intrusiveness of judicially imposed conditions to reflect the
seriousness of the offence, proportional considerations in sentencing can
be preserved.

Victim impact and input

Another issue that has arisen since the early scholarship on community
custody concerns the potential impact on victims. One of the most striking
transformations of sentencing in recent years concerns the role of the victim
(see Sebba, 1996). For many years crime victims were assigned the role of
complainant, and had no role in the sentencing hearing. Now, victims in
all Western nations have the opportunity to become an active participant
in the sentencing process. In most countries, the vehicle by which their
participation is achieved is the victim statement, or victim impact statement
(VIS) as it is known in North America. The VIS permits victims to express
their feelings about the crime to the court, and possibly to communicate
with the offender as well (Roberts, 2003c). Although most VIS schemes

attempt to focus the content of the statement on the harm inflicted or loss incurred, many victims insert material relating to the sentence that should be imposed, sometimes including direct sentencing recommendations.[41]

Victims of serious crimes of violence are sometimes dissatisfied with their treatment by the court and the severity of the sentence imposed on the offender. There are many reasons why this is so, having to do with the nature of sentencing in an adversarial system, the amount of information provided to victims and the way in which they are treated by criminal justice professionals such as prosecutors, and when testifying, defence counsel. It is important therefore to determine how much of this dissatisfaction may be due to the imposition of the community custody sentence, and how much is due to other factors. It is equally important to distinguish between the reactions of victims, and the policy positions taken by victims' advocates, or groups representing crime victims. These latter may not always reflect the views of all victims.

For crime victims, community custody carries advantages and disadvantages. Any sanction which permits the offender to keep working,[42] and therefore be able to pay compensation will be welcomed. Imprisoning an offender brings no tangible benefit to the crime victim. However, victims sometimes express objection to a sentence which in their eyes depreciates the seriousness of the crime. In jurisdictions in which there is a low ceiling on the length of sentence that can be imposed, or where there are statutorily excluded offences (which usually include serious crimes of violence), the opposition of victims may not arise. In countries such as Canada, where a community custody sentence can be and sometimes is imposed for a serious crime of violence, victims are at times upset. This is particularly likely if, as a result of living in a small community, the victim encounters the offender on the street as a result of a court-authorized absence from home. Indeed, throughout the brief history of the sanction in Canada, victims' advocates have opposed the use of the community custody sentence for crimes of violence (Young and Roberts, 2001).

The dissatisfaction springs from the perceived leniency of the sanction, as well from an perception that for a serious crime of violence, no community sanction, however severe, can adequately mark the crime. A vehicular homicide case that reached the British Columbia Court of Appeal in 2003 is typical of the kind of crime that causes additional pain to victims if the offender is permitted to serve his sentence in the community. The offenders were two young adult males, who were racing their cars at well over sixty miles an hour down a street on which the limit was fifty miles an hour. They were subsequently responsible for the death of a female pedestrian. An offence of this level of seriousness usually carries a custodial sentence in Canada. However, in recognition of some mitigating factors, the trial court judge imposed a sentence of community custody, of the longest possible duration (two years less one day). The sentence was appealed by the prosecution, but subsequently upheld by the BC Court of Appeal.[43] Upon hearing the outcome of the appeal, a relative of the family stated that 'It's a joke. She's in a box in the ground. They get the comforts of home.'[44] In another vehicular homicide case in Ontario, a man was sentenced to twenty-one months of community custody after being convicted of two counts of dangerous driving causing death. Upon hearing of the sentence, the husband of one of the victims said 'we feel like losers'.[45]

The reactions of victims are understandable. Criminal justice professionals are used to the complexities and seeming contradictions of the justice system. They are familiar with the concept of serving time in the community, and for them (or most of them) community custody is an accepted part of the penal landscape, if only in the context of parole. Victims of violence, however, may find community custody troubling in two ways. First, it may seem to violate truth in sentencing; and second, it may well be personally troubling for them to see the offender leaving the court room and going home, despite being told that he has been sentenced to a term of custody. They are responding to a term of community custody as though it were a form of probation.

Conclusion

To summarize, community custody should be seen as a distinct form of imprisonment, rather than just another community penalty. In order to ensure the rational application of the sanction, community custody must be located on a sanctioning scale. Harland (1998) proposes a multidimensional scaling scheme, by which different sanctions are scaled according to their ability to achieve a number of objectives.[46] Community custody can be scaled in such a fashion to ensure that it is roughly fixed within a rational scale of penalties. The sanction has the potential to promote a number of different sentencing objectives, many of which are beyond the power of prison to achieve.

At the same time, by virtue of the fact that this sanction is a form of imprisonment and a punitive state response to offending, it has a broader application than most other community-based or intermediate penalties, and addresses more sentencing objectives. However, whether in practice the sanction can achieve these goals and reduce the number of admissions to custody will depend in large measure upon the nature of the statutory framework. The form that community custody assumes varies considerably around the world, in terms of its structure and the conditions imposed on offenders. The next chapter reviews some representative regimes in different jurisdictions.

FOUR

Representative models of community custody

Many different models of community custody exist. No attempt will be made to describe them all; instead, a number of different versions will be examined, beginning with the conditional sentence of imprisonment created in Canada in 1996. The Canadian incarnation of community custody is particularly interesting as it represents one of the most ambitious forms of this sanction, with a broad ambit of application that includes offenders convicted of the most serious offences, including manslaughter and sexual assault. This feature of the sanction obviously increases the power of the sanction to reduce the number of admissions to custody, but also creates other problems. As well, the successes (and failures) of community custody as a sanction emerge most clearly with this model in this particular jurisdiction. The chapter is restricted to home confinement/community custody regimes pertaining to adults, although analogous sanctions exist in many countries for young offenders (e.g. Smykla and Selke, 1982).[1] For the purpose of elucidation, the Canadian sanction is presented in some detail; for brevity, counterparts in other countries are summarized more succinctly.

Canada: conditional sentence of imprisonment

The conditional sentence of imprisonment was introduced in Canada in 1996, as part of a broader sentencing reform initiative (see Daubney and Parry, 1999; Roberts and Cole, 1999). Although Canada has had a suspended sentence for many years, this is the first time that a community custody sentence has been available to sentencers. The conditional sentence is not an alternative to imprisonment; rather it is considered a form of imprisonment, the way an intermittent sentence is a form of, rather than an alternative to custody. The critical difference between the conditional sentence and other forms of custody (such as an intermittent sentence) is that the former is served in the community rather than a correctional institution.

Overall sentencing framework

The 1996 statutory reforms codified, for the first time in the country's history, the purpose and principles of sentencing. Section 718 of the *Criminal Code* identifies a fundamental purpose of sentencing and contains all the principal utilitarian sentencing objectives, including deterrence, rehabilitation and incapacitation. As well, the statement of purpose and principle includes acknowledgement of restorative objectives which have subsequently been the focus of several important judgments from the Supreme Court (see Roach, 2000; Roberts and Roach, 2003). Section 718.1 creates a 'fundamental' principle of sentencing, namely that sentences should be proportional to the seriousness of the crime and the degree of responsibility of the offender. Thus although the statement of the purpose of sentencing encompasses an eclectic mix of objectives, proportionality is central to the sentencing of adult offenders in Canada.

Statutory framework of the community custody sanction

According to s. 742.1 of the Canadian *Criminal Code,*

> Where a person is convicted of an offence, except an offence that is punishable by a minimum term of imprisonment, and the court
>
> (a) imposes a sentence of imprisonment of less than two years, and
> (b) is satisfied that serving the sentence in the community would not endanger the safety of the community and would be consistent with the fundamental purpose and principles of sentencing set out in sections 718 to 718.2,
>
> the court may, for the purposes of supervising the offender's behaviour in community, order that the offender serve the sentence in the community, subject to the offender's complying with the conditions of a conditional sentence order made under section 742.3.

Thus the statutory framework creates four pre-requisites: the offence may not be one carrying a minimum term of custody; the court must impose a term of custody under two years; the offender must not pose a risk to the community, and the imposition of such a sentence must be consistent with the statutory statement of the purpose and principles of sentencing (see above). The first two criteria are unambiguous; the others are more nebulous.

Table 4.1. *Percentage of sentences of imprisonment under two years, imposed for serious offences or offence categories, Canada.*

Offence or offence category	% of sentences of imprisonment within range of conditional sentence (up to 2 years less one day)
Assault	100
Burglary	90
Sexual abuse	87
Sexual assault	78
Major assault	66
Robbery	60

Source: Statistics Canada Data Shelf Table 2.11, available from author.

The first criterion eliminates from consideration the few offences in Canada that carry a minimum term of custody, including murder and impaired driving (second offence). The second criterion was introduced (a) to ensure that the sentence is used to replace terms of custody, and not other community-based sanctions such as probation, and (b) to restrict the conditional sentence to the less serious crimes, those resulting in shorter terms of custody (or at least shorter than two years; see Department of Justice, 1994). If judges were free to use the conditional sentence without first having to impose a term of custody, it may well be used for terms of probation – a classic case of widening the net (see discussion in chapter 6). The statutory 'ceiling' of two years less one day is, in reality, a permissive criterion, since almost all terms of custody in Canada are well under two years' duration. Thus few sentences of imprisonment are excluded from consideration on the basis of their length alone.

Table 4.1 provides an indication of the proportion of sentences of imprisonment falling within the ambit of the community custody sentence for a number of violent offence categories. As can be seen, most of the terms of custody imposed for serious crimes of violence fell within the range of the sanction. For example, almost 80 per cent of cases of sexual assault resulting in a term of custody during the period covered by the analysis were within the range of the community custody regime. This table demonstrates the broad reach of the community custody order in Canada. In 2002/3, the ninetieth percentile sentence length for crimes of violence in Canada was well under two years. In fact, the community custody 'ceiling' of two years less one day is significantly higher than community custody regimes in other parts of the world. For example, in Sweden, home detention (with electronic monitoring) can replace terms of imprisonment of three months or less.

The third criterion requires a court to undertake an assessment of the risk that the offender poses in terms of re-offending. In practice, the question of risk is usually restricted to consideration of the offender's criminal record and social circumstances. This usage of community custody provokes another question. If the offender is detained in such a facility, can he really be said to be serving a *community*-based sentence? I will return to this question in the concluding chapter. For the present it is simply worth noting that the courts in Canada have interpreted community custody to entail more than private residences. (This is consistent with developments in other jurisdictions.) The fourth criterion (that the imposition of the sentence must be consistent with the codified purpose and principles of sentencing) was added shortly after the legislation was passed (in 1997).

If the case before the court meets these four criteria, a judge has the discretion to impose a community custody order. No offences are excluded by the statute, as is the case in many other jurisdictions. Offenders convicted of some of the most serious crimes of violence and who are sentenced to very lengthy terms of imprisonment are eligible for a community custody sentence if they meet these four criteria. A relatively small number of such cases have received a community custody sanction, but they have received a disproportionate amount of attention from the media. This negative coverage of the sanction has alienated the public, and attracted considerable opposition from victims' advocates. The result has been considerable pressure on the government to further amend the community custody regime. A number of Private Member's Bills have been introduced to either repeal or restrict the sanction to non-violent cases. Most recently (in 2003), five provincial governments submitted a position paper to Parliament in which they proposed to restrict the application of the sanction.[2]

Statutory conditions
(A) COMPULSORY CONDITIONS
There are a number of compulsory conditions attached to all conditional sentence orders. According to section 742.3:

> The court shall prescribe, as conditions of a conditional sentence order, that the offender do all of the following:
>
> (a) keep the peace and be of good behaviour;
> (b) appear before the court when required to do so by the court; and

(c) notify the court or the probation officer in advance of any change of name or address, and promptly notify the court or the probation officer of any change of employment or occupation.

The offender is also required (a) to report to a supervisor within a specified period of time (and thereafter as and when required by the supervisor), and (b) to remain within the jurisdiction of the court unless written permission to leave is obtained from the court or the supervisor (section 742.3(1)(c)–(d)). The nature of the two additional conditions reflects, perhaps, the heightened concern with more closely supervising the offender placed on this sanction.

(B) OPTIONAL CONDITIONS

Before discussing the nature of the optional conditions permissible with respect to the two sanctions, it is important to understand the reasons for which optional conditions may be imposed for conditional sentences and terms of probation. It is reasonable to expect that the pattern of optional conditions attached to a probation order would differ from those ordered as part of a conditional sentence of imprisonment. First, the purpose behind, and theory underlying the two sanctions differs considerably. According to section 732.1(3)(h), the optional conditions of a probation order should be directed towards '*protecting society and for facilitating the offender's successful re-integration into the community*'. The conjunctive construction suggests that the optional elements should serve a dual function of protecting society *and* promoting the offender's rehabilitation.

In contrast, according to section 742.3(2)(f), the optional conditions of a community custody order should be aimed at '*securing the good conduct of the offender and for preventing a repetition by the offender of the same offence or the commission of other offences*'. In other words, probation conditions are aimed at promoting rehabilitation (within the context of protecting the community) while community custody conditions should attempt to prevent further offending. With such different underlying purposes, it might be expected that the kinds of optional conditions attached to the two sanctions would be quite different, although in the early days of the sanction this was not in fact the case (see Roberts, Antonowicz, and Sanders, 2000). Of course, some conditions may promote rehabilitation *and* reduce the likelihood of recidivism. Following a treatment program for a substance abuse problem is likely to promote rehabilitation by removing a risk factor from the life of the individual offender. On the other hand, other optional conditions serve very different purposes. Making restitution or performing community service may help to rehabilitate the offender, but it is harder to see how it will directly reduce the likelihood of the offender relapsing into criminality.

The enumerated optional conditions available to a court as part of a conditional sentence order do not differ substantively from the optional conditions of a probation order. There are two principal differences between the two sanctions. First, reporting to a probation officer and remaining within the jurisdiction of the court are not optional conditions of a community custody order since, as noted, they are already included as mandatory requirements (section 742.3(1)(d)(e)). Second, according to section 742.3(2)(e), the court may order the offender to attend a treatment program approved by the province in which the offender resides. In contrast, under the terms of a probation order, section 732.1(3)(g) permits the court to order the offender to actively participate in an official treatment program, but only with his consent. In practice, this distinction may make little difference, as judges seldom order treatment in the face of opposition from the offender.

Judicial powers in the event of unjustified breach of conditions
The Canadian legislation accords judges considerable discretion with which to respond to offenders found to have breached conditions without justification. After an allegation of a breach has been made, a breach hearing is conducted. If the Crown establishes, on a balance of probabilities, that the offender violated a condition of the order without justification, a sentencing court may (i) take no action (and perhaps simply admonish the recalcitrant offender); (ii) amend the conditions of the order (possibly by adding new conditions); (iii) suspend the order and commit the offender to prison for some portion of the time remaining on the order; or (iv) cancel the order, and place the offender in custody to serve the remainder of the sentence, subject to parole considerations.

The application of these provisions has resulted in relatively few offenders going to prison for breach of their orders. This, in turn, has contributed to the perception that the community custody regime in Canada is rather lax. (One cause of this perception is the nature of media coverage of community custody – see chapter 7.) If the image of Damocles is to ring true, the threat to people serving terms of custody in the community must be real; offenders must believe that a substantive and unjustified breach of their conditions will result in committal to prison. This is necessary to promote the deterrent value of the sanction as well as to maintain the integrity of the sentence in the eyes of the public and key criminal justice professionals such as judges. Of course there will be cases where an offender has wilfully violated a condition

Table 4.2. *Conditional sentences of imprisonment by offence category, Canada, 2000/1.*

	% PEI	% NS	% Ont	% Man	% Sask.	% Alberta	% BC
Violence	12	28	33	43	38	26	24
Property	52	30	38	28	37	46	37
Drugs	24	17	19	9	n/a	20	27
Other	12	25	10	20	25	8	12
Total	100	100	100	100	100	100	100

Source: Roberts (2002a).

but in a trivial way, yet has nevertheless been brought back to court, and judges need some flexibility to respond appropriately.[3]

Use of conditional sentence of imprisonment

The volume of conditional sentences imposed has nevertheless increased rapidly since its introduction. Within four years, almost 60,000 such sentences had been imposed (Hendrick, Martin, and Greenberg, 2003). Table 4.2 provides a breakdown of community custody sentences across Canada, for 2000–1. The first and perhaps most striking finding is the degree of variability across provinces with respect to the offences for which conditional sentences are imposed. As can be seen in Table 4.2, the proportion of conditional sentences imposed in 2000–1 for crimes involving violence varied from 12 per cent in Prince Edward Island, to fully 43 per cent in Manitoba. This suggests that different attitudes to the use of community custody have arisen among judges across the country, with the inevitable consequence that the probability of an offender receiving this sanction also varies considerably, depending upon the province in which he is sentenced. Aggregated across the country, crimes of violence accounted for one-third of community custody sentences.

Florida community control

The concept of community custody came to Florida much earlier than any of the other jurisdictions included in this survey. The Florida legislature enacted legislation in 1983 that created the sanction of community control. The sentence is a form of intensive supervised custody in the community. It includes surveillance on weekends and holidays, and is administered by officers with reduced caseloads, typically twenty-five offenders to one officer (Florida Corrections Commission, 2003). This caseload compares very favourably with other jurisdictions. In Canada, probation officers have mixed caseloads, supervising probation and community custody offenders. A typical caseload might be 100 offenders, with officers in some parts of the country supervising even higher numbers.

The community control sanction in Florida illustrates the variability of community custody schemes around the world. In light of the decade and state in which it was created, it is not surprising that the community custody sanction in Florida is more punitive, less restorative than any of the other regimes reviewed in this volume. Blomberg, Bales, and Reed (1993) characterize the sanction as 'a get-tough strategy that involves a series of offender surveillance and accountability measures' (p. 193). It was designed to reduce prison overcrowding and offer a punishment-oriented alternative to custody (Baird and Wagner, 1990). The maximum duration of a community control order is two years or the equivalent of the term of custody that could have been imposed according to the guidelines, whichever is less. The Florida model thus makes an interesting contrast with the Canadian version of community custody. The former stresses punishment and accountability, while the latter is far more 'restorative' in nature, reflecting the era and the statutory framework in which it was created.

Subsequent amendments to the original legislation create a number of statutory exclusions. An offender may not be placed on community control if he has been convicted of a forcible felony and has a previous forcible felony conviction. (Forcible felonies include manslaughter, robbery, aggravated assault, sexual battery, and a number of other enumerated serious offences as well as any other felony which involves the use or threat of force.)

Sentencing framework

The criminal punishment code in Florida establishes the legislative framework for sentencing. According to s. 921.002 (b), 'The primary purpose of sentencing is to punish the offender. Rehabilitation is a desired goal of the criminal justice system but is subordinate to the goal of punishment.' The next subsection states that 'The penalty imposed is commensurate with the severity of the primary offense and the circumstances surrounding the primary offense.' Punishment is therefore the purpose of sentencing in Florida and proportionality a leading principle. The influence of proportionality is clear from the fact that the conditions imposed as part of the community control sentence 'shall be commensurate with the seriousness of the offense' (Florida Statutes, Chapter 948.01 (4)). An additional principle directs judges to reserve custody for 'offenders convicted of serious offenses and certain offenders who have long prior records, in order to maximize the finite capacities of state and correctional facilities'.[4]

Statutory conditions

As with the Canadian (and other) community custody regimes, community control in Florida carries standard conditions which include: contact with a supervisory officer, mandatory public service, confinement to residence and electronic monitoring. Other conditions that may be imposed include restitution in 'money or kind', revocation of driving privileges, deprivation of non-essential activities or 'other appropriate restrictions on the offender's liberty' (Florida Statutes, Chapter 948 3(a)). As well, a 'basket clause' provides that the court may impose other such conditions that it deems appropriate. Every six months, offenders on community control are subject to a review by their supervisor. A similar review is conducted within ninety days of the offender's scheduled termination of the order. If the offender is returned to court on an allegation of a violation of the order, the court shall 'give the offender an opportunity to be fully heard' and in the event of revocation of the order, the response may be quite punitive. The court may impose 'any sentence that it could have imposed at the time the offender was placed on community control'. In addition, however, the court may modify or continue the order as it stands.

One characteristic of the community custody sanction in Florida is that offenders placed on community control must 'as a condition of any placement' pay the department [of Corrections] a total sum of money equal to the total month or portion of a month of supervision times the court-ordered amount (FS 948.09(1)(a)1.). There are a number of grounds on which the offender may be exempt from all or part of the payment.[5]

Use of community control in Florida

Since the sanction was introduced, almost a quarter of a million offenders in Florida have served a term on community control (Florida Corrections Commission, 2003). Unlike the conditional sentence of imprisonment in Canada, the volume of community control dispositions has been quite stable over the years. Although the number rose rapidly in the first few years (rising from 3,714 in 1984 to 12,967 in 1989), the volume has declined in recent years, from 16,230 in 1993 to 12,535 in 2001, a decline of 23 per cent (Florida Corrections Commission, 2003). In 1993, community control cases represented 17 per cent of the correctional caseload, falling to 11 per cent in 2000. Over the same period, prison admissions rose by 7 per cent. This

Table 4.3. *Offence breakdown, Florida community control program (2003).*

	Number	%
Violent crime, excluding robbery and burglary	2,988	23
Robbery	532	4
Burglary	1,500	11
Theft/Fraud	2,550	19
Drugs	4,133	31
Weapons	272	2
Other non-violent	1,340	10
Total	13,315	100

Source: Florida Corrections Commission, 2003.

decline reflects in part a shift in sentencing practices. Table 4.3 provides an offence category breakdown of the community control caseload in 2003. As can be seen, violent crimes account for a significant proportion (23 per cent) of all cases; 142 cases involved homicide and 672 offenders were on community control for a sexual offence (Table 4.3). In all 125,692 offenders were under correctional supervision in Florida as of 1 January 2003, and of these 10,106 were on community control.

New Zealand: home detention

Although a pilot scheme was launched earlier, full implementation of a form of community custody came to New Zealand in 1999 with the introduction of home detention (Gibbs and King, 2003a; Mitchell, 1999). As Mitchell notes 'Home detention is not a community-based sentence; it is a means of serving a sentence of imprisonment' (1999, p. 364).

Community custody therefore takes the form of a home detention sentence in New Zealand. Unlike the Canadian regime, offenders must pass a two-stage test. If they fall within the statutory framework of the home detention scheme, the sentencing court must grant or deny them leave to apply for home detention to the New Zealand Parole Board. This decision constitutes a sentence and as such is subject to appellate review. If granted leave, the offender may proceed to make an application to the Parole Board. The New Zealand regime also differs from most other community custody sanctions in that the offender will make his or her application for home detention from prison. Thus offenders granted leave to serve their sentences at home will have spent some time in prison, on average, forty-two days in 2001 (Spier, 2002).

This arrangement has advantages and disadvantages over a system in which the offender is sentenced directly to home confinement by a court. One advantage is that it provides offenders with a 'taste of prison', that may promote deterrence and provide an additional incentive to participate in a community custody sentence. Indeed, some offenders interviewed by Gibbs and King 'believed that a short time in prison was important to help them appreciate home detention' (2003b, p. 10). Offenders without previous custodial experience may be more inclined to adhere to their conditions after having been exposed to the back-up sanction which awaits them if they violate those conditions. In addition, critics of home detention may be more likely to accept the sanction, since some of these offenders will have served several months before being allowed home. An often-heard criticism of the conditional sentence of imprisonment in Canada is that it is called a term of imprisonment, yet offenders do not go near a custodial facility.

Finally, critics, and members of the public may be more supportive of release to home detention within a two-stage framework involving the judiciary and the parole board; such a structure means that the offender has to convince two decision-makers who are applying two sets of criteria.[6] The oft-heard misperception of parole – that it is granted to all who ask for it by a single decision-maker – should not arise in this context. These features of the New Zealand community custody regime may help to explain why home detention has been 'accepted by New Zealanders generally' (Gibbs and King, 2003b, p. 15), while in Canada there has been more public, professional and media resistance to the concept of offenders serving sentences of imprisonment at home.

On the other hand, requiring the offender to (a) make the application from prison, and (b) to convince both judge and parole board has drawbacks. It means that the sanction more closely resembles a form of accelerated parole release, and therefore may not have the same status as a community custody sentence in other jurisdictions. Home detention in New Zealand might be seen to be more a correctional program, applicable to a relatively small number of prisoners, than an autonomous sanction designed to replace custody. And of course, if the offender is required to make an application from prison, and to spend on average several weeks there, the whole purpose of community custody, namely to spare the offender the pains of imprisonment, is undermined. In those weeks of custody awaiting the decision of the parole board, the offender may lose his or her job, and suffer other adverse consequences of admission to custody.

Another distinguishing feature of the New Zealand regime lies in the fact that prisoners must apply for home confinement. This feature of the regime may bolster the perception that community custody is an 'offender-friendly' form of imprisonment, rather than routinely imposed like institutional imprisonment. Ultimately this feature of the New Zealand regime may therefore affect public perceptions of home detention as a sanction. In 1999, Mitchell predicted that 'it is inevitable that the credibility of the scheme as a form of imprisonment will be challenged' (p. 364). If this form of imprisonment is perceived by the public to be a privilege that should be accorded few prisoners, then the ability of this 'modern form of imprisonment' (Mitchell, 1999, p. 363) to make significant inroads into the volume of custodial admissions will be compromised.

In Canada, a court considering the sentencing of an offender may, having decided that custody is inevitable, choose between imposing, say three months' imprisonment or six months' community custody. This flexibility of approach has been the object both of criticism and praise. It has been praised for recognizing that the two sanctions do not carry the same 'penal value', and are accordingly almost never interchangeable on a one-to-one ratio. On the other hand, critics have argued that courts should impose a fixed term (say six months) and then proceed to determine whether the six months will be served in custody or the community. These commentators have feared that judges may protract community custody orders well beyond the term of imprisonment that would otherwise have been imposed, to reflect unreasonable judicial perceptions that community custody is a lenient sentencing option. In New Zealand this issue does not arise, as judges do not have the jurisdiction to impose home detention. All they can do is authorize the prisoner sentenced to less than three years to make an application to the parole board.

Statutory framework

Section 97 (1) of the Sentencing Act 2002 sets the ambit of the home detention scheme. As with the Canadian conditional sentence of imprisonment, the limit of home detention in New Zealand does not extend beyond a sentence of two years' duration.[7] According to section 97(3), if the offender is sentenced to a term of custody of not more than two years, the court *must* grant the offender leave to apply to the New Zealand Parole Board for home detention unless the court is satisfied that this would be 'inappropriate to grant leave'. The legislation specifies a number of criteria to be considered in making this determination:

(a) the nature and seriousness of the offence; and
(b) the circumstances and background of the offender; and
(c) any relevant matters in the victim impact statement in the case; and
(d) any other factor that the court considers relevant.

Elsewhere the Sentencing Act specifies the purpose and principles of sentencing, which reflect a desert-oriented sentencing philosophy (Roberts, 2003b). It is not surprising therefore to see crime seriousness listed as the first factor for the court to consider in determining whether leave may be granted to the offender to apply for home detention. A noteworthy departure from many other community custody regimes is the statutory reference to the victim impact statement. This presumably directs judges to consider whether the victim will be adversely affected if the offender is allowed to serve a term of home detention rather than institutional custody. Most importantly, there is a statutory exclusion: offenders convicted of one or more of a list of serious violent offences are excluded from the home detention scheme. The ceiling of two years encompasses a smaller proportion of custodial sentences than the Canadian equivalent; however, the vast majority of custodial sentences imposed in 2001 (84 per cent) fell within this range[8] (Spier, 2002).

Review by parole board

If the court grants the offender leave to apply for home detention, the individual may then apply to the parole board which will commission a 'suitability report' prior to making its decision. The board has a statutory obligation to consider a number of factors, including the likelihood of recidivism, the nature of the offence, the question of whether the offender will benefit from home detention, the welfare of other people occupying the residence in which the offender will be detained, and submissions made by victims. The obligations upon the probation officer are made clear by section 34(2) of the Parole Act which requires the probation officer to:

> ensure that every relevant occupant of the residence where it is proposed that the offender be detained is aware of the nature of the offender's past and current offending; and

> (b) tell every relevant occupant that the reason for giving that information is to enable the occupant to make an informed decision about whether to consent to having the offender reside at the residence; and

> (c) tell every relevant occupant that the information provided about the offender must not be used for any purpose other than that described in paragraph (b); and

> (d) see the consent of every relevant occupant to having the offender reside at the residence.

Although the statute does not state it explicitly, the last provision implies that the failure of any relevant[9] individual to provide his or her consent will prove fatal to the application for home detention. In this sense, family members effectively exercise a veto over the application. Clearly, the interests of an offender's family must be considered by any authority considering imposing home confinement. However, it may create a quandary for family members who may feel ambivalent about their role regarding the court order. On the one hand there may well be a strong desire to help the offender avoid imprisonment; on the other, family members may be apprehensive about his continual presence at home, the impact of the conditions upon their lives, or about their obligations regarding the conditions that must be respected. As Mitchell (1999) points out, families may well exercise control over the decision to place the offender on home detention, but there is no provision in the statute by which they may withdraw that consent. The offender may at any time request that the board return him or her to a penal institution.

Pre-requisite conditions
Assignment to home detention in New Zealand requires a two-step approval process involving the judiciary and an administrative body. The consequence is that only a small minority of eligible offenders are released to serve their sentences at home. Only some offenders will be eligible for home confinement. Of these, only a minority will be granted leave to apply, and of these, many will be turned down by the parole board. Less than one-third of prisoners who have applied for home confinement have been granted release to the program (Gibbs and King, 2003a). An even smaller percentage of all prisoners within the range of sentence length will serve part of the sentence in the program. In 2001, only 10 per cent of offenders sentenced to a prison sentence of two years or less (and therefore within the ambit of the home detention regime) were actually released to serve their sentences at home (Spier, 2002).

Statutory conditions
Offenders released to home confinement must remain at home except for approved excursions to work (or to find work), to seek medical treatment, to attend approved rehabilitation programs, to attend a restorative justice conference or 'other process relating to the offender's offending', to carry out any undertaking arising from any restorative justice process; or any other purposes authorized by the probation officer responsible. It is noteworthy that in this way the New Zealand regime relates the conditions of detention

directly to the offending behaviour giving rise to the sentence in the first place. This creates a salutary reminder to the offender of the reason for his detention. All home detention offenders are subject to a form of electronic monitoring, and house arrest. If the offender leaves his residence, the Community Probation Service is alerted. In addition, random checks of the property are made by the responsible probation officer.

Consequences of breaching conditions

Unlike the Canadian (and other home) confinement regimes, violating a condition of home detention in New Zealand constitutes a fresh criminal offence, punishable by up to three months in prison. However, there is some discretion allowed the court: minor (but unjustified) breaches can result in amendments to conditions. If an offender commits an offence while on home confinement, and the fresh offence is punishable by imprisonment, the court 'must order that the offender be returned to a penal institution, unless the court considers that, because of the nature or circumstances of the offence or the circumstances of the offender, it would be unjust to do so' (s. 99(3)(a)). This is a better approach than that which is found in some other jurisdictions; the court's discretion is highly constrained, but not eliminated. In most cases in which an offender re-offends, he or she will be committed to custody, although the court retains the power to act otherwise in exceptional circumstances. In the event that the new offence is not punishable by imprisonment, the court 'may, but is not required to, order that the offender be returned to a penal institution to serve the remainder of his or her sentence' (s. 99(3)(d)).

Cases given leave to apply for home detention and actually released

In 2001, approximately one eligible case in five that was granted leave to apply for home detention involved a crime of violence; almost a third were property offenders, 12 per cent drug offenders, while the category representing the highest proportion of cases was traffic offences (32 per cent; see Spier, 2002). Courts were least likely to grant leave in cases involving the administration of justice (17 per cent granted leave, 83 per cent declined leave). Violent offenders also had a relatively low success rate, with cases more much likely to be denied than granted leave (66 per cent denied, 34 per cent granted). These statistics reflect the exercise of judicial discretion. The pattern changes somewhat when the decisions of parole authorities are examined, reflecting the board's different mandate and statutory considerations.

What kinds of cases are actually granted release to home detention in New Zealand? In light of the statutory framework, it is not surprising that a relatively small percentage of releases to home detention involve an offender convicted of a crime of violence. Statistics for 2001 reveal that 16 per cent of successful home detention applications were for violent offences, 31 per cent for property crimes, 17 per cent for drug crimes, 4 per cent for offences against the administration of justice, 31 per cent for traffic offences and 1 per cent for 'other' offences (Spier, 2002). It is noteworthy that applications from offenders convicted of violent crimes had the lowest success rate: only 42 per cent of applications in 2001 were approved, compared to 68 per cent of drug offender applications and 77 per cent of offenders convicted of an offence involving the administration of justice.

In New Zealand, the number of offenders on home confinement never rose above 200 per month between 2000 and 2002 (Clark, 2002). However, with the passage of the Sentencing Act 2002 and the Parole Act 2002, both of which commenced on 30 June 2002, the number of home detention cases began a steep rise. Nevertheless, they still represent a relatively small percentage of all convictions, or even admissions to custody. In 2001, 594 offenders were released from prison to home detention, which represents less than 3 per cent of all custodial sentences imposed[10] (Spier, 2002).

New South Wales: home detention order

A pilot scheme involving the home detention of certain offenders has been operational in this jurisdiction since 1992. The Home Detention Order (HDO) was subsequently placed on a statutory footing with the Home Detention Act 1996 (NSW). The legislation was introduced with the explicit purpose of reducing the use of imprisonment as a sanction and not simply adding to the existing range of intermediate punishments (Keay, 2000; Law Reform Commission, New South Wales, 1996).

Statutory framework
The HDO carries a statutory ceiling of eighteen months. Offenders placed on an HDO are subject to surveillance by means of electronic monitoring as well as visits from probation officers. One of the most striking features of the New South Wales community custody sanction is the way that it is structured to screen out offenders convicted of the most serious offences, as well as those with the more serious criminal histories. The legislation contains a lengthy list of offences that are subject to a statutory exclusion. Section 76 of the Crime (Sentencing Procedure) Act 1999 explicitly states that an

HDO may not be made for any of a number of offences, including: murder, attempted murder, manslaughter, any sexual offence (whether involving an adult or child victim), armed robbery, any offence involving the use of a firearm, serious assaults (occasioning bodily harm), stalking or intimidation offences, certain drug offences and any domestic violence offence committed against a person with whom it is likely that the offender would reside, or continue or resume a relationship, if a home detention order were granted. As well, offenders with a particular criminal history profile are also excluded from consideration, including anyone with a previous conviction for many of the enumerated offences.

Thus the legislation screens out the most serious cases by means of a ceiling on the limit of the sentence that may be served on home detention, as well as statutory considerations relating to the offence of conviction and the offender's previous convictions. While other jurisdictions (like Canada) leave much to the exercise of judicial discretion, legislators in New South Wales clearly had a different vision of community custody in mind. This issue will be explored in more detail in a subsequent chapter; for the present it is sufficient to note that this more restrictive regime is likely to prove less effective in reducing admissions to custody (as a result of the many cases excluded by the statute). There is also a less obvious, symbolic consequence of prescribing so many exclusionary grounds: it undermines the power of community custody as a sanction, by restricting its application. On the other hand, such a regime will protect the sanction from the inevitable media scrutiny and public condemnation that so often follows (and has followed, in Canada), when an offender convicted of a particularly serious crime of violence is sentenced to serve his or her sentence of custody at home.

Determining suitability

The home detention provisions in New South Wales provide a number of criteria that need to be fulfilled before a home detention order may be imposed. The court must be satisfied that: the offender is a suitable person to serve such a sentence; that such a sentence is appropriate 'in all the circumstances'; that the persons with whom it is likely that the offender will reside have consented in writing to the making of such an order; and that the offender has signed an undertaking to comply with the obligations of the order (s. 78(1)).

The legislation then prescribes other factors that the court must consider, including: the contents of an assessment report on the offender and evidence from a probation or parole officer. The assessment report is critical, as a court may make a home detention order 'only if an assessment report states that, in the opinion of the person making the assessment, the offender is a suitable person to serve a term of imprisonment by way of home detention' (s. 78(2)(4)). Finally, a home detention order may not be made if the court considers it likely that the offender will commit any sexual offence or any offence involving violence while the home detention order is in force. The legislation adds that the court may arrive at this determination 'even though the offender may have no history of committing offences of that nature' (s. 78(6)).

The guidance provided by the statute is not directed to judges alone; a number of provisions contain guidelines for the probation and parole service. In compiling the assessment report for the court, this service must 'take into account, and specifically address, the following matters':

(i) any criminal record of the offender, and the likelihood that the offender will re-offend,
(ii) any dependency of the offender on illegal drugs,
(iii) the likelihood that the offender will commit a domestic violence offence,
(iv) whether any circumstances of the offender's residence, employment, study, or other activities would inhibit effective monitoring of a home detention order,
(v) whether the persons with whom it is likely that the offender would reside, or continue or resume a relationship, understand the requirements of the order and are prepared to live in conformity with them, so far as may be necessary,
(vi) whether the making of the order would place at risk of harm any person who would be living with or in the vicinity of the offender,
(vii) any matter prescribed by the regulations.

Home Detention Offenders are subject to a series of standard conditions, as well as any additional conditions imposed by the sentencing court and the Parole Board. The Probation Service may also indicate in its assessment report the kinds of conditions deemed to be appropriate in the event that a home detention order is made. Finally, another provision directs the Probation and Parole Service to find suitable accommodation, in the event that the offender is homeless.

Use of home detention in New South Wales
In light of the somewhat lower ceiling, and the numerous statutory exclusions, it is perhaps not surprising that the home detention order is imposed in only a relatively small number of cases in New South Wales. Heggie (1999)

reports that 366 offenders were placed on home detention in the first eighteen months of the scheme. Consistent with the statutory framework, these offenders were convicted of less serious offences than community custody offenders in other jurisdictions. The category of offender accounting for most admissions was 'driving offences',[11] while only two per cent of the offenders had been convicted of an assault (Heggie, 1999).

Finland

Community custody has long been a feature of the Finnish criminal justice system. Called conditional imprisonment, it has proved a success in that jurisdiction, and, as will be seen in a later chapter, has played an important role in reducing the use of incarceration as a sanction. Chapter 6 of the Criminal Code of Finland establishes a desert-based framework for sentencing: 'The sentence shall be passed so that it is in just proportion to the damage and danger caused by the offence and to the culpability of the offender manifest in the offence' (c.6 s.1).

The upper limit of the sanction is two years, comparable to the ceiling on the Canadian version of community custody. This high ceiling may explain the effectiveness of the sanction in reducing the use of custody over the past few decades. Under the Finnish regime, committal to custody will be activated in the event of further offending; violation of conditions alone will not result in committal to custody. The use of the conditional sentence of imprisonment is explicitly guided by this principle: a prison sentence within the statutory range can be made conditional provided that 'the seriousness of the offence, the culpability of the offender manifested in the offence, or previous convictions of the offender manifested in the offence, or previous convictions of the offender do not require an unconditional imprisonment'. Crime seriousness plays a critical role: the more serious the offence, the longer the period of conditional imprisonment, and the lower the probability of this form of custody rather than committal to a correctional facility (Lappi-Seppala, 2001).

Use of conditional sentence of imprisonment

Over the past fifty years, the volume of conditional sentences imposed in Finland has increased dramatically. In 2000, 13,974 such dispositions were imposed, representing just under two-thirds of all prison sentences. Finland remains the jurisdiction that has employed this sanction to the greatest extent. In 1950, conditional imprisonment accounted for 2,812 sentences, under a third of all sentences of imprisonment. The volume increased

Table 4.4. *Use of community custody sanction in Finland.*

	%
Traffic offences	54
Violent crime, including robbery	18
Theft and related offences	11
Drugs	4
Offences against the administration of justice	2
Other offences	11
Total	100

Source: Data provided to the author by Lappi-Seppala.

steadily and exceeded the number of immediate custody sentences by 1980. This total rose steadily to a high of 17,000 in 1990 (Lappi-Seppala, 2002). In 1950, most sentences of imprisonment were immediate; in 2000, conditional imprisonment terms exceed the number of institutional sentences. Conditional sentences accounted for 22 per cent of convictions, immediate custody for 13 per cent of convictions ((Lappi-Seppala, 2002). Table 4.4 provides a categorical breakdown of offences resulting in a conditional sentence of imprisonment in Finland for the most recent year for which these data are available. As can be seen, over half the convictions were for driving related offences, with less than one-fifth of these dispositions being imposed for a crime of violence.

England and Wales: suspended sentence of imprisonment

After the Halliday Review of sentencing in England and Wales, the government introduced a sweeping reform bill which was eventually proclaimed into law in 2003. This legislation places the purposes of sentencing on a statutory footing for the first time. According to section 189(1) of the Act, a court which passes a sentence of imprisonment of at least twenty-eight and not more than fifty-one weeks may sentence the offender to a suspended sentence of imprisonment. This sanction is composed of several elements. First there is a custodial term, which falls within the limits stipulated and which is suspended. The second element is a period of supervision during which the offender will have to comply with a number of requirements such as unpaid community work, a curfew, or various treatment conditions. Third, there is an 'operational' period, during which the initial custodial term may be activated if the offender fails to comply with one of the conditions of the supervision period, or if the offender commits another offence within the jurisdiction of the United Kingdom. The supervision period and the operational period must each be a period of not less than six months, and not more than two years in duration.

A concrete example will illustrate the structure of the sanction. A court sentences an offender to nine months' custody, and then makes this sentence a suspended term of imprisonment. The offender is then required to comply with the conditions of the supervision order, for a one-year period, and the entire sanction is framed within a two-year operational period. Thus after one year, the supervision requirements would have been met, and at the end of the two-year operational period, the suspended sentence itself would elapse, absent further offending, or failure to comply with conditions during the supervision period. The requirements of the suspended prison sentence order were described by the White Paper as representing a 'demanding programme of activity' (Secretary of State, 2002b, p. 93). The possible requirements are enumerated in clause 190 (1) of the Act, and include (but are not restricted to): unpaid work; prohibitions on certain activities; curfews; and treatment requirement of various kinds. The onerousness of the conditions will be determined by judicial practice, and will of course vary from case to case.

A suspended sentence was introduced in England and Wales in 1967 and has been the focus of considerable scholarship over the years (e.g. Bottoms, 1981; Dignan, 1984). Since its heyday, the use of the suspended sentence has declined precipitously and by 2001, the sanction was effectively on life support. Cavadino and Dignan (2002) observe that 'the measure is now hardly used at all' (p. 152). Indeed, recent sentencing statistics reveal that for the past five years, only one per cent of offenders convicted of an indictable offence received a suspended sentence (Home Office, 2002). Whether the suspended sentence of imprisonment defined in the Criminal Justice Act will resuscitate interest in, and use of, this form of imprisonment remains to be seen.

The White Paper employed the term 'Custody Minus' for this new sanction. The shift in terminology illustrates once again the importance of the public image of community custody. Dropping all references to the name 'custody minus' has several advantages. First, the term implied a weaker form of imprisonment, and this may have created public image problems (the American equivalent might be 'Custody Lite'). Second, the new name discourages consideration of the two sanctions as stronger and weaker forms of the same sanction (imprisonment). The 'plus' and 'minus' suffixes implied that one is always more severe than another. In reality, the suspended sentence of imprisonment can be much more punitive than Custody Plus.

A Custody Plus order could be as brief as twenty-eight weeks in total duration, with only two weeks served in custody. In contrast, a suspended sentence of imprisonment can comprise fifty-one weeks' custody (suspended) accompanied by two years of supervision (with onerous requirements) and a two-year operational period. Failure to comply with the requirements may result in committal to custody for the full fifty-one weeks. Members of the public, and indeed offenders, might reasonably have asked what the tags 'plus' and 'minus' mean in this context, as the 'plus' sanction is by no means more severe than its 'minus' counterpart. In reality, the two sanctions exist in parallel and are conceived with different penal aims, and different offenders in mind.

Ambit of the suspended sentence of imprisonment in England and Wales

Sentence length statistics show that approximately two-thirds of immediate receptions into prison in England and Wales 2000 were under twelve months and accordingly within the range of the new suspended sentence of imprisonment (Home Office, 2002, Table 4.6). Thus, most serious offence/offender combinations, which attract the longest one-third of all custodial sentences, are excluded from consideration for a suspended sentence of imprisonment. The lower maximum limit in England and Wales (compared to other countries) will protect the new sanction from the inevitable negative media commentary arising when a very serious personal injury offence results in a sanction which does not entail the imprisonment of the offender. It may also help to preserve proportionality in sentencing, by preventing the imposition of a suspended sentence for a very serious crime.

Relationship between suspended sentence of imprisonment and statutory purposes and principles of sentencing

Another lesson from the Canadian experience concerns the importance of linking the use of a potentially controversial sanction such as the suspended sentence of imprisonment, to the statutory principles of sentencing. Before the Canadian Parliament amended its conditional sentencing legislation (in 1997, only six months after the original legislation came into force), judges were free to impose a conditional sentence without regard to the codified principles of sentencing, including the fundamental principle of proportionality. The result was that a non-custodial sentence (the conditional sentence) could be (and was) imposed for some very serious crimes of violence, in potential violation of the principle of proportionality. In order to correct this problem, Parliament expeditiously amended the conditional sentence provisions.[12] As noted, the amendment created another statutory pre-requisite: before imposing a conditional sentence, judges had to be satisfied that the imposition of such a disposition would be consistent with the codified purpose and principles of sentencing.

No such provision is contained in the Criminal Justice Act in England and Wales. For better or worse, section 189 simply creates the power of a court to make a suspended sentence of imprisonment order in the place of committing the offender directly to custody. It is a surprising omission, particularly in light of the fact that general sentencing provisions relating to the purposes of sentencing are placed on a statutory footing for the first time by the Criminal Justice Bill (in clause 126). The authors of the Act may have considered directing judges' attention towards circumstances that would make a suspended sentence particularly appropriate (or inappropriate). As Cavadino and Dignan (2002) note, one of the design flaws of the suspended sentence was that there was a failure to 'provide sentencers with sufficiently clear guidance as to the circumstances in which the sentence was to be used' (p. 151).

This absence of a link between these new sanctions and the principles of sentencing may well undermine their effectiveness in terms of reducing the number of admissions to custody. In their review of the three sanctions as described in the white paper, Cavadino and Dignan (2002) draw some pessimistic conclusions. They anticipate that the new sanctions will be used to target persistent offenders convicted of relatively low seriousness crimes: 'As a result, the new measures will almost inevitably drive the prison population to new heights' (pp. 154–5).

Judicial involvement in the administration of the suspended sentence of imprisonment

In Canada, there is no statutory authority for the involvement of the sentencing judge in the administration of the conditional sentence of imprisonment. Nevertheless, judges sometimes require offenders placed on the community custody sentence to return to court to report on their progress. This requirement focuses the offender's attention on the sanction, is probably of assistance to probation officers attempting to ensure compliance with conditions, and also permits the court to vary (or delete) conditions that have become problematic for reasons beyond the offender's control.

The suspended sentence provisions of the Criminal Justice Act go much further than this ad hoc arrangement, and provide courts with the authority to review the suspended sentence order as well as fairly detailed guidance on the purpose and nature of the review. Section 191 states that:

A suspended sentence order may –

(a) provide for the order to be reviewed periodically at specified intervals,
(b) provide for each review to be made, subject to section 192(4), at a hearing held for the purpose by the court responsible for the order (a 'review hearing'),
(c) require the offender to attend each review hearing, and
(d) provide for the responsible officer to make to the court responsible for the order, before each review, a report on the offender's progress in complying with the community requirements of the order.[13]

Being required to attend frequent reviews may be resented by some offenders. The Act also authorizes courts to dispense with a hearing. If the responsible officer's report indicates that the offender has made satisfactory progress, the court may recognize this and waive the hearing, relying on the report alone to monitor compliance. The review provisions therefore offer the offender some incentive to comply with his or her conditions; compliance will reduce the number of court appearances. At the same time, the consequences for non-compliance are serious.

Consequences of non-compliance

The White Paper was somewhat ambiguous about the consequences for the offender of breaching the conditions imposed as part of its 'custody minus' sentence. At one point it states that 'Any breach will lead to immediate imprisonment' (Secretary of State, 2002b, p. 93), but elsewhere the text notes that failure to comply with the community supervision component '*could* result in immediate imprisonment' (Secretary of State, 2002b, p. 97; emphasis added). Clarification has been provided by the Act itself.

Powers of the court

Section 8(1) of Schedule 12 provides courts with a range of options: (a) order that the suspended sentence be served with its original terms and custodial period unaltered; (b) order that the suspended sentence take effect but for a lesser term; (c) amend the order by imposing more onerous community requirements consistent with the authorization for the original conditions; (c) extend the period of supervision; (d) extend the operational period. As with the Canadian statute, then, the Act provides judges with a number of options with which to respond to unjustified breach or re-offending. Unlike the conditional sentence of imprisonment in Canada, however, the statutorily-defined options in England and Wales are more rigorous.

Breach of conditions or fresh offending can result in the imprisonment of the offender for the entire period that was suspended. This means that an offender who breaches his conditions twelve months into an eighteen-month period of supervision on a six-month suspended term could be committed to custody for the full six-month period that was initially suspended; a year of compliance on the part of the offender would be all for naught. In such a scenario, courts are likely to recognize the offender's period of compliance. A more likely judicial response would be to substitute a briefer period of imprisonment, perhaps for three months. This would punish the offender for breaching the condition, yet simultaneously recognize that a considerable period of the supervision period had been completed without incident.

Warning the offender

Section 4 of Schedule 12 of the Act creates a statutory obligation on the probation service to issue a warning to the offender, and to record this fact. The direction in paragraph 3(2) of the schedule is very precise with respect to the admonition:

> A warning under this paragraph must –
>
> (a) describe the circumstances of the failure,
> (b) state that the failure is unacceptable, and
> (c) inform the offender that if within the next twelve months he again fails to comply with any requirement of the order, he will be liable to be brought before a court.

The reasoning underlying the more punitive court responses to breach (than the analogical provisions regarding breach of a conditional sentence order in Canada) would therefore appear to be that the offender has presumably already received an official warning. This arrangement is superior to the Canadian statute which accords far more discretion to probation officers, members of the prosecution service and judges with resulting variability of response.

Sub-paragraph 8(3) of Schedule 12 does create an 'escape hatch' for what is otherwise a rather tough set of breach provisions. A court is compelled to make an order in response to a breach or re-offence, 'unless it is of the opinion that it would be unjust to do so in view of all the circumstances'.

The next sub-paragraph identifies two important circumstances for consideration: 'the extent to which the offender has complied with the community requirements of the suspended sentence order', and (in the event of subsequent re-offending), 'the facts of the subsequent offence'. Thus an offender who complies with the conditions of his order for almost the entire order, but who falls at one of the last hurdles, may well receive an understanding response from the court, and be spared either incarceration or any of the punitive, community-based responses to breach. In the event that a court assumes this sympathetic response to an offender in this position, there is a statutory obligation to provide reasons.

To summarize, Schedule 12 of the Act provides courts with a flexible, yet rigorous set of responses with which to deal with offenders who violate their conditions. The breach arrangements constitute a superior response to their analogical provisions in the Canadian *Criminal Code* pertaining to the conditional sentence of imprisonment. Offenders sentenced to a suspended term of imprisonment in England and Wales will have clear reason to see their sentences as forms of imprisonment (rather than a kind of enhanced probation), and a strong prudential incentive to comply with the conditions. The result may well be of benefit to the justice system and offenders.

Conclusion

This chapter has revealed the diversity of sanctions found under the general rubric of community custody. The forms of this sanction reviewed here generally share a number of common features: offenders serving these sentences are all deemed: to be serving a term of custody; required to comply with a number of statutory conditions, including either home confinement (with or without electronic monitoring) or a curfew; subject to additional conditions tailored to their specific circumstances and facing the threat of committal to a correctional institution in the event of non-compliance. Aside from these basic elements, the sanctions differ widely in their scope of application, the extent of impact on the offender's life (and that of his or her family), and the ultimate consequences with respect to breach of conditions. The next chapter explores the reactions of offenders and their families to this unique alternative to custody.

FIVE

Coming home to prison: offender perceptions and experiences

> The views of offenders were not often considered in studies of the criminal justice system. There appears to be a certain unspoken agreement that having been sentenced . . . the views of the individual so dealt with are irrelevant.
>
> (Mair and Nee, 1990, p. 52)

This chapter approaches the phenomenon of community custody from the perspective of the people most affected by the sanction: offenders and their families. The voluminous international literature on sentencing has paid insufficient attention to the perceptions of prisoners at home. As Mair and Nee rightly observed over a decade ago, it is a regrettable oversight; many stereotypes about imprisonment and other sanctions have developed and been perpetuated in the absence of systematic research. Nevertheless, the limited research literature on offender perceptions does offer insight into the evolving punishment of community custody. This chapter reviews findings from focus groups and interviews with community custody offenders in Canada, and places this research in the context of similar research in other jurisdictions (e.g. Aungles, 1994). In addition, this chapter summarizes the experiences of family members and spouses of offenders who have been ordered to serve a sentence of custody at home. The research that has accumulated to date suggests that community custody carries many benefits for offenders, although its full potential has yet to be fully realized.

Public stereotypes of crime and justice

Members of the public subscribe to a number of myths about crime, offenders and prisons. Most people under-estimate the severity of the sentencing process. This can be seen in the estimates that people make about criminal justice statistics such as sentencing trends and parole grant rates. The public underestimates the percentage of offenders who are imprisoned, as well as the average sentence length (see Roberts and Hough, 2001; Roberts and Stalans, 1997, for a review). As well, the public tends to underestimate the severity of prison life (see Roberts and Hough, forthcoming, for a review). When a sample of Florida residents were asked about prison conditions, almost nine out of ten believed that prisoners in that state were housed in air-conditioned cells, when in fact only a few correctional facilities have this feature (Florida Department of Corrections, 1997).

These misperceptions of the reality of prison life lead people to dismiss a sentence of years in prison as 'a slap on the wrist', one that the offender can do 'standing on his head'.[1] Even lengthy prison sentences are decried as evidence of leniency by people who do not stop to imagine what a year in custody is actually like. Misperceptions of community custody are also likely to abound. One public stereotype[2] of community custody is that offenders serving sentences at home enjoy all the benefits of home life, and the conditions they must obey – going to work or school, attending medical appointments and the like – are simply those obligations that confront any law-abiding citizen on a daily basis. This somewhat naive (and cynical) view of community custody accounts for the widespread public opposition to the use of community custody for offenders convicted of serious crimes of violence. For this profile of case, the public expect a more severe response from courts (see chapter 7). Being confined to one's home simply fails to impress the public as a sanction severe enough to represent an adequate response to violent crime.

The perception is not entirely without some foundation in some jurisdictions. In the early days of the community custody regime in Canada, offenders on whom this sentence was imposed had few conditions to follow. House arrest, for example, was practically unheard of (Roberts, Antonowicz and Sanders, 2000). Curfews were rare and many were very flexible, for example requiring the offender to be home only after 10 pm and until 7 am. In some respects, the sanction was little different from a term of probation. However, since then, community custody orders have become tougher: house arrest is more frequent and curfews tend to be more restrictive, beginning shortly after the offender has finished work for the day (Roberts, 2002a).[3] In some jurisdictions such as Florida, it is an onerous sentence by any definition. An accurate idea of the true impact of any sanction can only be gained from understanding the perspective of the people who experience it. Where, then, do offenders stand?

Many difficulties confront the researcher trying to draw conclusions about the experiences of offenders confined to their home. First, the nature of conditions imposed on community custody offenders varies greatly across jurisdictions, making it hard to draw general conclusions. Second, other confounding variables must be taken into account. The offender population eligible for community custody also varies considerably. If the sanction is reserved for only non-serious property offenders with a stable family environment and employment history, offenders' reactions are going to be very different from those of offenders in a jurisdiction in which home confinement offenders come from a more serious, higher risk population.

As well, the administration of the sanction will have an important impact upon offender reactions. If sponsors receive support and assistance from the state, and if probation officers are able to devote a significant amount of time to supervising each offender, breach rates will be low, and this will emerge from research upon offender perceptions. But if the justice system fails to provide even sufficient information for family members – to say nothing of support – and if probation officers have high caseloads that prohibit more than a perfunctory telephone inquiry every few weeks – the sanction will fail. This failure will also be clear from interviews with offenders and their parents and families.

Offender perceptions of community custody are critical to the success of the sanction from another perspective as well. If prisoners at home regard the sentence as little more than 'enhanced probation', non-compliance with conditions is likely. Widespread violation of conditions will eventually spell the demise of the sanction. Judges will be less likely to impose the sentence if they have to deal with a high number of breach hearings, or see the same offenders re-appearing before their court having served terms of community custody. If high breach rates are publicized by the news media, members of the public will perceive the sanction as being little more than probation, and cynicism with the sentencing process will worsen (see chapter 7). High breach rates will also lead to the incarceration of offenders for whom this alternative form of imprisonment was originally conceived. This will defeat the principal objective of the sentence, namely reducing the number of individuals committed to prison.

There are two principal seams of research that bear upon the experience of serving custody at home: studies that explore the perceptions of offenders regarding the relative severity of different sanctions, including community custody, house arrest, and prison, and, more importantly, studies conducted on offenders who have served, or are serving terms of custody in the community. Before reviewing this research, it is worth noting the findings from three studies that have reported the experiences of people other than offenders who have tried to understand the impact of a community custody sentence.

Simulating the experience of home confinement

Judges are probably quite familiar with the conditions of prisons to which they sentence offenders. Some members of the judiciary will have visited prisons in the course of representing accused persons and offenders before being appointed to the bench. As well, individual judges sometimes take the time to visit correctional facilities. In recent years, judicial education programs have also included presentations on life in prison, or actual tours of correctional facilities. No similar initiative of which I am aware has focused on home confinement, although it would make considerable sense in light of the proliferation of community custody sanctions. In determining the appropriate conditions, and in order to know what is a fit length of sentence to impose, judges need to have a good understanding of the impact of the sanction on offenders and their families.

A few enterprising judges have placed themselves on electronic monitors, in order better to understand the impact of the sanction (e.g. Carlisle, 1988; Abrahamson, 1991). Carlisle's early report understandably explored the impact of the devices themselves, and failed to consider the wider psychological consequences of home confinement. However, Abrahamson summarizes the experience of a judge in California who spent a weekend under house arrest conditions, including having to wear an electronic monitoring device. Over the weekend the judge found the experience claustrophobic, and had wanted to remove the monitoring device after a very brief period.

Stinchcomb (2002) reports the findings from an 'experiment' involving students in a Corrections class. One of their course assignments required them to spend the weekend under conditions that simulated the experience of house arrest. Since the experiment was restricted to forty-eight hours, the conditions were constructed to be more restrictive than those imposed on offenders.[4] Although the experience was obviously artificial, carried no penal consequences and the 'prisoners' were not obliged to participate, Stinchcomb reports that the students' attitudes changed; they developed a better appreciation of the restrictions on liberty created by house arrest. After reviewing the students' journal entries, Stinchcomb concluded that 'for the majority of participants . . . the experience had been a significant emotional event' (p. 476), and was not the easy ride that they may have anticipated.

Offender perceptions of the relative severity of sanctions

One of the most striking (and significant) findings in the field is the gap between popular conceptions of the relative severity of punishments, and the perceptions of offenders who actually experience criminal punishment. Misconceptions exist here as well. First, many people believe that community sanctions generally, including community custody, are pretty 'easy' sentences; the offender just has to stay out of trouble, and drop in occasionally to report to a probation officer. This is why the public in many countries has such a jaundiced view of parole: it is not perceived as a portion of the term of imprisonment served in the community, but rather as 'time off' the sentence. The gulf between the experience of life in prison and life on parole is too great for most people to consider the latter in any way a continuation of the former. This perspective probably extends to community custody sentences, and explains some of the public opposition to the sanction when applied in certain cases.

The most lax community custody regime makes considerable requirements of offenders, and even the Canadian version – which is relatively indulgent in theory and practice with respect to a breach of conditions (see chapter 4) – carries the threat of committal to custody if the offender violates the conditions of the order. Members of the public tend to take for granted their freedom of movement. If they were to consider the effect of house arrest more carefully they might appreciate that being denied pleasures such as taking one's child to a football match or joining the family on a bank holiday trip to the seaside is a real punishment. And unlike a fine or some other sanctions, house arrest has social consequences for the offender. His or her status as an offender is apparent to all other people with whom he or she shares a residence.

Choosing between incarceration in a prison or at home

Another public stereotype about the relative severity of punishments is that prison is perforce much more punitive than any community-based alternative. Prisoners and ex-prisoners don't always share this view. This conclusion reflects the findings from systematic research into offender perceptions as well as anecdotal accounts from criminal justice professionals in several countries. Crouch (1993) for example, asked a sample of prisoners to choose between being sentenced to either prison or probation. Not surprisingly, the percentage of respondents who stated that they would elect to go to prison rather than be placed on probation increased as the anticipated time on probation lengthened. However, even when asked to consider one year in prison and three years on probation, approximately one-third of the sample chose imprisonment over probation (Crouch, 1993, Table 1).

The testimony of some criminal justice professionals in Canada with respect to this issue also suggests that offenders frequently avoid community custody by expressing a preference for prison. I have heard several defence counsel express the view informally or in their sentencing submissions that their client would be better off going to prison, as the conditions of the proposed community custody order were so onerous. Joel Pink, a leading defence counsel in Canada has noted that 'as a defence lawyer, I often recommend against [a community custody sentence] because the punishment is more severe than if they did straight jail time' (see Hayes, 2002). Partly this is defence counsel rhetoric, in the 'well, they would say that wouldn't they?' tradition. Defence counsel seek to convince judges that a community custody order is a tough sanction, and therefore can replace institutional imprisonment.

However, I have also been told by offenders that they would prefer to 'get the sentence over with' and are worried that breaching the order will land them in jail anyway, and possibly for a longer period than would have initially been imposed.[5] Some judges in Florida have made the same point: the community control sanction is so restrictive that offenders have 'actually turned down community control in favour of going to prison' (Flynn, 1986, p. 68). As well, in some jurisdictions, community custody offenders cannot benefit from 'good time' or remission off community custody; this makes a prison term more appealing, particularly if the conditions of release on parole are less onerous than those of home confinement (see discussion in Payne and Gainey, 2000).[6] (This is another reason for incorporating some comparable form of incentive for home confinement offenders, an issue that will be explored further in the concluding chapter of this volume.)

There is something wrong with an alternative sanction if offenders prefer instead to go to prison. The criminal justice system should encourage the imposition of punishments that spare offenders the pains of imprisonment, and which elicit the positive steps towards rehabilitation that are possible under a community custody order. If, despite these efforts, offenders are effectively imprisoning themselves (by electing instead to go to prison), we probably need to re-think the sanction, or educate offenders about its advantages in relation to institutional imprisonment.

Maidment (2002) reports the findings from women in Canada who had been subject to electronically monitored house arrest. She found that a number of the women reported that serving their time at home had been more difficult than a term of imprisonment, principally as a result of the increased stress associated with the sanction. Prison was easier, they found, because they had less to do; they did not have to worry about the day-to-day challenges of raising children and running a household greatly complicated by the restrictions of the court order.

A limited number of studies have been conducted upon offender perceptions of the relative severity of different sanctions. This literature has yet to explore perceptions of home confinement in a systematic manner. However, Petersilia and Deschenes (1994) asked a sample of Minnesota offenders to rank a number of sanctions on the dimension of severity, with results that would surprise many members of the public. These authors concluded – a decade ago – that it was no longer necessary to equate punishment exclusively with the use of imprisonment. When a number of conditions are 'packaged' together, the resulting composite sanction often becomes less preferable than imprisonment to many offenders (Petersilia and Deschenes, 1994). Reviewing these studies more recently, Martinovic (2002) comes to a similar conclusion, and questions the popular view according to which incarceration is inevitably the most punitive sentencing option.

Although community custody was not one of the sanctions rated by the offenders in this study, three years of intensive probation, a less severe sanction than community custody, was rated as the equivalent of one year in prison. Spelman (1995) also obtained severity ratings from a sample of offenders and his results confirm the relatively high ranking of home detention conditions. For example, one year with a late curfew (10 pm) was rated as being more severe than two years on probation, one year of mandatory alcohol or drug treatment, or one year of unannounced home visits by probation officers. Thus on the severity continuum, community custody is likely to rank relatively high. Similarly, research by Blomberg, Bales and Reed (1993) with offenders in Florida's home confinement program found that most individuals found the experience to be punitive, largely because of the many restrictions placed upon their freedom.

In light of the limited number of studies on the issue, it is hard to isolate the components of a community custody sanction that determine offender reactions. Researchers have yet to establish the elements of community custody that make it a tough sentence. Is it the residence restriction, the electronic monitoring (where this is a condition) or some other element(s) of the sanction? Some research suggests that it is the electronic monitor that drives perceptions of the severity of home confinement, although this begs the question of why this condition is perceived to be so aversive (see discussion in Martinovic, 2002). Is it the technological intrusion into the home, the presence of a device worn on the body, or some other aspect which make it so punitive?

Offender attitudes to community custody

'It is like being with the people that I love, and doing my time with them, but it's not easy. Actually, I think it's tougher than being in jail.'[7]

As noted, the reactions of offenders serving community custody sentences are likely to vary depending upon the nature and intrusiveness of conditions imposed, and perhaps also the severity of judicial response to violations of those conditions. Offenders wearing electronic monitors and/or subject to tight curfews are likely to be less positive about the experience of life in the virtual prison; in contrast, offenders with less restrictive curfews will find the experience of home detention less onerous. It is important therefore, in considering the research into this issue to bear in mind the conditions under which the respondents lived when they participated in the study.

In the research by Beck, Klein-Saffran and Wooten (1990) for example, the participants were federal parolees in the USA who, being serious offenders, were fitted with leg transmitters for relatively long periods of time. These offenders found the experience of community custody with electronic monitoring to be more punitive than living in a halfway house, with the restrictions imposed being the most important cause of stress. Nevertheless, they were keenly aware of the alternative (prison), and Beck et al. observe that most participants were only too happy to be at home rather than in a correctional institution. Similar reactions from home confinement offenders are reported by Rubin (1990).

Interviews conducted as part of Home Office research into curfews enforced by tagging (Home Detention Curfews) indicated that offenders were equally positive: 90 per cent were in favour of the program.[8] Offenders viewed the experience as a necessary cost; the intrusiveness of the sanction was an acceptable price to pay for getting out of jail early. Fully four out of five offenders on HDC cited getting out of prison as the principal advantage of the scheme (see Dodgson, Goodwin, Howard, Llewellyn-Thomas, Mortimer, Russell and Weiner, 2001; Mair and Mortimer, 1996). This finding is common to all studies that explore offenders' reactions to community custody; however intrusive the conditions may be, almost all offenders are aware that if they were confined inside a prison, life would be worse. As one offender on a tight curfew order in England put it: 'Being in at eight and having to stay in for 12 hours is nothing compared to being locked up for 23 hours and seeing my girlfriend and baby [only] every two weeks' (Walters, 2002, p. 33).

Another source of the appeal of community custody is that offenders tend to be aware of the more individualized treatment associated with community custody. A clear advantage of community custody is that offenders supervised in the community are treated more as individuals rather than prisoners. Although there are rules common to the supervision of all such offenders, supervisory personnel provide individual rather than group attention. This bodes well for the future of these offenders. Research has demonstrated that offenders report that being treated as an individual is one of the most important determinants of 'going straight' (e.g. Leibrich, 1994).

In New Zealand, community custody is not a sanction imposed on offenders, but a form of release from a sentence of imprisonment for which prisoners have to apply. Some prisoners elect not to apply for home detention, seeing less attraction to living at home. It depends in large measure on the nature of home life. In the words of one prisoner who was granted home confinement: 'If I didn't have my kids I would have preferred to go to jail' (cited in Gibbs and King, 2003b, p. 8). The experience in New Zealand has been very positive, from the perspective of offenders and their sponsors. Gibbs and King (2003b) summarize their research into the reactions of these individuals in the following way: 'Sponsors and detainees were overwhelmingly positive about the concept of home detention' (p. 12). No prison will ever generate such a response from the people detained therein, or their families. Church and Dunstan (1997) report that of the thirty-three detainees in their research, fully twenty-six perceived home detention to be superior to prison in every respect.

The reactions of offenders in several countries seem to be contingent upon their perception of whether community custody is a substitute for imprisonment, or a highly intrusive community sanction. People who see it as a prison substitute appear far more positive; those who had expected to receive a much less punitive sanction like probation were more likely to have difficulty with the restrictions of home confinement. This brings home yet again, but from a different perspective, the importance of constructing community custody as a sanction to divert prison-bound offenders, rather than as a punishment for the more serious cases that might otherwise be sentenced to probation or a fine.

Institutional versus community custody

Many people may be surprised to learn that offenders will on occasion choose prison over an intermediate sanction, but this surprise is founded upon the notion that prison is always and everywhere more punitive than its alternatives. In addition, research that examines the nature of the impact of conditions such as electronic monitoring and home confinement demonstrates that there are important parallels: many (but by no means all) of the pains of imprisonment can be reproduced in the home. Payne and Gainey (1998) provide a fascinating comparison between the pains of imprisonment and those of life on electronic monitoring. They point out that many of the traditional pains of imprisonment, including loss of personal autonomy, deprivation of liberty and goods are endured by people on electronic monitoring.

It is interesting to note that several individuals in the Canadian study commented that while community imprisonment was clearly better than prison, it was not necessarily easier; living on a conditional sentence created challenges and difficulties not encountered in prison. In one sense prison was the easier sanction, because they simply had to 'wait out' the sentence: 'I didn't like being behind bars, but being out is harder than being in jail.' Another offender described life on a community custody order in the following words: 'You have to think about what you are doing in the world.' Some individuals expressed pride at having lived through the absolute house arrest. One said: 'It's been a long haul but I'm proud of what I've done.' Such statements are seldom heard from people leaving prison, or ending a period on parole.

Perceptions of active vs. passive sentencing

'In jail you know what you got. What you're doing. You may as well sit there for six months.'

As noted in Chapter 3, prison creates a passive environment; prisoners react and respond to instructions from the institutional authority. In contrast, a community custody sentence is a far more active disposition; the offender can (and should), actively take steps towards rehabilitation and restoration. Some judges impose obligations on offenders to actively change their lives. This contrast between the two forms of imprisonment was brought home by one offender in Canada, who said: 'I've been in jail and there's nothing to do, you just eat. If you don't want to eat, you sleep. You stay the whole day sitting down. Being outside is preferable because I can prove to myself that I'm not that kind of person. I can prove to [other] people that I'm not that kind of person.' This illustrates the positive potential of the community custody order.

A term of imprisonment has an undeniable degree of clarity; for a number of reasons, the same cannot be said for community custody. First, in jurisdictions such as Canada, it is a relatively new sanction with which most people are unfamiliar. Few people know about the statutory conditions imposed on all community custody offenders. Second, community custody is a highly protean disposition, the nature of which varies from cases to case depending upon the number and nature of conditions imposed, as well as judicial reaction to any breach of those conditions. Most prisoners serving sentences are subject to the same conditions as a result of the level of security to which they have been assigned; the only critical variable is therefore the duration of the sanction.

These critical differences between community custody and imprisonment may explain why a number of offenders had some difficulty explaining the meaning of the community custody sentence that they were serving. There was general agreement among all participants that the sentence involved following certain rules to stay out of jail. Several participants agreed with one woman's statement that it didn't really matter what the conditions were, you were just happy not to go to jail. One offender stated that: 'If I went to jail, I would come out worse.' The offenders interviewed in Canada were keenly aware of the destructive nature of custody, but this awareness is not restricted to Canada. An offender on the home detention program in New Zealand observed that 'Home detention is heaps better [than prison]. You're mixing with a different type of person. I'm amazed the justice system hasn't twigged to that earlier. If you want to turn people like myself into criminals, throw us into prison' (cited in Church and Dunstan, 1997, p. 11).

Knowledge of the community custody order
Few offenders going to prison (even for the first time) need to be provided with information about prison life in advance; they are informed of institutional regulations on arrival, and correctional officers are ever-present to ensure that these rules are understood and obeyed. Community custody is rather different; offenders need to have a clear sense of the nature of the order, its conditions, and, most importantly, the consequences of violating those conditions. This was accordingly one of the issues explored in focus groups conducted with community custody offenders in Canada (Roberts et al., 2003). Not surprisingly, perhaps, the offenders displayed a wide range of knowledge about the sentence they were serving.

Some individuals were very sophisticated with respect to the way that the sentence had been imposed, as well as its conditions and the consequences of non-compliance. On the other hand, a small number appeared to have very little idea what the nature of purpose of the sentence was; they were just 'doing time' at home. Few offenders reported receiving information about the sentence from the court or the prosecutor. This is to be expected, as it is not the function of the prosecutor to provide this information, and while an explanation from the bench may be useful in terms of bringing home to the offender the consequences of breach, most judges simply do not have the time.

More surprisingly, a significant number of offenders stated that their counsel had told them little about the sanction beyond a perfunctory 'you're not going to jail'. According to these offenders, their defence counsel generally had little to say about the conditions imposed, either in court during submissions on sentence, or afterwards to their clients. Those offenders who had received information reported that it had been provided by the probation officer. One of the people who claimed not to have received any information stated that 'Nobody explained anything to me.' In the absence of any information, she assumed the consequences of breaching were that she would be going back to jail. She also claimed never to have signed anything, as did a number of other offenders, although all community custody offenders are required to sign a form. Some individuals said that they would have liked to have heard more from the judge at sentencing regarding the order that he or she was imposing. When asked why they had not asked any questions in open court when given a chance to speak, one provided a simple explanation: 'you're not going to question a judge when he's letting you go free'.

Ambiguity surrounding the conditions of community custody orders

Many people to whom we spoke (including family members and probation officers) described the ambiguity surrounding their obligations. Offenders reported being unsure whether particular acts or omissions would trigger a breach allegation. While certain conditions of the sanction were clear – for example, offenders knew when they lived under house arrest – several did not know the exact limits. One offender stated that he was unclear about what constituted a breach: 'If I stop at the seven-eleven [neighbourhood corner store] and grab an ice cream, am I breaching [conditions]? If I take the wrong bus and have to find my way back, am I breaching?' Sometimes this ambiguity provoked inquiries to the supervising officer, yet even these individuals were on occasion unsure exactly how much discretion they could exercise for certain kinds of alleged breaches.

In addition, some offenders seemed unaware that they could apply for a variance in conditions, if a particular condition was creating exceptional hardship or difficulties. One offender noted the fact that a tight curfew had interfered with his ability to fulfil his role as a parent; he believed that in this respect the curfew was counterproductive.[9] He had served the entire sentence with this restrictive condition without knowing that he could have applied for an amendment. This is another example of the importance of the offender taking an active part in the sentence in order for the disposition to achieve its full potential as a sanction. The offenders also reported some ambiguity on the part of the court. One offender stated that the judge in his case had imposed an absolute curfew and then questioned his own order, wondering whether this permitted the offender to go to work.

Daily life in the virtual prison

'I was working in the kitchen while in remand, that was the only thing worthwhile in prison . . . the community is the better way to go. It's also a lot harder, it teaches you [to make] a lot of sacrifices.'

'I have a bit of a problem sitting at home on a beautiful day when the 7–11 is five steps away.'

'The hardest part would be dealing with your friends and family, explaining why you couldn't go out.'

'The hardest for me was absolute house arrest, it's hard when . . . you've gotta do something, and you can't. For example, our lease is up . . . and I got to go find another place, and I can't do it.'

What is it like to live under a tight set of court-ordered conditions, including house arrest or a strict curfew? As noted earlier, much will depend upon the nature of those restrictions as well as the length of time that they have to be observed. However, many offenders in Canada and also elsewhere (e.g. Church and Dunstan, 1997), found – like the judges and students who simulated the experience – that living under home confinement conditions was harder and the conditions more intrusive than they had anticipated. The conditions that are hardest to respect are likely to account for the most breaches. The one issue on which all the Canadian offenders agreed was that the most difficult part of serving a community custody sentence was complying with house arrest or a very restrictive curfew. This result is consistent with Petersilia and Deschenes (1994) research wherein offenders were asked to rate the perceived difficulty of a number of community correctional conditions: house arrest with electronic monitoring was rated as the most difficult condition (see Figure 3).[10]

Many of the offenders interviewed in Canada had been sentenced to absolute (i.e. 24-hour) house arrest. The consequences of this condition included the following: preventing offenders from participating in social activities; interfering with family outings and special occasions; creating stigma when other people realized that the offender was serving a sentence. For one offender, the hardest condition was performing community service on top of his job. Nevertheless, he found it a rewarding experience: 'When you're working 50 hours week, it makes for some very long days. But it wasn't just a punishing experience, it was a rewarding experience.'

Impact of community custody on children of the offender

An important consideration in imposing community rather than secure custody is the presence of a family. There is an additional incentive for courts to avoid incarcerating the offender if he or she has dependants, and many of the offenders who spoke to us about the experience of community custody had families, often with small children. The most punitive element for these offenders was the impact that the sentence had upon their children, whose interactions with their parents and daily lives were affected for the duration of the sentence. One offender noted that the sentence was 'especially hard on the kids to accept what has happened'. She added: 'It's hard on the kids, because we used to go out, especially in the summer. Every time they ask me I say I can't.' Several offenders complained of the restrictions that absolute house arrest introduced upon their children's lives.

A female offender discussed the house arrest condition in the context of other conditions imposed: 'the absolute curfew is the hardest thing. I can't go anywhere without telling my PO [probation officer]. Absolute curfew is like house arrest. My daughter wants to go the park, but I can't take her.' She added that it put a lot of strain on her when she had to try and explain why they couldn't go to the park: 'Sometimes I'd say, "oh, I'm tired" or "we just can't do that today". It's hard because I don't know what to say. [pause] I have to make excuses.' However, she added that staying home was easier than going to jail. She would rather stay home and be with her kids, and believed that if she did not have kids she would have been sent to jail.

Effect on relationships: the intensification hypothesis
One must be wary of generalizations with respect to the effect of home detention on issues such as relationships; close confinement for long periods will have different effects depending upon the personalities of the individuals involved, the nature of the relationship and the home environment. Although it has yet to be formally tested, it may well be that an *intensification* effect exists: home environments characterized by conflict and tension are likely to become worse as a result of the domestic confinement of the offender. Walters (2002) found that offenders on curfew orders in England

and Wales reported that the curfew placed a strain on their relationships; it was hard to 'walk away from arguments' (p. 32). It is worth noting that these offenders were on curfew orders for a relatively short period of time. The maximum term of the order is six months; fully 70 per cent were serving curfew orders of under four months. Facing a curfew order of two years would be a far more daunting proposition, which would create even more stress upon relationships.

Partners were also affected by the community custody sentence. One said: '[It has] been very hard on my girlfriend. She felt strapped down. She couldn't go nowhere, I couldn't drive her anywhere . . . it was also hard for her because she didn't want to tell her friends that I was on a conditional sentence . . . My girlfriend often tells me how it affects [their relationship]. All we can do is cook some supper if I get groceries on Sunday. All we can do is watch movies if she goes and gets them. I don't have problem with [the other conditions imposed] but the twenty-four hours at home are too much.'

On the other hand, home detention in generally positive environments may well enhance human relationships. There is certainly evidence from the Canadian research that this is the case; young adult offenders confined to homes that they shared with loving parents reported that the sentence had been a positive experience. The restrictions on the offenders' movements can help rupture anti-social contacts, and prevent these individuals from being drawn into criminogenic life patterns.

In general, the limited research on the effect of home confinement on co-residents is topic has found that offenders report that relationships with co-residents improved. Research reported by Dodgson et al. (2001) is an exception. These researchers interviewed offenders on the Home Detention Curfew and found that the experience of being on the program had made no difference to their relationships with others. However, it must be recalled that these offenders were on the program for a relatively short period of time (a maximum of sixty days) which is probably insufficient time to affect these relationships. Moreover, of those who had noticed a change, twice as many said that matters had improved rather than worsened (Dodgson et al., 2001).

The necessity to dissemble about the sentence

Few members of the public stop to think about the impact of a community custody sentence on the ways that people react to the offender. However, these reactions can amplify the stigma associated with the sentence. One individual noted that when his 'in-laws' heard of the sentence, they terminated any further contact with him; in his words, they 'shunned' him. Other offenders talked about the stigma that they had felt when they had told their co-workers about the court order and its associated restrictions. And some offenders expressed concern about potential 'whistle-blowers' – people who might call the police if they believed that the offender was violating some condition of his or her order. This is illuminating because it underlines the important reality that surveillance is not the exclusive domain of probation officers. If it were, ensuring compliance would be impossible, as probation officers in most jurisdictions simply have too many clients to monitor their behaviour adequately. The negative reaction of others appears to create pressure on community custody offenders to passively hide their status, or actively deceive other people.

Offenders sentenced to community custody and obliged to wear an electronic monitor will often have to explain their status to people with whom they have some relationship. In Canada, most offenders sentenced to a community custody sentence are not subject to electronic monitoring, since the equipment is not currently available in most provincial correctional systems.[11] However, the restrictions on their movements meant that most offenders had to confront the question of how much to disclose to other individuals. Fearful of the consequences, many offenders elected to dissemble, particularly with respect to the workplace. In the case of employers, some offenders said nothing rather than explain the true state of affairs. As one individual noted, 'I think I'll get fired if I tell my employer.' In some cases, however, it was impossible to hide the fact of the sentence, as there were occasions when they were invited to stay after work and this had compelled them to explain why this was not possible.

Explaining the community custody order to other people – particularly to children – was a source of considerable anxiety for many offenders. In the case of relatively young children, some offenders resorted to deception, or simply said (in response to requests to go out) that they 'couldn't go out right now'. Other offenders explained matters more fully, and explained why:

> 'My son is fourteen . . . I sat down with him this summer and I told him what I did and what had happened. The main reason I told him is because he's approaching that age I told him I don't want him to follow in my footsteps.'

Lifestyle changes

In Canada, the optional conditions that a court may impose should reduce the likelihood of the offender re-offending. In pursuit of this objective, courts order offenders to follow treatment, abstain from consuming alcohol and other such conditions. The popular discourse regarding community custody tends to overlook this purpose of the sanction, but there is a substantial body of evidence, albeit unsystematic, that offenders do change their lifestyles when confined to home. A number of offenders interviewed in Canada reported that their life patterns had changed while on the sanction, and that several of these changes, particularly with respect to drugs and alcohol, had persisted afterwards.

For some offenders, community custody creates an inverted lifestyle. For example, some offenders have jobs which require them to work far from home.[12] One truck driver interviewed in Canada whose community custody order permitted him to drive his truck across the province noted that work had become pleasurable: while working, he was able to go to roadside restaurants, and move around relatively freely. However, once he was at home, his life became constrained, and he was unable to leave the house, even to visit the local newsagent. For this individual, life at work had become far more attractive than home life.

Research with home confinement offenders reported by Rubin (1990) found that respondents showed a reduction of drug and alcohol use after being on home confinement. This finding contradicts the view that community custody offenders spend much of their time drinking or taking drugs, safe in the knowledge that their behaviour cannot be monitored while home, merely their presence (Harkins, 1990). The explanation for the more abstemious conduct of these offenders appears to be that their alcohol consumption had been associated with spending most evenings in pubs. Even when this was once again possible (after the sentence was over), the desire to do so was not as strong.

Loss of spontaneity

Being on a community custody order clearly means that daily life has to be planned far more carefully. Offenders have to consider whether particular acts will constitute a breach of the order, and they have to contact their sentence supervisors in order to apply for permission to attend particular events. For older offenders, making an application to a younger probation officer was a 'humbling' experience, as one such individual remarked. In order to join people for a coffee after one of his group therapy meetings he had to obtain the permission of his probation officer, otherwise he would have been in breach as the order required him to return directly home once the meeting had ended. Gibbs and King (2001) also report that the necessity to plan excursions from home created psychological pressure on detainees.[13]

Most, but by no means all offenders seemed concerned about the consequences of breaching the order by returning home late. One offender noted that 'I never actually ran out of time [returning home after a court authorised shopping trip] but I was always worried about running out of time.' Time pressures were a source of considerable stress for these offenders (see also Beck and Klein-Saffran, 1991). This was compared to the leisurely pace of shopping without such a constraint to which members of the public have become accustomed. For the general public, the worst consequence of dawdling while shopping is missing the bus home; for community custody offenders, being late home may result in arrest, and, ultimately, committal to custody.

Experiences and perceptions of family members and other sponsors

'I don't think the judges understand when they hand down this sentence, that they're handing down the same sentence to the family.'

There are important reasons for needing to hear from these individuals. First, their lives are dramatically affected when their loved ones are placed under a condition such as house arrest or a strict curfew. Imprisonment affects the lives of people other than the offender, but only indirectly. When an offender is sentenced to community custody, many of the conditions imposed are shared with his or her family members. This is particularly true when electronic monitoring is used. This creates a zone of surveillance which encompasses the offender's co-residents. Aungles noted this a decade ago in her landmark study of the prison and the home in Australia: 'The surveillance of the prisoner in the home must inevitably be control and punishment shared by both the prisoner and his wife or parent' (1994; p. 69).

Second, family members and partners play a vital role in ensuring the success of a community custody order. In most jurisdictions, probation caseloads do not permit more than perfunctory monitoring of most community custody offenders, except for the higher risk cases. Whether an offender respects conditions such as an absolute curfew, a non-association order or a prohibition against the consumption of alcohol, will depend more upon the support of his or her family or partner. If community custody works as a sanction, it will be more a consequence of the vigilance and support of family members than even the most draconian threats from the court or the most intrusive surveillance by probation officers. This explains why detainees in New South Wales identified family and social support as the most important contributors to successful completion of a home detention order (Heggie, 1999).

The literature on co-habitants or sponsors of community custody offenders is far from extensive, and like the research on offender experiences, draws upon small samples of subjects, who are always volunteers (see Quinn and Holman, 1991; Holman and Quinn, 1992). Nevertheless, in an important sense family members and partners (or sponsors, in jurisdictions such as New Zealand where they have a formal role) of people serving a community custody sentence have also been sentenced by the court. Few jurisdictions have recognized this, with a notable exception being New South Wales where there was considerable concern, as the Home Detention Bill was being debated, about the impact on the families and partners of detainees (see Heggie, 1999).

Family members and partners of community custody offenders in Canada and elsewhere were acutely aware of the impact on their lives. One family member noted that: 'We felt like we were kind of being judged too.' King and Gibbs (2003) report the same reaction from sponsors of offenders on home detention in New Zealand. This is one of the costs of community custody: sponsors' lives are directly and indirectly affected by the conditions imposed on the offender. And, to a degree, they become an extension of the administration of the sentence; family members play a vital role in ensuring compliance with the conditions of the court.

There was some resentment among family members in Canada that the court had seemed unaware that a sentence was effectively being imposed on the entire family, and not just the offender. This lack of consultation resulted in the parents feeling left out of the process. They were passive bystanders at the sentencing hearing as the court imposed a sentence that would change their lives for up to the next two years. One man attended the sentencing of his son and said that while the judge was reading each of the conditions he had been thinking about each of them and how they would affect his family: '[After] each condition I'm thinking, ok, how am I going to do this, how am I going to do that? I certainly felt that I walked out of there with a bigger burden.'

Offenders, too, were well aware of the impact of their sentence on the people with whom they lived (see also Payne and Gainey, 1998, who found that almost two-thirds of their sample of electronically monitored offenders described negative effects upon their families). A typical comment was the following: 'My parents feel like they're the ones being punished; they feel like they're on a sentence.' This offender remarked that in his view, his parents have been turned into 'his jail-keepers'. Another said: 'It's been hard on my family, very hard, since I have missed family gatherings, religious ceremonies, and other important family events.'

In addition to the anxiety regarding the possibility that the detainee will violate conditions and be returned to court, and then possibly to prison, parents carry the responsibility of assisting the offender in complying with conditions. Sponsors sometimes feel conflicted in this respect: confronted with an offender who is about to violate a condition, what should they do? Remonstrate with him, and if that fails, report the individual to the proba-tion authorities? It is an invidious position in which they find themselves as a result of the sanction. Gibbs and King (2003b) report the same phe-nomenon with the sponsors of home detainees in New Zealand. Sponsors and other family members 'felt the weight of expectation placed upon them by Prison Board members and probation officers: to supervise detainees informally and let probation officers know if things were not working out' (p. 206).

As noted in chapter 4, in some jurisdictions, prior to the imposition of a community custody sentence the court orders an inquiry into the question of the impact of such a sentence on third parties, namely those sharing the residence in which the offender will reside. This includes a consultation with family members. In Canada, a conditional sentence of imprisonment is imposed without any such consultation, and for up to two years less one day in length. The pre-sentence report may address the suitability of the offender for a conditional sentence, but it does not explore the reactions of, and consequences for, family members, nor does it solicit any input with respect to the kinds of conditions that might (or might not) promote the purpose they are designed to serve.[14] Thus family members and partners are expected to play an important role in the administration of the sentence (by encouraging compliance), yet are given no input into the way that sentence is constructed.

Until their son or daughter was sentenced, as with most members of the public, the parents to whom we spoke in Canada had heard almost nothing about the community custody sentence, a finding consistent with findings from public opinion surveys on the issue (see chapter 7). Many under-estimated the intrusiveness of the restrictions that would be placed on the offender's (and their) freedom of action. This was true in Manitoba in 2003 and also in British Columbia a decade earlier (Doherty, 1995). Once sponsors became involved, there was a sense that they were not sufficiently implicated in matters. One noted: 'They don't give you much opportunity to speak up.' Another commented that 'We didn't have any say. You just were told what they were going to do.' The exclusion of parents in particular seems curious in light of their obvious importance in helping to assure the offender's compliance with the court-ordered conditions. The label of leniency applied to this sanction in Canada also affected family members' reactions. Some couples had been told by the defence counsel not to get involved, as their son had 'gotten a break'. This seems an inappropriate position to adopt; surely parents should not be expected to be *grateful* for assuming the burden of helping an offender cope with his or her court-ordered conditions.[15]

The primary response of the sponsors interviewed in Canada encapsulated two emotions: relief that their family member had not been sent to prison, and anxiety that he or she may nevertheless end up there through non-compliance with conditions. A general finding of the research literature is that families and partners welcome the sentence if it spares the offender from being imprisoned (see Doherty, 1995; Walters, 2002; Church and Dunstan, 1997). This is true even if the home confinement necessitated wearing an electronic monitor (Mair and Mortimer, 1996). It was clear to the parents that in light of the offence (and criminal record) of the offender, committal to custody had been a very real possibility. Accordingly, they were most appreciative of the fact that their son or daughter had been able to come home (most had been in remand at the time of sentencing) rather than being sent to prison. Thus one family member described the imposition of the community custody sentence as 'the best thing that ever happened'. Sponsors of home detainees in New Zealand had a similarly upbeat view of the program. One mother noted that 'I just think home detention is a wonderful thing . . .' and identified the constructive nature of the program in the following way: '. . . it gives people a chance to change their ways, change the people they mix with' (Gibbs and King, 2003b, p. 207).[16]

Several parents made statements that illustrate the positive elements of a community custody sentence. For example, some of the conditions that had been imposed – notably abstinence and non-association orders regarding certain individuals – had proved to be hugely beneficial and had succeeded in rupturing destructive links between their sons and other offenders. In this respect, it was clear that court-ordered conditions had achieved something that had proved beyond the power of the offender's parents. One family noted that one of the conditions imposed on their son was to avoid all contact with a co-defendant, and that this court-imposed stricture had proved 'a godsend'. Over time, the offender had come to realize what a bad influence the individual had been on his life. The participant seemed unsure whether or not their son would have come to this realization had he not been ordered to avoid contact as part of the conditional sentence, or had he been sentenced to prison.

This is an illustration of the complementary relationship that exists between the judicial sentence and the offender's social milieu, notably his or her family. Both elements play a critical role in ensuring compliance with conditions and promoting the offender's rehabilitation. One family member in Canada summed up his experience in the following way: 'It was very difficult at first, but it has turned out to be very rewarding. Or at least, a lot of good has come of it.'

Another couple stated that although they had found the sentence difficult, it also had had a very positive impact on their son. Because of the conditions attached to the order, these parents found that they gained a greater degree of influence over the course of their son's life. Where his peer groups would influence him to his detriment, the parents now had a greater say than in the past. This couple needed no convincing of the advantage of community custody over a term of imprisonment. The families to whom we spoke offered clear evidence that some of the conditions imposed as part of the court order, as well as the fact that the offender had been spared an institutional prison term, had contributed to re-establishing relationships among family members (see also Church and Dunstan, 1997). To some degree this was also acknowledged by the offenders themselves; one young adult recognized that his relationship with his mother had improved during the time that he had served on the order.

When an absolute curfew is imposed on the offender, his or her spouse has a choice: they can continue to come and ago as they had done before the order began, or they can remain at home. Most individuals to whom we spoke in the Canadian research had made the decision to remain with their partner, effectively assuming the restrictions of the court order upon their own lives. Doherty (1995) reports that most of the spouses of electronically monitored offenders in her BC study responded the same way, disengaging from social activities while their partners were obliged to be at home. This can create resentment among family members, and in some cases provoked tension in the household. Far from promoting a healthy environment, one young woman reported that the absolute house arrest condition represented a threat to her relationship, which she felt could not withstand the 'cabin fever' atmosphere.

One of the most striking characteristics about prison is the stigmatizing effect it has upon prisoners. Their families however are not adversely affected in this respect beyond the discomfort they may feel visiting a correctional facility. But with community custody, the sentence is shared to a greater degree. Families and partners sometimes report feeling some embarrassment about the sentence being served under their roof. This emerged from interviews with families in Canada as well as New Zealand, where Gibbs and King report that sponsors 'were more likely than detainees to describe feeling stigmatised by home detention' (p. 80).

Conclusion

The literature on offender perceptions of home confinement is admittedly rather sparse, employing small numbers of participants whose reactions may not be representative of all offenders. As well, the variable nature of home confinement/community custody regimes makes it hard to draw general conclusions. These studies need to be supplemented by more comprehensive research using larger samples of subjects. Nevertheless, some tentative conclusions may reasonably drawn.

Offenders serving their prison sentences at home are subject to numerous constraints that change their life in a dramatic manner. As well, there is little discussion in the case law – and none in news media accounts of community custody – of the impact on innocent third parties, or the role that family members play in helping to 'administer' the sentence of the court. One of the strengths of this sanction is that it draws upon the resources of the community – the social networks of the offender – to achieve some of its objectives. This penal strategy comes with a cost, however: the effect of the sentence is amplified through these networks, and other peoples' lives are affected in significant ways. Of course, this is true of imprisonment as well. When an offender is committed to custody, his partner and his family suffer the loss of their loved one, and have to accustom themselves to the inconveniences of visiting hours. The isolation of a prison sentence, however, has a destructive effect upon social relations; this is why such a high percentage of relationships fail to survive a lengthy term of incarceration. Community custody strengthens the links between people.

The reality of home confinement bears little resemblance to the popular conception of the sentence. Offenders see many conditions such as house arrest and tight curfews as being very restrictive, and in that sense punitive. The detainees in the home detention program in New South Wales are a good illustration of this. Although they were well prepared for the experience of home detention (having been given considerable amount of information beforehand), most respondents to the exit survey were 'shocked at how tough the scheme actually was' (Heggie, 1999, p. 79). House arrest carries unforeseen consequences for the people with whom these offenders share their residences. Their liberty is subject to many restrictions. As well, these sponsors bear the at times heavy responsibility of ensuring that their co-resident complies with conditions.

Families and partners of offenders sentenced to community custody have an onerous task thrust upon them, and in most jurisdictions, no institutional support is provided. This reality has consequences for the construction of home custody regimes which will be explored more fully in the concluding chapter of this volume. Yet despite all this, there is ample evidence in the research to date that offenders and their families see a positive element to community custody, and not simply because the sanction spares them the experience of prison. Although on occasion home detention caused tension among family members or between partners, there is more evidence to suggest that the increased time at home has a salutary effect on relationships. Many (but by no means all) recognize that community custody creates opportunities for them to change their lifestyle, and to preserve social relations that otherwise would be threatened or ruptured by incarceration. In this sense, offenders perceive the sanction as a novel form of custody. Whatever other people may feel about this new form of custody, offenders seem well aware of the potential of the sanction.

SIX

The effect of community custody
on prison admissions

Although as noted in chapter 3, community custody aims to achieve multiple sentencing aims, home confinement regimes have usually been introduced in order to reduce the number of prisoners in custody (e.g. Law Reform Commission of New South Wales, 1996; Daubney and Parry, 1999). This chapter explores a critical question regarding community custody: can the sanction actually achieve this goal? Will creation of this sentence result in a widening of the net, as a result of being applied to offenders who otherwise have received a non-custodial sanction? The experience with some other alternatives to imprisonment has been disappointing – the trends with respect to the use of imprisonment reviewed in chapter 2 attest to this fact. However, the limited data regarding community custody are more positive. In jurisdictions such as New Zealand it is too early to know whether community custody is an effective tool to reduce the number of admissions to custody. In these countries, community custody either is too new an innovation, or has not been sufficiently widely implemented to make a difference to custodial populations. The experience in Canada and Finland yields the clearest (and most positive) findings in this regard, and accordingly will be explored in more detail.

Although no comprehensive international review has been conducted, researchers have concluded that there is little evidence that decarceration is a consequence of the creation of a community custody sanction. For example, Vollum and Hale (2002) in their recent research review of electronic monitoring and house arrest across the USA address the question of whether this sanction does divert offenders from prison, and conclude that 'the jury is still out' (p. 3). Reviewing the international literature on this question however, reveals a more positive response. Although community custody has failed to reduce the number of prison admissions in some jurisdictions, in others there is evidence of a decarceration effect.

The introduction of any new alternative is designed to reduce admissions to custody while simultaneously avoiding 'widening of the net', or 'up-tariffing'. These terms refer to the application of an alternative sanction to offenders who were not at risk for a term of custody in the first place (see McMahon, 1990, for discussion). In the most recent review, Holman and Brown conclude that 'programs designed to be "alternatives to incarceration" and alleviate prison crowding lead nearly half a million people into American prisons each year' (2004, pp. 206–7). Net-widening has proven to be the bane of many alternative sanctions introduced over the past twenty years. This has led to warnings from many scholars of the potential dangers of creating new sanctions, particularly those that carry a punitive element, or that impose stringent conditions on the offender.

Apprehension about the net-widening effect of a new sanction has included home confinement schemes and community custody in general. Thus in 1996 Michael Tonry expressed the view that 'There seems little reason to believe that house arrest is any less vulnerable to net widening [than other intermediate sanctions]' (p. 120). Writing of community custody in Canada, Pierre Landreville describes what he refers to as the 'l'éscalade du controle pénal': 'Ce type de surveillance pourrait être imposé, craint-on, à des personnes qui auraient eu une simple probation'[1] (1999, p. 115). There was clear evidence to justify these views in the earlier years of home confinement regimes. However, as we shall see, more recent evidence suggests that the problem can be contained.

The potential for community custody to 'net widen' is certainly present; there is a tendency for members of the public and some criminal justice professionals to see community custody as an enhanced form of probation. If judges see the sanction as a form of 'Probation Plus', then it assuredly will be used for some cases that would not otherwise have been sent to prison – the more serious cases from the probation caseload. Other commentators have adopted a more optimistic view regarding the introduction of community penalties, arguing that the problem of net-widening has been overstated (see Cusson, 1998).

Defining net-widening

It is important to clarify what is meant by net-widening. According to one definition, net-widening occurs when a new alternative sanction is imposed on an offender who previously would have received a less severe sanction.

The sentencing process is uniquely responsible for this kind of widening of the net. In this chapter I refer to this outcome as 'direct' net widening. The offender may have avoided prison, but is nevertheless now subject to more rigorous social control than would previously have been the case. In the context of community custody, an example of this would occur when an offender who previously would have been sentenced to probation now receives a term of custody to be served at home. If this were the case, these offenders would be punished more severely than in the past, and a certain percentage of them would inevitably end up in prison, having violated their conditions, a clear case of net-widening as a result of 'up-tariffing' (see Brownlee, 1988).

The most likely sentence that would give place to a community custody sentence under a net-widening scenario is probation. Indeed, this was the experience in England and Wales following the introduction of the partly suspended sentence. Although there was a decline in the use of unsuspended terms of imprisonment, there was also a decline in the proportionate use of other non-custodial sanctions such as probation (see Dignan, 1984). Bottoms (1981) found that suspended sentences were imposed on offenders who would not have been at risk for custody in the first place. In his historical review of community penalties in England and Wales, Nellis describes the experience using language that also applies to several other jurisdictions: 'Thus, despite the availability of new alternatives, sentencers were not always using them as policy-makers intended' (2002, p. 24).

Another form of net-widening occurs when violation of the conditions imposed leads to the incarceration of the offender for breach. The danger of this kind of 'indirect' net-widening occurring is even greater for community custody, since many regimes require courts to provide a rigorous response to breaches; usually this means incarceration for some period, if not the time remaining on the order. For this reason, the success of a community custody sanction is crucially dependent upon the nature of the conditions imposed on the offender. If the conditions are too demanding, breach will become almost inevitable, resulting in the incarceration of the offender.

However, assuming that the conditions are not unreasonable, and the offender has been supervised appropriately, if an offender who *otherwise would have gone to prison* receives a term of community custody and is eventually admitted to prison for violating his conditions, it is harder to describe this latter scenario as a case of pure net-widening. In this example, the offender has played some role in widening the penal net. The Alberta Court of Appeal recognized this when it discussed the Damocles image associated with this kind of sanction. The Court likened the threat of imprisonment to the sword hanging by a rope over the individual's head, and noted that 'the *only* way that this rope can break is if *the offender himself cuts it . . .*' (emphasis in the original).[2] At the very worst, the individual has been spared at least part of the custodial sanction (the portion under supervision in the community prior to breach of conditions).

Experience in other jurisdictions

Florida

Although Florida's community control program was, as noted, designed to reduce prison overcrowding, analysis of sentencing trends before and after introduction of the sanction suggests that the proportion of offenders sent to prison did not decline significantly following introduction of the new sanction (Baird and Wagner, 1990). However, this finding reflects the influence of other factors rather than the failure of the program. Baird and Wagner (1990) report that more than half the community control placements in the period studied were individuals who otherwise would have been committed to prison. Blomberg et al. (1993) conclude that the introduction of home confinement 'enabled the state to supplement probation sanctions rather than alter its increasing reliance on prison sanctions' (p. 195). Thus it is not community custody *per se*, but the way in which the sanction has been incorporated into the Florida sentencing system that accounts for its failure to reduce the use of institutional imprisonment.

Finland

Lappi-Seppala (2001) describes the community custody sanction as the country's 'most effective alternative to imprisonment' (p. 113). The reason for this view is that in Finland, the conditional sentence of imprisonment has had an important impact on prison populations in that country, although this success story has not achieved the attention that it deserves. At the start of the 1950s, the number of prisoners in Finland was four times higher than in neighbouring Nordic countries (Lappi-Seppala, 2003).[3] In 1950, less than one-third of sentences of imprisonment were conditional sentences of custody, served in the community. By 1990, this form of community custody was accounting for 60 per cent of all sentences of imprisonment (Lappi-Seppala, 2003). Significant reductions in the number of prisoners were achieved in the period 1950–89, due in large measure to the application of this form of community custody (see Lappi-Seppala, 2003, Figure 11–10).

Thereafter, the number of prisoners declined at a modest rate, as the use of the sentence sanction remained stable. This dramatic shift from institutional to community custody was achieved without appearing to generate widespread public opposition. Lappi-Seppala (2003) identifies what he refers to as 'attitudinal readiness' on the part of the judiciary as an important explanation of the country's ability to lower the number of people in prison. The experience in Finland therefore demonstrates that community custody can make significant inroads into the prison population, so long as it is supported by judges, and imposed sufficiently frequently.

New Zealand

As noted in the previous chapter, in New Zealand, home detention is an option for two categories of offenders: (i) offenders who have been sentenced to imprisonment for two years or less and who have been granted leave to apply for home detention and (ii) prisoners serving sentences in excess of two years. When the sanction is applied in these ways, net-widening is not an issue. The only way that the program can expand the web of penal control would be if judges, cognizant of the offender's likelihood of obtaining release to the program, were more likely to sentence the individual to custody in the first place, and this seems unlikely. The New Zealand methodology ensures that home confinement is not imposed on offenders who would otherwise be sentenced to a less severe sentence such as probation, but at the same time, the nature of the regime is unlikely to effect a major reduction in the prison population.

In the first eighteen months of the regime, a total of 897 offenders were placed on home confinement. This represents less than one-third of the number of people who applied, and an even smaller percentage of eligible offenders (Gibbs and King, 2003a). The figure of 897 must be seen in the context of the volume of offenders on whom a custodial sentence was imposed. In 2001, 26,366 offenders were sentenced to continuous or intermittent (periodic) custody (Spier, 2002). Community custody will have to become far more common before it significantly reduces the use of custody in New Zealand. Nevertheless, the experience to date shows that widening of the net has been avoided in New Zealand, even if the reduction in the number of admissions to custody has to date been modest.

England and Wales

As noted in chapter 4, the Criminal Justice Act of 2003 created a form of community custody sanction, the effects of which will not become apparent for some years. However, the experience with curfew orders reveals some positive findings. The curfew order, which originated in the 1991 Criminal

Justice Act, was the subject of pilot projects in addition to an evaluation of the national application (Walters, 2002). This order represents a modest form of community custody. It has a comparatively limited application of six months for adult offenders, and carries a curfew period that can be as little as two hours per day. For this reason, its impact on the overall prison population in excess of 70,000 is likely to be minimal. However, the critical question addressed here is whether the order has become an 'add on' sanction or has actually served to replace admissions to custody.

Walters (2002) reports the findings from the first thirteen months after 'roll out', during which time 4,600 orders were imposed. In light of its restricted ambit, it is not surprising that the order was applied to a population of less serious offenders: less than 10 per cent of offenders placed on these orders had been convicted of a crime of violence, while fully one quarter had been convicted of a theft-related offence (Walters, Table 2.3). Determining the decarceration effect of the curfew orders is complicated by a number of factors, including the likelihood that this sanction was being imposed as a response to breach of a community sentence. However, it seems reasonable to conclude that approximately one-fifth to one-quarter of these orders had been imposed on offenders who otherwise would have been committed to custody (see Walters, 2002, p. 40). As noted, this is unlikely to reduce the prison population in England and Wales either dramatically or quickly. Nevertheless, with usage growing rapidly, the difference is likely to become more apparent. In addition, as Walters (2002) observes, the cost savings generated by the first year of the orders amounted to a sum in excess of a million pounds. After reviewing findings from a number of studies, Mair (2001) concludes that approximately half those offenders sentenced to home confinement with electronic monitoring represented true diversions from custody, the other half being cases that would previously have attracted a less severe disposition such as a fine or probation. Thus widening of the net remains a live issue with respect to the use of home confinement in England and Wales.

Impact of community custody sanction on admissions to prison in Canada[4]

As noted earlier, a community custody sentence (the conditional sentence of imprisonment) was introduced in Canada in 1996. It is now possible to come to some definitive conclusions regarding the impact of the sanction on admissions to prison in that country. There are two central questions of interest:

- to what extent have admissions to prison declined in the period following the introduction of community custody? This question refers to the *decarceration* effect.
- to what extent have community custody orders been imposed on cases which prior to 1996 would have received a non-custodial sentence (such as a fine or probation). This question refers to the *widening of the net* effect.

If widening of the net has occurred, the combination of custody plus community custody orders will exceed the previous custodial rate. If the opposite has occurred, if the combination of custody plus community custody orders falls below the number of custodial admissions pre-1996, then a more general shift away from sentences of imprisonment is present.

The following graphic with three theoretical scenarios illustrates the logic of the subsequent net-widening analysis. Scenario A shows the decarceration effect of community custody, with no evidence of widening of the net. All the conditional sentences have been drawn exclusively from the custodial caseload.

Scenario (A) Reduction of admissions to custody, no widening of net

	Pre community custody	Post community custody
Number of custodial sentences	100	80
Number of community custody sentences	–	20

In Scenario B, the introduction of 20 conditional sentences has resulted in a reduction (10 per cent) in the number of custodial admissions. However, not all of the conditional sentences replaced a term of custody, and must have drawn from other sanctions; this is clear evidence of widening of the net.

Scenario (B) Reduction of admissions to custody, with some widening of the net

	Pre community custody	Post community custody
Number of custodial sentences	100	90
Number of community custody sentences	–	20

In Scenario (C), community custody has reduced the use of incarceration as a sanction, but other factors have also contributed to the reduced incarceration rate. As will be seen, there is evidence of both scenarios (B) and (C) in the community custody data in Canada, although widening of the net represents a small fraction of the decarceration effect.

Scenario (C) Reduction of admissions to custody in excess of the number of conditional sentences

	Pre community custody	Post community custody
Number of custodial sentences	100	70
Number of community custody sentences	–	20

Table 6.1 summarizes trends with respect to the impact on admissions to custody for a number of provinces[5] over the period 1993/4 to 2000/01 (see Roberts and Gabor, 2004, for further information). In order to control for influences such as changes in the volume of convictions, or shifts in the use of different sanctions, the analysis uses the rate of admissions to custody per 10,000 charges heard in court. The analysis controls for changes in the crime rate, and changes in the use of other sanctions.

Decarceration

With respect to decarceration, Table 6.1 demonstrates a significant drop in the rate of custodial sentences between the pre and post-conditional sentence periods included in the analysis. Nationally, rates of admissions to custody declined by 13 per cent over the period, with eight of the nine jurisdictions experiencing declines in custodial admissions. A decline of this magnitude represents almost 55,000 admissions to custody over the period covered by the analysis. There was a significant negative correlation ($r = -.45$; $p < .05$) between changes in the rate of custody and the volume of conditional sentences imposed. This represents the *decarceration* effect. In general, the provinces with the highest rates of community custody orders also experienced the greatest reductions in admissions to custody. It is interesting to note, however, that the correlation between the volume of community custody orders and the decline in admissions is not greater. This means that a proportion of the drop in custody rates is explained by variables *other* than the introduction of conditional sentencing. Exploring these factors

Table 6.1. *Impact of community custody sentence in Canada.*

	% change in custody rate per 10,000 adults charged, pre to post implementation
Quebec	−5
Prince Edward Island	4
British Columbia	−14
Ontario	−5
Nova Scotia	−18
Alberta	−19
New Brunswick	−32
Newfoundland and Labrador	−37
Saskatchewan	−47
All provinces in analysis	*−13*

Source: adapted from Roberts and Gabor (2004).[6]

is beyond the scope of this chapter. It is clear, however, that independent of the introduction of community custody, judges have been using some alternatives to custody more often in recent years. The use of probation, for example, increased significantly over the period (Roberts and Gabor, 2004).

Increased use of probation as a sanction
The declining prison admission statistics in response to the introduction of community custody are in fact only part of the story. Examination of the probation admission statistics over the period encompassing the introduction of community custody reveals that there was a significant increase in the use of probation as a sanction. The rate of probation terms per 10,000 charges increased by 10 per cent nationally from the pre-reform period to the post-reform period. There are a number of possible explanations for the increased use of probation as a sanction. One explanation concerns the codification of the purposes and principles of sentencing in 1996. As noted, these principles encourage judges to employ alternatives to custody wherever possible and appropriate. Sensitizing judges to the principle of restraint may have provoked a renewed interest in an alternative to imprisonment such as probation.[7] This may explain the fact that in 2000/1, probation was the most widely used sanction in Canada, imposed in 44 per cent of cases (Thomas, 2002), up from 34 per cent in 1993–4 (Roberts, 1999b).

Interest in restorative justice may also have played a role in stimulating the use of both probation and community custody. Although Canada has not pursued restorative goals with quite the enthusiasm of other jurisdictions such as New Zealand (see Morris, 2004), the sentencing purposes codified in 1996 contain several elements that are restorative in nature (see Roach, 2000). For example, one of the statutory sentencing objectives is 'to provide reparations for harm done to victims or to the community' (s. 718.(e)). Reparation is impossible while the offender is imprisoned. Community service, the principal means by which offenders can make reparation to the community, is often ordered as a condition of a probation order.

In addition to these statutory reforms, several judgments of the Supreme Court in Canada in recent years have given fresh impetus to restorative considerations at sentencing (see Roach, 2000; Roberts and Roach, 2003). In light of these developments, perhaps it is not surprising that judges have increasingly turned to probation as a sanction. Finally, the inception of community custody itself may have stimulated judicial interest in alternatives to imprisonment, and it would be natural for this interest to focus on probation.

Direct net-widening

Across all provinces there has been a small degree of net-widening (relative to the decarceration effect). This means that some of the offenders sentenced to a community custody order over the period covered by the analysis were not drawn from the custodial sample. Prior to the creation of this sanction, these individuals would have been sentenced to a non-custodial sentence.[8] Approximately 5,000 offenders over the course of the period covered by the analysis would have been sentenced to a non-custodial sanction. However, this widening of the net effect must be set against the decarceration effect already described, in order to arrive at a 'net' decarceration effect. The result is still impressive, as the decarceration effect is much larger than the widening of the net effect.

Net-widening as a result of admission to custody following breach of conditions

One other consideration must be taken into account in evaluating the impact of community custody in Canada, and that is the outcome of community custody orders. If a high percentage of orders resulted in the offender breaching his or her conditions and being sent to prison, this would seriously undermine any movement towards fewer admissions. Since community

Table 6.2. *Percentage of successfully completed community custody orders, three Canadian provinces (1997–2001).*

	% 1997/8	% 1998/9	% 1999/00	% 2000/1
Ontario	88	90	89	89
Manitoba	78	79	71	63
Saskatchewan	87	85	80	78

Source: Roberts and Gabor (2004).

custody orders in Canada are frequently longer than the terms of custody that they replace, a high incarceration rate in response to breach could threaten the effectiveness of the entire regime.[9] As it happens, there has been very little of this kind of 'indirect' net widening. The breach rate to date of community custody orders has been very low, and only a minority of the founded breaches have been committed to prison.

Table 6.2 provides the outcomes of community custody orders for the three provinces for which these data are available. As can be seen, only a small percentage of community custody orders to date have resulted in revocation for a breach of conditions. In the most recent year for which data are available in Ontario, almost 90 per cent of orders were completed successfully. A breach is the first pre-requisite for admission to prison. The second requirement is a committal order from the court (in response to an unjustified breach). Since Canadian courts have considerable latitude in responding to offenders who have breached their orders, it is perhaps not surprising that judges do not always or often send the recalcitrant offender to prison.

Table 6.3 provides data regarding judicial response to breach in two provinces. Several trends are significant. First, as can be seen, the judicial response differs across the two jurisdictions. In Ontario, in 2000/1, less than one-quarter of the cases in which a breach is found to have occurred (without reasonable excuse) the community custody order was cancelled and the offender sent to prison for the balance of the time remaining on the sentence. (This is the most punitive response to breach possible permitted by the *Criminal Code.*) Courts in Manitoba, however, are far more likely to activate this response, as it was recorded in over half (53 per cent) the founded breaches in the most recent year (Table 6.3).

Expressed as a proportion of all community custody orders, the number of offenders who were ultimately committed to custody for breach is very

Table 6.3. *Judicial response to breach of community custody orders, two Canadian provinces, 1997–2001.*

	% 1997/8	% 1998/9	% 1999/00	% 2000/1
Ontario				
No action taken; offender remains in the community	33	28	25	28
Conditions amended and offender remains in the community	24	30	20	22
Offender is committed to custody for a portion of the time remaining on the sentence	16	23	25	27
Offender is committed to custody for the duration of the sentence	26	19	29	23
	100	100	100	100
Manitoba				
No action taken; offender remains in the community	30	18	5	6
Conditions amended and offender remains in the community	5	18	22	16
Offender is committed to custody for a portion of the time remaining on the sentence	11	19	24	25
Offender is committed to custody for the duration of the sentence	53	45	50	53
Total	100	100	100	100

Source: Roberts (2002a).

Table 6.4. *Breakdown of community custody sentence lengths, Canada,
2000–2001.*

	% Up to 6 months	% >6 to <12 months	% 12 to <18 months	% 18 to <24 months
New Brunswick	82	8	8	2
Prince Edward Island	80	8	10	2
Newfoundland	77	14	7	2
British Columbia	68	10	14	7
Ontario	60	14	16	10
Manitoba	52	15	22	11
Nova Scotia	50	27	15	8
Quebec	46	14	27	13
Saskatchewan	44	19	24	13
Alberta	41	14	27	18

Source: Statistics Canada.

small, around 2 per cent. Thus although some offenders eventually entered
custody having been sentenced to community custody, the number pales
beside the number of offenders in the community who would otherwise
have begun their sentences in prison. In addition, as noted, it is harder to
consider admissions for breach as an example of true net widening, since
the offender him or herself has been responsible for the outcome.

One final important point is worth making about the reduction in admissions to prison across the country. As would be expected,[10] community custody sentence lengths are not evenly or normally distributed up to the limit
of two years less one day. Shorter community custody sentences are far more
frequent. Table 6.4 provides a distribution of community custody sentences
for the provinces in 2000–1. These data are significant because they demonstrate that a statutory limit as high as two years less one day is not necessary
for the sanction to achieve a significant reduction in admissions to custody.
Indeed, the ceiling on the length of a community custody order could be
lower, with little appreciable impact on the extent to which the sentence
reduces admissions to custody. If the ceiling were eighteen months instead
of two years less one day, it would eliminate only a small percentage of
conditional sentences imposed.

This point carries great significance for other jurisdictions contemplating
the creation of a conditional sentence of imprisonment. It demonstrates that
it is possible to restrict the ambit of the sanction (and thereby prevent many

of the most controversial cases involving very serious offences which attract lengthy terms of custody) without significantly affecting the sanction's ability to reduce the number of admissions to prison. (This issue will be explored further in the final chapter of this volume.)

To conclude, the data from Canada reveal that the volume of admissions to custody did decline in the years following the introduction of a community custody sentence.[11] Moreover, only a modest number of individuals who previously would have received a community-based sentence (such as a fine or probation) were sentenced to the new form of custody. In some jurisdictions, notably England and Wales, the introduction of a form of community custody did not reduce admissions to custody. How, then, was the Canadian version of community custody successful where others have failed?

One of explanations for the success in Canada lies in the nature of the statutory framework. As noted earlier, a court must first decide to impose a term of custody before it may sentence the offender to community imprisonment. This essentially makes the conditional sentence of imprisonment in Canada a form of custody, and not an intermediate sanction lying between prison and probation. If community custody is inserted into the array of sanctions, between probation and prison, it will inevitably will be used by judges for serious probation candidates, which is widening the net. As well, lying beneath prison on a scale of severity, judges will be reluctant to impose community custody for some offences: *it will lack the status of imprisonment.* The lesson seems clear: in order to be effective in terms of reducing admissions to prison, community custody should be created as a form of custody, and not an intermediate sanction.

The nature of judicial reaction to the sanction has also played a role in achieving a reduction in the number of admissions to custody. Judicial confidence is critical to the success of any new sanction; in Canada, judges have embraced the new sanction, and applied it to a wide range of offences. This has occurred even in the context of considerable negative media commentary (see chapter 7). One cause of the judicial enthusiasm for the sanction is the strong endorsement community custody received from the Supreme Court in a guideline judgment in 2000 (*R. v. Proulx*). Without this decision, the 'uptake' of the new sentence may have been much slower.[12]

Conclusion

Many ways of reducing the number of individuals sent to prison have been attempted. In a jurisdiction with formal sentencing guidelines – such as many US states – reductions in admissions to custody can be achieved by moving specific offences out of the incarceration zones of the sentencing guidelines matrix. Common law countries without formal numerical guidelines may use statutory language to reduce the use of incarceration. Legislatures in these jurisdictions devise detailed criteria that must be met before an offender may be sent to prison. For example, the 2003 Youth Criminal Justice Act in Canada obliges judges to proceed through a number of steps before a young person may be committed to custody.[13] Legislatures can thus make it harder for judges to impose a term of custody.

Introducing a single new sanction such as community custody is one of the least effective ways of lowering prison populations when judges have a wide panoply of dispositions from which to choose when sentencing offenders. The reason for this is that no single disposition is going to account for a very high percentage of sentences imposed. This helps to explain the rather ambivalent response of sentencers in Britain to the introduction of new non-custodial options (see Hough et al., 2003). However, the experience in Canada and some other countries at least demonstrates that community custody can reduce the number of offenders sent to prison, and in a relatively short space of time. It also carries the potential, once the public and the judiciary become more supportive of the sanction, to have a more dramatic impact on prison populations by being used for a wider range of offences and offenders.

SEVEN

Public attitudes to community custody

Although there is now an extensive literature on public attitudes towards sentencing, and alternatives to traditional imprisonment, most of this research focuses on alternative sanctions other than community custody: far less is known about public reaction to terms of imprisonment served at home. One reason for this is the relative novelty of this sanction in many jurisdictions. Researchers have explored public reaction to some elements of community custody, such as home detention, electronic monitoring, and curfews; this work sheds light on public opinion regarding community custody, and will be examined here. As well, researchers in Canada have surveyed the public with respect to the community custody sentence, with interesting results.

After discussing public reaction to alternative sanctions in general terms, this chapter explores the extent of public knowledge, and nature of public opinion regarding community custody. The research findings suggest that if community custody is properly conceived, and fully explained to the community, it is seen as a satisfactory substitute for institutional imprisonment for a wide range of offences. Public support for community custody seems to increase as the conditions imposed on the offender become more restrictive. However, for the present at least, the public appear to draw the line at using this sanction for the most serious personal injury offences. For these crimes, the public continue to regard penal sequestration as the only appropriate criminal justice response.

Any history of penal policy development over the past few decades needs to devote a chapter to the role that public opinion has played in the evolution of policies. The views of the public have been responsible, directly or indirectly, for many sentencing and sentencing-related reforms, including mandatory sentencing, the abolition of parole, sex offender registries, and capital punishment. These reforms have been introduced to respond to the pressure of public opinion, as punitive measures of this kind prove popular with the public, particularly in the USA (Reitz, 2001, p. 229). However, the public alone cannot be blamed for all the punitive excesses that we have witnessed. To a large degree, the voice of the people has been appropriated by politicians who have exploited public apprehension over crime and dissatisfaction with justice in support of these (and other) penal reforms (see discussion in Roberts et al., 2003).

In addition, public attitudes reflect the fact that people are often encouraged to believe that harsher sentencing options such as mandatory sentences will appreciably lower crime rates. In this sense, politicians in a number of jurisdictions have misread *and* misled the public. At the same time that penal populists have devised ever more stringent sentencing policies, criminal justice researchers have been accumulating a substantial literature that demonstrates public support for concepts such as proportionality, rehabilitation and reparation (see Cullen, Fisher and Applegate, 2000; Roberts, 1992; Roberts and Stalans, 1997). Researchers in a number of jurisdictions have also demonstrated that the public are less punitive than is often assumed (e.g. Bondeson, 2002; Mande and Butler, 1989; English, Crouch and Pullen, 1989).[1]

The methodology employed to measure public opinion plays a role in determining the outcome of the study; many researchers have discovered that the degree of public support for punitive responses to crime depends in large part on the kinds of questions put to the public, and the amount of information provided to respondents. Provided with minimal information the public responds rather punitively; when given the opportunity to consider issues in more depth, or when they are provided with more information, the public are far less likely to demand harsh punishment, and more likely to accept community-based sanctions (e.g. Zamble and Kalm, 1990).

Perceptions of leniency in sentencing and confidence in the courts

This said, there is no mistaking the fact that the top-of-the-head reaction of the public to general questions about sentencing is relatively negative. Most people believe the criminal justice system favours the interests of the offender and is tilted against those of the victim; this conceptual imbalance is seen to pervade the sentencing process. Reactions to questions about sentence severity make the point clearly. Examining public responses to polls about sentencing trends over the past thirty years reveals that whenever the question is posed, most people respond that sentences are too lenient.

In Canada, for example, the most recent poll containing this question found that approximately two-thirds (63 per cent) of the public believed that sentences were too lenient; less than one-third were of the opinion that sentences were 'about right'. Twenty years earlier, the percentage responding that sentences were too lenient was almost the same (65 per cent; see Sanders and Roberts, 2004).[2] According to the 2000 administration of the BCS, 75 per cent of respondents believed sentences were too lenient; less than one-quarter thought they were about right (Mattinson, 2002). These trends emerge in all Western nations in which representative polls have been conducted (Cullen et al., 2000; Roberts, 1992). Since the result is the same regardless of whether crime rates are changing or stable, and independent of changes to the severity of the courts, opinions must derive from a source other than actual criminal justice trends, presumably the news media.

This perception of leniency contributes to the low levels of public confidence in the courts. Comparative research across several Western nations demonstrates that of all components of the criminal justice system, courts (and sentencers) receive the most negative ratings. For example, repeated administrations of the British Crime Survey have revealed that respondents have less confidence in the courts than the police, and assign the least positive ratings to judges. The 1998 BCS found that 26 per cent of respondents rated judges as doing a poor or very poor job, while only 6 per cent held this view of the police (Mattinson and Mirrlees-Black, 2000).[3] In Canada, although 67 per cent of the respondents to a national poll rated the police as doing a good or excellent job, only 50 per cent had this view of judges (Hough and Roberts, 2004b).

As for the USA, over thirty-five years ago, pollster Louis Harris wrote that 'Courts are criticized rather severely across this land today. I think it is not an overstatement to say that there is a crisis of confidence about them, especially those courts dealing with criminal justice . . . less than a third believe that the courts have been generally fair in dealing with criminals. Forty nine per cent say the courts have been too lenient' (1968, p. 10). In 2002, just over two-thirds of polled Americans held the view that the courts were not harsh enough (Sourcebook of Criminal Justice Statistics, 2003; for trends between 1970 and 2000, see Cullen et al., 2000). Similar results emerge in most other Western nations (Hough and Roberts, 2004b, for a review). Mirrlees-Black (2001) among others has demonstrated that people who express the least confidence in the courts are also more likely to see the courts as being too lenient. The perception of leniency and low levels of public confidence in the courts go hand in hand.

Confidence levels of this kind create pressures upon the criminal justice system. As Davies notes: 'public opinions and sentiments cannot be ignored if public confidence is to be maintained in the criminal justice system' (1993, p. 25). In the area of sentencing, the views of the public are important to the success or failure of any new sanction, including and especially community custody. Indeed, it is clear that public opinion played a critical role in the demise of the suspended sentence of imprisonment, introduced in England and Wales in 1967. The disposition came to be regarded as a 'let off'; all the offender had to do was stay out of trouble and punishment was waived, or so it appeared to the public eye.

Influence of public opinion

The influence of public attitudes can be seen in a number of contexts. A national survey of judges in Canada in 1985 found that most believed that the community was an important factor in determining sentence (Brodeur, Roberts, Mohr and Markham, 1988). More recently, other surveys of the judiciary in Canada produced evidence that community views influence sentencing practices, most judges acknowledging that they considered the impact on public opinion before imposing a community custody sanction (Doob, 2001; Roberts, Doob and Marinos, 2000). This is further evidence of the complex relationship between the practice of the courts and the views of the community (see Bondeson, 2002, for discussion of the relationship between criminal policy and community views).

Community sanctions have often been represented by the news media and some politicians as lenient sentencing options. This image problem has long plagued alternative sanctions in several countries. Tonry, among others,[4] has described the perceived leniency of intermediate sanctions as 'the most difficult obstacle' to greater implementation of these sanctions (Tonry, 1996, p. 128). This view is sustained by the results of numerous polls. For example, in 1996 a poll revealed that over half the American public agreed with the statement that 'community corrections are evidence of leniency in the criminal justice system' (Flanagan, 1996). A similar result emerged from a 1998 poll conducted in Arkansas (University of Arkansas, 1998).

The public may tar all community sentences with the same brush in this respect, but research on offender perceptions (see chapter 5) fails to sustain this perception of all community based punishments. Some community custody sanctions impose very stringent conditions on offenders, and are certainly not experienced as lenient. Speaking of intensive probation, a sanction which falls short of community custody in severity, Petersilia and

Deschenes (1998) note that 'the balance of sanctions between probation and prison appears to have shifted, and at some level of intensity and length, intensive probation is the more dreaded penalty' (p. 157). This reality has yet to permeate the public consciousness, and reflects the gap between received wisdom about serving a sentence in the community, and the actual experience of offenders.[5]

Scholars working on the suspended sentence in England and Wales in the 1960s were aware of the potential public criticism that this sanction would be seen as evidence of leniency towards offenders. Writing of the early versions of the suspended sentence, Ancel (1971) noted that 'another threat to the suspended sentence can be that uncontrollable factor, public opinion and its panic reaction to certain types of offence' (1971, p. 24). And, as noted, this perception contributed to the demise of the sentence, which in recent years has accounted for less than 1 per cent of sentences imposed for indictable offences (Home Office, 1999). A similar public perception has bedevilled the community custody of imprisonment introduced in Canada a quarter of a century later. This version of community custody has repeatedly come under attack from the populist media, particularly when a term of community custody has been imposed on an offender convicted of a serious crime of violence. News stories encourage the perception that community custody is often imposed for a serious crime of violence, and that judges are determined to make life easy for offenders, by sending them home rather than to prison. The result is that the concept of community custody is brought into disrepute through media coverage of a relatively small number of controversial cases.

Public support for rehabilitation in prison

A number of elements of community custody are likely to appeal to the public. Although public support for imprisonment as a sanction is strong, the public around the world clearly want the prison to educate, treat and otherwise improve the lives of prisoners. This is true even in states such as Florida, where attitudes to offenders are probably more punitive than elsewhere. A state-wide survey of Florida residents found that 92 per cent approved of providing inmates with education, and almost as high a percentage (87 per cent) supported the provision of substance abuse programs (Florida Department of Corrections, 1997). Finally, 96 per cent approved of inmates working while in prison (Florida Department of Corrections, 1997). Similarly, in Britain, while 73 per cent believed that 'keeping prisoners secure' was an absolutely essential function of prisons, almost as high a percentage saw 'helping to prepare prisoners to live law-abiding lives on release' as essential (MORI, 2003).

Although the public sees security and rehabilitation to be almost equally important functions of the prison, they are under no illusions about the extent to which these functions are accomplished. Thus 90 per cent of the sample were confident that prisons kept prisoners from escaping, but only 44 per cent were confident that prisoners were helped to prepare for a law-abiding life upon release (MORI, 2003). Americans share this pessimism regarding the effectiveness of imprisonment: when asked to rate the performance of the prison system in achieving various goals, rehabilitating offenders was the task on which the system received the worst ratings. Only 14 per cent thought the system was doing a good job, while half the sample rated the system as doing a poor job in this respect (Gallup, 2000). Similar findings emerge from public opinion polls in Canada (see Hough and Roberts, 2004a).

Public opinion and community custody in Canada

As noted in an earlier chapter, the Canadian community custody sentence has a broad range of application (up to two years less one day in duration), encompassing approximately 95 per cent of all sentences of imprisonment. This means that it can be imposed for the most serious offences short of murder, but including manslaughter, aggravated assault and aggravated sexual assault, and robbery. In practice, it is seldom imposed for a very serious crime of violence.

News media coverage of community custody

The fate of any penal sanction (and many penal reforms) lies in the hands of the news media, who have the power to shape public opinion, which then influences judges, policy-makers as well as politicians. With respect to sentencing, the media have typically presented an image of capricious decision-making, founded upon individual cases that resulted in particularly lenient sentences for serious violent crimes. Indeed, the public perception of unprincipled leniency on the part of the courts derives from newspaper coverage of sentencing decisions. Stories that conform to the media image and that reinforce popular stereotypes about crime and punishment, are likely to prove popular with newspaper editors. The result is that the public receive a very distorted view of sentencing decisions, and indeed of the entire criminal justice system.[6]

Box 7.1. *Examples of community custody headlines in Canadian newspapers (2000–3).*

Law on Sentencing Far too Lenient (*Globe and Mail*)
Molester Show's Law's Weakness (*Edmonton Sun*)
Sentence Sparks Outrage (*Calgary Herald*)
Sex offender walks free (*Ottawa Citizen*)
Fake Doctor Dodges Jail (*Toronto Star*)
No Justice in House Arrest for Child Molester (*Toronto Star*)
House Arrest for Rapist Upsets Victim Counsellors (*Toronto Star*)
Man confined to home for sex assaults on boy (*Toronto Star*)
Paralyzed Teen lashes out at free-ride sentence (*Toronto Star*)
House arrest in fatal hit and run (*Toronto Star*)
No jail for sex with student (*Ottawa Citizen*)
Hockey duties score lighter sentence (*National Post*)
We bring 'em in, judges send them back out (*Edmonton Sun*)
Rioter dodges Jail (*Edmonton Sun*)
Cushy Sentence a Miscarriage (*Toronto Sun*)
Pimp given 2 years house arrest: 3 sold as sex slaves (*Toronto Star*)

The experience with electronic monitoring in the USA and community custody in Canada confirm this rather pessimistic view of media coverage of criminal justice. Almost from its inception (in 1996), the Canadian news media have represented the community custody as a form of probation, a non-penalty, and have used terms such as 'get out of jail free card' to describe the sanction. News media stories inevitably emphasize the element of community custody that suggests it is a lenient sanction[7] – the fact that the offender is at home. In the first few years of the community custody regime, offenders had relatively few conditions to observe, and this was responsible for many of the adverse news stories. As noted in an earlier chapter, the community custody regime changed in 2000 with a Supreme Court guideline decision (*R. v. Proulx*). Thereafter, the more rigorous conditions imposed (including house arrest with electronic monitoring, tight curfews and the like) were either overlooked by journalists, or underplayed. The consequence is that the true severity of community custody has not been communicated to the public in Canada.

A review of newspaper stories about community custody published over the period 1996 to 2002 reveals that most articles emphasized elements of the sentence likely to inflame public opinion. Box 7.1 provides some typical headlines from recent (2000–3) stories.[8] At the time that this volume goes to press, a lengthy article in Canada's national newspaper decried

Figure 7.1. House arrest for plotter © the *Ottawa Sun* and Errol McGihan.

the imposition of a community custody sentence by describing it as a non-custodial sentence 'wherein [the offender] is essentially free'.[9]

News media coverage is about more than just headlines and stories. A message about criminal justice can be powerfully conveyed by means of an image. One example of this can be seen in Figure 7.1. This image covered almost the entire front page of a major newspaper in Canada and depicts the reaction of an offender to the imposition of a community custody order. In light of the seriousness of the offence (she had tried to have her parents murdered), the offender may have been anticipating a custodial sentence. Her joy at receiving a community custody sentence is clear. Without the caption ('House arrest for plotter') a reader might wonder whether she had won the lottery rather than been sentenced to a term of imprisonment. This kind of image feeds the perception that community custody is anything but an aversive experience. The caption also undermines the integrity of the sentence by implying that the offender merely had to remain at home, when in reality a number of other conditions were imposed.

How then, do the public react to community custody as a sanction? Although there is a voluminous research literature on public opinion and alternatives to imprisonment (see Roberts, 2002b, for a review), only a few studies have explored public reaction to this specific alternative sanction. However, what we have learned from these studies is encouraging. Before considering the research that has focused on community custody, several studies on related issues are relevant. As with so many issues in criminal justice, it behoves us to first consider what people know about community custody before considering the nature of their opinions. Attitudes towards this sanction can only be evaluated in light of the extent of public knowledge. Let us begin then by reviewing the findings from surveys that have measured public knowledge of community custody.

Public knowledge of community custody sentence in Canada

In one survey using a representative sample of the public, we tested public awareness of the new sanction in the following way: respondents were provided with three descriptions and asked to identify the one that correctly identified the sentence of community custody. The two incorrect definitions described judicial interim release (bail) and discretionary release from prison (full parole). Since only three options were offered, approximately one-third of the sample should be correct on the basis of chance alone. The results demonstrated poor levels of public knowledge: fewer than half the respondents (43 per cent) chose the correct definition. This statistic is not significantly different from chance ($X^{(1)} = 1.6$, p. > .05). Almost as many (38 per cent) chose the definition of parole, while 13 per cent selected bail (6 per cent responded 'don't know'; see Sanders and Roberts, 2000).

Clearly then, the intense media coverage of community custody since it was introduced had not resulted in widespread awareness of the nature of the new sanction. This knowledge question was repeated on a poll conducted three years later, with the same outcome: less than half the respondents could accurately identify the community custody sentence (Sanders and Roberts, 2004). These findings are consistent with research on community penalties in general; few members of the public are aware of their existence (see Roberts, 2002b). In research conducted with surveys of the Scottish public, only one respondent in a hundred claimed to know a lot about sentencing options available to the courts (Rethinking Crime and Punishment, 2002).

Implications for critics and advocates of community custody

The results of these surveys suggest that there is a considerable lag between passage of a criminal justice reform and public awareness of the legislation. Fully six years after the creation of the community custody sanction (in 2002), during which time the sentence was frequently in the news, most people are still unaware of the nature of the new disposition. Moreover, the test of public knowledge in these surveys was a relatively easy one: respondents had one chance in three of guessing correctly and the wrong options did not include a definition of probation. Since a term of probation is quite similar to a conditional term of imprisonment, had we included probation as a response alternative, the percentage of respondents with the correct answer would have diminished considerably. An important challenge for the criminal justice system is therefore to improve the extent of public knowledge with respect to the new sanction. If this is accomplished, community custody will attract greater support from the community and judges will feel more confident in imposing such sentences.

The knowledge question tested public awareness of the definition of the sanction. Even if people are aware of the nature of community custody, and are able to distinguish it from parole or regular probation, this does not mean that they fully understand the phenomenology of imprisonment at home. As noted by Gibbs and King (2003a) 'The public . . . do not know the "real" impact of home detention' (p. 209). That is why it is vital to explore the experiences and reactions of people who are actually serving sentences of imprisonment at home (see chapter 6). Most people have an image of life in prison, and in many cases this image may not be that discrepant from reality. The public know that prisons impose restrictions and routines, that prisoners occupy small cells – often with another prisoner – and are restricted in their movements. The number of television programs about prison life alone ensures that most people can probably imagine what it is like to be locked up in prison.

However, understanding the effect of restrictions such as absolute house arrest requires more imagination than many people may possess. There is a natural human reaction to see the kinds of constraints that are imposed on others as being quite trivial; if they were imposed on us, we might feel differently. House arrest may not seem like a particularly onerous condition – after all the offender can enjoy the freedom of his own house – but being denied the freedom to attend Christmas parties, to take one's children to football games, to participate in sports, visit pubs, take summer holidays – may be harder to bear than many people realize.

One example illustrates the problem. Interviews with offenders serving community custody sentences in Canada revealed that the sanction provokes numerous ethical challenges. Should the offender explain the court-ordered restrictions to his or her children? Are they old enough to understand such explanations, and, if quite young, will imparting this information have a negative psychological effect? Many of the offenders interviewed acknowledged that this was a problem, and one that they resolved by means of deception: they invented reasons why they could not take their children out at any time of the day (Roberts et al., 2003; see also Mainprize, 1995).[10] These kinds of restrictions weigh heavily on offenders, and increase the penal value or punitiveness of the sanction. It is unlikely, however, that many members of the public stop to consider such issues when evaluating the severity of a sanction that restricts a person's social interactions in these ways.

The public's lack of familiarity with community custody must be borne in mind when considering the effect of the sanction on community views. When people lack confidence in an institution such as criminal justice, and view justice stories through a lens of scepticism, they are unlikely to be particularly receptive to a potentially creative sanction of this kind.

Support for community custody in specific cases

In order to explore the extent of public support for the community custody sentence as an alternative to imprisonment, respondents to a national survey in Canada were asked to sentence offenders described in a number of scenarios (see Sanders and Roberts, 2000). The six offences used were: sexual assault; impaired driving causing bodily harm; fraud by an employee; fraud by a lawyer; spousal assault; assault. Prior to being asked to make a choice between the imposition of a prison term or a term of community custody, subjects were provided with a description of a community custody. As well, respondents were given a clear description of a term of imprisonment, including the effect of release on parole. In this way, respondents were able to make an *informed* choice between a community custody sentence and a conventional term of imprisonment. Respondents were then given (at random) two of the six crime scenarios, and were asked to choose between imposing a term of imprisonment or a community custody of imprisonment. Figure 7.2 summarizes the results for the six offences.

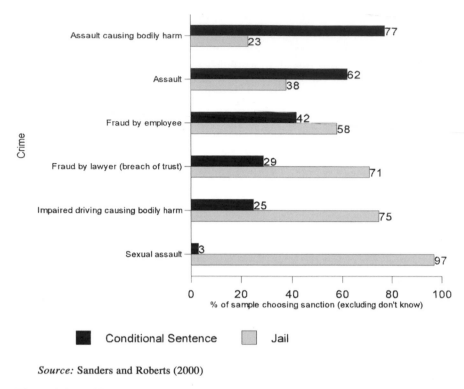

Source: Sanders and Roberts (2000)

Figure 7.2. Public support for conditional sentencing for six crimes.

As can be seen, support for the community custody sanction (rather than imprisonment) varied from a low of 3 per cent in the sexual assault case to a high of 77 per cent in the case of assault causing bodily harm. It is not surprising that there was so little support for community custody in the sexual assault scenario, as crimes of sexual aggression are generally regarded by the public as among the most serious. However, there was considerable support for imposing community custody in the other cases. It is noteworthy that the majority of respondents who were asked to sentence the offender convicted of spousal assault favoured the imposition of a community custody order sentence rather than a term of imprisonment. Domestic violence is also an offence which attracts considerable public condemnation, yet almost two-thirds of the sample rejected sending the offender to prison, and favoured the imposition of a community custody. This result suggests that the public see community custody as applying to more than just offenders convicted of crimes involving property.

Table 7.1. *Public sentencing preferences, prison vs. community custody for assault case, three surveys.*

	% 1997	% 2000	% 2002
Prison	29	22	15
Community custody	71	76	81
Don't know	<1	2	4
	100	*100*	*100*

Sources: Marinos and Doob (1999); Sanders and Roberts (2000); Sanders and Roberts (2004).

Replicating previous findings

In order to test the reliability of public support for community custody, one offence scenario was used repeatedly across three representative surveys with independent samples of subjects, in 1997 (Marinos and Doob, 1999), 2000 (Sanders and Roberts, 2000) and 2002 (Sanders and Roberts, 2004). The case involved an assault in which the victim suffered a broken nose. Respondents were given a choice between imposing a term of imprisonment, or community custody. As can be seen in Table 7.1, there was significantly more support for the community custody option on all surveys. The fact that the level of public support for the community custody was nevertheless so similar across surveys suggests that there is considerable public support for the community custody sanction, for this profile of offender at least. Three data points is insufficient to establish a trend; however, it is interesting to note that support for the community custody sentence rose across the three surveys. This may suggest growing public acceptance as the sanction became more used: the volume of such sentences tripled from 1997 to 2002 (Roberts, 2002a).[11]

These studies demonstrate both the limitations and the possibilities of community custody. The limitations on public acceptance of the sanction clearly relate to crimes of sexual aggression, to the most serious crimes. The public appear to be almost unanimous in their rejection of a community custody for the more serious forms of sexual violence. What is not clear from this research is whether this public opposition is founded upon a perception that offenders convicted of such crimes should be excluded on grounds related to desert or dangerousness. Is community custody inappropriate for serious crimes of violence because these offenders represent a threat to the community (in terms of re-offending) or because they simply deserve to be imprisoned?

Public attitudes towards house arrest

One of the few polls to address the issue of house arrest was conducted in Arkansas in 1998. Respondents were asked to evaluate the effectiveness of house arrest as a strategy to 'protect citizens from crime'. As a group, respondents were marginally more positive than negative: excluding respondents with no opinion, 53 per cent of the sample believed house arrest would be effective, 47 per cent were of the view that it would be ineffective (University of Arkansas, 1998). This ambivalence probably reflects public cynicism about community custody. The survey also asked respondents about electronic monitoring, and found much more positive perceptions: almost three-quarters perceived EM as an effective way of protecting the public (University of Arkansas, 1998).

Research addressing comparable sanctions in other jurisdictions shows widespread public support for community custody in less serious cases. For example, Elrod and Brown (1996) explored reactions to electronically monitored house arrest (hereafter EHA) using a sample of New York residents. They found that support for EHA was relatively high for the less serious property crimes: 57 per cent of the sample endorsed the use of EHA for theft under $1,000; this percentage declined to 22 per cent if the value of the property stolen exceeded $1,000. Similarly 38 per cent of the sample supported imposing EHA for a personal injury offence if medical attention was not required; only 13 per cent supported EHA if the offence resulted in injuries requiring medical attention (Elrod and Brown, 1996, Table 1; see also Marinos and Doob, 1999).

Britons, too, appear to be supportive of electronic monitoring. Dowds (1995) reports that a 1990 poll found that 58 per cent of the public supported electronic monitoring. Frost and Stephenson (1989) report the findings from a survey using a convenience sample in the United Kingdom and a limited range of offences. 'Tagging' (electronic monitoring) was seen as a more appropriate sentence for the less serious offence of car theft than burglary. Being subject to monitoring was rated as being significantly less harsh than prison.

Research by John Doble in several US states sheds important light on public reaction to house arrest as a sanction (see Doble Research, 1995a,b). In a series of studies conducted in several states, Doble and his colleagues have asked members of the public to evaluate various alternatives to imprisonment, including house arrest. A consistent finding in the literature on

Table 7.2. *Percentage of respondents in favour of community based sanctions.*

	% Oklahoma	% North Carolina
Community service	98	98
Restitution	97	97
Boot Camp	95	97
Restitution centres	92	91
Strict probation	92	89
Half-way houses	84	88
Day reporting centres	83	88
House Arrest	77	80

Source: Adapted from Doble Research Associates, 1995a; 1995b.

attitudes to sentencing is that people favour the use of alternative sanctions rather than incarceration for non-violent offenders. Respondents in two states were asked whether they favoured or opposed the use of these alternatives for non-violent offenders. Table 7.2 demonstrates the widespread public support for alternatives when considering this profile of offender, but it also suggests that house arrest is less popular than some of the other community-based sanctions.

This is confirmed by responses to a subsequent question where respondents were asked to identify which of these sanctions should be used most often. House arrest was the sanction preferred most by only 5 per cent in both states (Doble Research Associates, 1995a,b). It is easy to understand why: house arrest was described for the respondents in the following terms: 'where offenders must, by electronic monitoring, stay at home except to go to work or school'. While this is an accurate description of house arrest, it implies that all the offender has to do is remain at home at the specified times. Properly conceived, community custody should involve more than just passively sitting at home, leaving the house for court-authorized functions. If the sanction does not include more than this, community custody will not attract as much public support. As Table 7.2 makes clear, when the offender is actively engaged in reparative steps – whether involving community service or restitution to the victim – the non-custodial option becomes far more acceptable to the public as a sanction.

Sigler and Lamb (1996) explored public (and professional) perceptions of the effectiveness of electronic monitoring and house arrest. Respondents were asked to rate these programs on a number of dimensions, including the ability to deter, punish and to promote community safety. Since the survey asked about a number of programs, it was possible to make comparisons among nine types of community correctional programs, and between these programs and prison. The results showed that EM and house arrest were ranked sixth and seventh in terms of most dimensions. Prison was seen as being the most effective sanction at achieving community safety, deterrence, and punishment, and was also rated as the most severe. However, prison was also ranked as the least cost-effective option. As with a number of other studies in which comparisons were made between public views and professional expectations of public views, the general public was more supportive of community alternatives and less supportive of prison than the criminal justice professionals believed (see also Gottfredson and Taylor, 1984).

These findings carry a lesson for jurisdictions contemplating introduction of a community custody sentence. They suggest that public support for community custody will decline as the seriousness of the crime increases. This reflects the power of prison; no other sanction is deemed sufficient to reflect the inherent seriousness of crimes of sexual aggression.[12]

Effects of providing information about community custody

If the public know little about community custody, what happens to their views when they are given more information? A general finding in the public attitudes literature is that people become less punitive when given sufficient information on which to base an opinion. This finding has been demonstrated in large-scale tests of the hypothesis such as the British Deliberative Poll, as well as in experiments involving small numbers of participants. In the Deliberative Poll, the opinions of a large, representative sample of the public were measured before and after they attended a weekend during which they were exposed to a number of presentations about crime and justice. Views on a number of criminal justice issues became (and stayed) more liberal after the weekend experience (see Hough and Park, 2002).[13]

The Deliberative Poll experience lasted a full weekend; few members of the public have the time to participate in such an event. However, Gainey and Payne (2003) provide clear evidence that public attitudes to community custody (home detention with electronic monitoring) change after a much briefer educational experience. University student subjects in the USA were given a short (thirty-minute) presentation on electronic monitoring that included discussion of the positive and negative potentials of the sanction. Attitudes to the sanction were measured before the presentation and one week later. Comparison of attitudes pre and post presentation revealed a statistically significant shift in opinion: attitudes became more positive towards EM.

Participants regarded Electronic Monitoring as tougher, more likely to deter and more useful in promoting rehabilitation after the presentation. It is important to note that this was not an attitude change study; by including information relating to both perspectives on EM the researchers avoided the charge that they were simply providing pro-EM propaganda. Although some previous tests of the information-attitude hypothesis have generated mixed results (see discussion in Gainey and Payne, 2003), this study demonstrates that the increasing public knowledge levels promotes support for an alternative sanction.

This same hypothesis was directly tested in Canada with respect to the community custody sanction. The experimental hypothesis tested in the present context was that public support for community custody would be greater if respondents were made aware of the specific conditions imposed on the offender. Respondents were provided with a description of a typical case of burglary committed by an offender with several previous convictions for the same crime. In Canada, an offender convicted of this offence with this criminal record would almost certainly be imprisoned (see Roberts and Grimes, 2000).

To test our hypothesis, respondents were randomly assigned to one of two experimental conditions. In one condition, subjects were given a choice between imposing six months in prison or six months' community custody. Specifically, they were told that 'The judge is trying to decide between a 6-month prison sentence or 6 months to be served in the community as a community custody. Which do you think is appropriate, a 6-month prison sentence or a 6-month community custody?' Subjects assigned to the second condition were given the same choice, except that the specific conditions attached to the community custody were identified. Respondents were informed that if the offender received the community custody sentence, he would have to report to authorities, obey a curfew, make restitution and perform some work for the community. (These are typical conditions imposed in community custody orders.)

Of the sample provided with the minimal description of the community custody (without the actual conditions specified), almost three-quarters (73 per cent) of the sample favoured the imposition of a conventional term of custody. This finding is consistent with previous research in which members of the public were asked to sentence an offender convicted of this crime (Canadian Sentencing Commission, 1987). However, the trend in sentencing preferences is almost completely reversed in responses from the subjects in the second condition (where the conditions imposed on the offender were made salient): support for the community custody rose from 28 per cent to almost two-thirds of the sample (64 per cent), with a corresponding decline in support for institutional imprisonment. The difference between conditions is statistically significant ($X^{(1)} = 26.6$, p. $< .001$).

This finding sheds some important light on the source of public opposition to community custody. It suggests that it is not the presence of the offender in the community to which members of the public object, but rather the perception that the offender is merely spending the time at home, without being expected to do more than refrain from further offending. Simply making the conditions explicit to subjects resulted in an almost complete reversal of support for the two sanctions (community and institutional imprisonment). Finally, it is worth noting that the home confinement option placed before respondents to the survey did not include electronic monitoring; if the offender had been monitored in this way (as is often the case in the USA, public support for this sanction (over imprisonment) would undoubtedly have been even stronger (Sanders and Roberts 2000).

The appeal of the community custody order (over imprisonment) is clearly related to the conditions attached to the order. If the public have confidence that the sanction carries restrictions – as was the case for the subjects in this experimental condition – then community custody becomes an attractive sentencing option. The reaction of Canadians is similar to that of US residents. Turner, Cullen, Sundt and Applegate (1997) explored public tolerance for community-based sanctions using a sample of people from Ohio. These researchers found that the public was reluctant to endorse community-based sanctions that did not entail the close monitoring of offenders. When asked to choose from among a range of sanctions, regular probation attracted little more support than the 'no punishment' option. However, there was significant tolerance for house arrest (see Turner et al., 1997). A similar pattern emerges from the survey conducted by Brown and Elrod (1999) in which respondents were asked to identify the characteristics that are reflective of a good house arrest program. The option 'frequent contact with corrections officer' was the most popular, attracting significantly more support than reducing costs associated with incarceration and making the offender pay for the program.

Since a number of elements of the community custody sentence were made salient to subjects, including a curfew, restitution, community work and reporting conditions, it is hard to know which was most responsible for the reversal in public support for this sanction over imprisonment. In all likelihood it is the combination of conditions that made the sanction more attractive to respondents. However, previous research suggests that the restorative elements of restitution and community work probably had the most influence, and this highlights one of the clear advantages, in terms of public perceptions, of community custody over institutional imprisonment.

Conditions of community custody and effect upon perceptions of effectiveness

Making the conditions of the order more restrictive also affects public ratings of the effectiveness of the sanction. This can be demonstrated in the following way. Respondents were asked to consider a specific case. For example: 'A woman shot and killed her husband and is convicted of manslaughter. At the trial she testified that her husband physically, sexually and emotionally abused her.' They were then asked to rate the effectiveness of a community custody sentence or a term of imprisonment (between subjects design). As with the previous question, however, the conditions of the community custody order were specified: 'The judge sentences the offender to a 2 years less one day community custody. The sentence includes house arrest: the offender may leave her house only for work, community service, or medical appointments. She must also continue to receive counselling, maintain employment, and perform 200 hours of community service.'

All respondents were asked to rate (using a ten-point scale) the effectiveness of the sanction (prison or community custody) in achieving the goals of sentencing. Critics of community custody often argue that the sanction lacks sufficient penal bite, or severity, to deter other offenders or adequately denounce serious crime.

Table 7.3 provides effectiveness ratings for three crimes (manslaughter; possession for the purposes of trafficking and sexual assault), and three sentencing objectives[14] (deterrence, denunciation and rehabilitation). As can be seen, there are surprisingly few differences in perceived effectiveness of the two sanctions to achieve the traditional goals of sentencing. Where statistically significant differences did emerge, they were actually in the direction favourable to the community custody sanction. Thus in the cases of trafficking and sexual assault, the community custody sanction was perceived as being more effective at achieving rehabilitation and denunciation. These findings clearly demonstrate that in the eyes of the public, community custody can achieve the objectives of sentencing to the same degree as imprisonment, if the sanction carries conditions that restrict the lifestyle of the offender, and these conditions are made clear.

Table 7.3. *Public ratings of relative effectiveness of community custody and prison.*

	Manslaughter: community custody	Manslaughter: imprisonment	Sexual assault: community custody	Sexual assault: imprisonment	Possession for purposes of trafficking: community custody	Possession for purposes of trafficking: imprisonment
Sentencing objective						
Deterrence	4.86	4.97	4.42	4.51	4.75*	4.27*
Denunciation	5.09	5.31	4.66	4.87	5.46*	4.97*
Rehabilitation	5.73	5.35	4.72*	4.24*	5.49*	4.29*

* = significant difference between two sanctions, $p < 0.5$

Question: 'On a scale of 1–10, with one being not at all effective and 10 being very effective, how effective do you feel this sentence is in meeting the following goals of sentencing?'

Source: Adapted from Sanders and Roberts (2004).

The results summarized in Table 7.3 also make an interesting contrast with judicial perceptions of the effectiveness of community custody compared to prison (see chapter 2, Table 2.6). Although the questions posed to the public and the judiciary were not exactly the same, they were close enough to draw some limited conclusions about the perceptions of the two groups. Comparing the findings from Tables 7.3 and 2.6 suggests that the public have somewhat more confidence in the effectiveness of community custody. For example, while one-third of judges were of the view that community custody could almost never be as effective as imprisonment in achieving denunciation (Table 2.6), the public saw the two sanctions as equally effective in this regard (Table 7.3).

Potential for rehabilitation: prison versus community custody

Prison has not achieved its iconic status as a punishment by convincing the public of its utility to change offenders. Members of the public harbour no illusions about the ability of imprisonment to improve offenders and turn them back to a law-abiding lifestyle. Consider the findings of surveys in which people are asked about the effects of imprisonment on offenders and on recidivism rates. Doble Research Associates (1998) asked members of the public in New Hampshire whether alternatives or prison were more likely to rehabilitate offenders. Fully three-quarters voted for alternatives, less than one-quarter believed that prison was more effective in this respect.

The issue was approached in a different way in Oklahoma where respondents were asked 'For every ten offenders who go to prison, how many are successfully rehabilitated?' Almost two-thirds of the sample estimated that three in ten or fewer were rehabilitated (Doble Research Associates, 1995a). Views regarding the rehabilitative potential of alternative sanctions were more positive (see Doble Research Associates, 1995a, Table 34). Similarly, when the Florida Department of Corrections asked the public whether inmates are more or less likely to commit crimes 'than before they served their time', approximately six respondents in ten believed more crime was the likely result of spending time in prison; only 7 per cent held the view that prison would make prisoners less likely to re-offend (Florida Department of Corrections, 1997).

In this respect, community custody has a clear edge over prison in the eyes of the public: people know that imprisonment does not make prisoners better, and that offenders are better off remaining in the community. If the public knew that the vast majority of prison admissions were under three months – with time actually served being even shorter period – they would have even less faith in the ability of prisons to effect real change in prisoners' lives. This finding would have little relevance for the debate on the future of imprisonment if the public cared only to punish, deter or incapacitate. But as Cullen et al. (2000) and other researchers have repeatedly demonstrated, there is a bedrock of support among members of the public for rehabilitation. The principal reason why public support for community alternatives falters when considering violent or recidivist offenders is that alternative sanctions are seen to lack the denunciatory power or severity sufficient to reflect the seriousness of the criminal conduct. This perception may be true for conventional probation, suspended or community custody and even some intensive supervision programs, but far less accurate when applied to a *properly constructed* community custody order.

The social significance of the prison

Why is the public so attached to institutional imprisonment? The prison is clearly a unique sanction that carries a significance beyond the single dimension of severity. If the severity of prison explained the deep attraction of the sanction, the use of alternatives could be promoted simply by making them more punitive. In most jurisdictions, the average sentence of custody is around a month.[15] It is possible to construct a fine the value of which would be seen as more severe than thirty days in prison. If the offender had not the means to pay a fine of sufficient magnitude to achieve the penal equivalence of thirty days' custody, the time to pay could be protracted over a longer period of time, or his or her wages could be garnered. But there is empirical evidence that the public reject the use of alternatives to custody in the more serious cases, no matter how high the fine.

Doob and Marinos (1995) for example, found that even when the public were able to impose a fine of any magnitude, this disposition was not seen as being capable of achieving the goals of sentencing to the same extent as custody. They found that different punishments were perceived to achieve different sentencing objectives, and that with respect to denunciation, no fine, however high, was the equivalent of imprisonment.

It would appear then, that while increasing the punitiveness of community sanctions such as community custody will enhance their image in the eyes of the public, simply making these sanctions tougher will be insufficient to displace custody from its central role in popular conceptions of punishment. It will take something of a paradigm shift involving a transformation of popular views of the concept of imprisonment, a subject that will be pursued further in the concluding chapter of this volume.

This paradigm shift will require the public to embrace a new form of custody. Part of the explanation for society's attachment to institutional custody as a sanction lies in the mere familiarity of prisons, and of the ceremony of someone being admitted to an institution. This may change as people become more familiar with the alternative versions of custody. Although no public opinion research exists on the subject, it seems likely that when weekend or intermittent custody was introduced, the public found the concept strange and interpreted it as evidence of leniency; until that point people went to prison for fixed periods of time at the end of which they would return to society. Yet intermittent terms are now routinely imposed in many jurisdictions. Moving from institutional to community custody is admittedly a more radical transition, but one which may still be accepted by the public.

Pedagogical effect of the sentencing process

Whatever the nature of public opinion with respect to community custody, it is possible that the use of this sanction by the courts – judicial practice – may have an influence upon community perceptions. Although most people expect the sentencing process to achieve several goals simultaneously (to deter, to denounce and to rehabilitate), there is clear public apprehension about re-offending. Part of the public's opposition to community custody is founded upon people's fears that the offender will take advantage of his relative freedom to re-offend. The comparatively low breach rates of community custody offenders in Canada (see Roberts, 2002a) may ultimately reassure the public that imprisonment at home does not put the community at risk. But it is also possible that continued use of the sanction by judges may change public opinion, as over time, people become more comfortable with the concept of community imprisonment. Mere use, in Hamlet's words, may well 'change the stamp of nature'.

EIGHT

Making community custody sentences work

This final chapter draws upon the accumulated experience in different jurisdictions to propose ways in which community custody can be used to promote the purposes of sentencing, and attract the confidence of key criminal
justice professionals (such as judges and prosecutors) as well as members of
the public. These suggestions relate to the way the sanction is constructed,
its range of application as well as its administration.

Locate the sanction on a scale of severity

Several steps are necessary to fix the position of the sanction on a scale of
severity. First, the sanction must carry a clear ensemble of statutory conditions applicable to all offenders on the sentence. Second, although courts
should have the discretion to impose additional conditions crafted to the
individual circumstances of offenders, there should be limits on these discretionary conditions. Otherwise a judge could impose a raft of additional
conditions and thereby move the particular sanction up the severity scale
and rupture the principle of proportionality. These limits are also necessary
to ensure that judges do not impose oppressive or demeaning conditions,
that can be lifted only after a time-consuming delay associated with a review
by an appellate court.

Third, a clear ratio should be established between time in custody and
time on community custody. Judges have to ensure that the order is roughly
commensurate in severity with the term of custody that otherwise would
be imposed. This can be accomplished by modulating the length of community custody to reflect the less severe experience of living at home, even
under an absolute house arrest condition. An appropriate rule of thumb

might be the two for one ratio established in many jurisdictions to recognize time spent in custody pre-trial. Most jurisdictions accord offenders credit for pre-trial detention on a ratio of two to one; an offender who has spent three months is credited with six months off the term of custody ultimately imposed. The logic behind this arrangement is that the conditions of pre-trial custody are more severe than those in which sentenced offenders serve their time. This same reasoning justifies a longer term of community custody. Fourth, in practical terms, it will be necessary to place a 'cap' on the length of a community custody sentence. A three-month prison term may be replaced by a six-month community custody relatively easily, but doubling a two-year prison sentence and creating a four-year community custody order makes little sense, and creates great hardship for family members of offenders.

These steps do more than simply curb judicial discretion. They help to achieve interchangeability between different forms of custody. This interchangeability is likely to promote the greater use of the 'substitute sanction', which in this case is community custody (see discussion in Tonry, 1998). As well, these steps also help to ensure parity in sentencing, one of the requirements of ordinal proportionality (von Hirsch, 1993). In many countries, the offender may not be sentenced to community custody if the court considers that he or she represents a risk in terms of re-offending. If two equally culpable offenders are sentenced to, respectively, prison and the community on the basis of their risk level, proportionality will be violated unless the two sanctions are roughly comparable.

Ordinal proportionality also has implications when two equally culpable offenders are both sentenced to community custody. As von Hirsch notes, 'Persons convicted of crimes of like gravity should receive punishments of like severity' (p. 18). The second challenge is harder; courts must also ensure that comparable offenders both sentenced to custody at home experience approximately equally severe dispositions. Establishing a common set of statutory conditions applicable to all offenders sentenced to imprisonment at home is one step. The experience around the world is variable in this respect; in some countries the compulsory conditions are fairly minimal. But this only goes part of the way towards ensuring parity. No control is possible over the home environment in which offenders will be confined.

Make the sanction an autonomous, multidimensional disposition

In order for community custody to realize its potential, the sanction must consist of more than simply a restriction on an offender's liberty. Creating a curfew order, or ordering the offender to remain at home under house arrest may constitute a punitive sentence, but will achieve little more than punishment. Curfews and house arrest should be *conditions* of community custody, imposed to hold the offender accountable, protect the public from re-offending and to assist the offender in complying with other restrictions such as non-association orders. But there should be more to the sanction than simply staying home, just as prison should involve more than simply confinement in a cell. Offenders should be encouraged to pursue treatment (if necessary), to make compensation to the victim (where possible), and where appropriate, take steps towards restoration to the community. Community custody should encourage offenders to pursue law-abiding lives. In this way, offenders can actively participate in, rather than simply discharge the sentence of the court. Home confinement should be a condition, but not the only or defining condition of a sanction that is conceived to accomplish much more than simply 'ground' the offender.

Defining 'community' for the purposes of a community custody order

When most people think of home confinement or community custody orders, they envisage the offender serving his or her sentence in a private residence. However, the essence of a community custody order is that it is served in the community rather than prison, not that it is served in a home or flat. An illustration of this can be found in the *Knoblauch* judgment from the Supreme Court of Canada. The appellant pleaded guilty to a series of charges involving explosives, and had a previous conviction for possession of a weapon. The man had been found in possession of an arsenal capable of inflicting great harm. The background to these offences was a lengthy history of mental illness consisting of deeply ingrained personality difficulties and fantasies of violence. On the face of it, such an individual would not appear to meet the statutory criterion of not representing a threat to the community. However, the Supreme Court took the position that if he were confined to a secure mental health facility, the level of risk would be manageable. This gives rise to the question of whether such a facility is any different from a prison.

Can being ordered to serve a sentence in a secure facility such as a locked psychiatric ward be considered a community-based sanction? The question cuts to the heart of definitions of community custody. The minority position in Knoblauch was that confinement in a locked psychiatric institution is tantamount to imprisonment because it 'shares many of the attributes of a custodial sentence'. However, this does not make it a custodial sentence any more than the conditional sentence becomes a term of probation because it shares some of the characteristics of probation. Although in practice a community custody order may not restrict an offender's lifestyle to the same extent as a term in prison, the degree of constraint alone is not what distinguishes community custody from imprisonment. If this were the case, a very intrusive community custody sentence, constructed to restrict the offender's movements to a greater extent even than prison, would lose its status as a community-based sanction, even though the offender resides at home.

Community custody is about holding offenders accountable without imposing a term of penal confinement. Prison exists to isolate, punish and, latterly to rehabilitate. In contrast, the purpose of a secure psychiatric institution is to isolate and to heal. Penal confinement consists of sequestration from society in an institution, the primary – some would say the exclusive – purpose of which is to punish. In the event, the Court upheld the imposition of the community custody order, with the condition that the offender be detained for the duration of the order in the secure psychiatric facility. In so doing the Court expanded the range of the community custody order in Canada (*R. v. Knoblauch*; see Roberts and Verdun-Jones, 2002). Community custody need not be restricted to the offender's residence.

Ensure that community custody is clearly distinguishable from probation

One of the problems created by the community custody legislation in Canada is its similarity to probation.[1] In order to find its place in the range of sanctions available to a sentencing court, a community custody must be clearly distinguishable from other sanctions (such as probation). A community custody sentence must be both distinguishable from, and more severe than, a term of probation. If it is similar to probation, judges may use the two sanctions interchangeably, resulting in widening of the net. As well, if the sanction is no more punitive than probation, judges are unlikely to use the new sentence as a replacement for imprisonment, thereby undermining the effect of the reform upon prison admissions.

Legislators in Canada had to create a sanction that was tougher than probation, but which did not involve committal to custody. In this respect at least, they appear to have failed. The only study to make a comparison of the conditions imposed on probation offenders and community custody offenders found that the patterns were very similar (see Roberts et al., 2000).

In the first two years at least, before the Supreme Court handed down a judgment that specified the way in which a conditional sentence should be constructed, some of the community custody orders contributed to the image of the sentence as being little more punitive than a term of probation. Community custody orders have changed considerably since then as a result of the Supreme Court judgment (*R. v. Proulx*), but had the two sanctions (community custody; probation) been more carefully distinguished from the outset, the confusion could have been avoided.

The community custody sentence and probation share a similar statutory platform in Canada (see Roberts, 1997; 1999a for discussion). Both sanctions carry compulsory conditions and allow courts to craft individual conditions for the specific needs of particular offenders. Both sanctions carry the threat of imprisonment in the event of violation of conditions, and violating a probation order in fact constitutes a fresh offence, whereas violating a community custody order merely triggers a breach hearing. And both categories of offenders are supervised by the same criminal justice professionals (probation officers).

The principal difference between the two sanctions with respect to the critical issue of conditions imposed is that judges may order an offender to attend an approved treatment program as part of a community custody order, whereas treatment can only be ordered as a condition of probation if the offender gives his consent. But even this distinction is more apparent than real; in practice, ordering offenders to attend treatment without their consent is almost never attempted since it makes little sense from a therapeutic perspective. A court may have the power to order an offender to attend a treatment of psychiatric therapy, but it cannot compel disclosure to a therapist. Other jurisdictions have created a community custody sanction that is more clearly distinguishable. Custody should carry conditions that clearly distinguish it from sanctions such as probation. The issue of conditions will be discussed later in this chapter.

Require judges to impose a term of custody before imposing a community custody order

The experience in a number of countries suggests that the sanction should be constructed as a form of custody (rather than an alternative to imprisonment lying somewhere between probation and prison). Courts should be required first to impose a term of custody before making a community custody order. This would mean that judges would have to overcome any statutory pre-requisites in this regard. The success of the

Canadian sanction in reducing the number of admissions to prison can be directly attributed to the fact that the statutory framework compels a court to employ the sentence *after first having resolved to commit the offender to custody.*

This pre-requisite needs to be clearly located in a statutory framework that contains the principle of restraint with respect to the use of incarceration as a sanction. Research conducted in several jurisdictions makes it clear that reductions in prison populations are best achieved by reducing the number of admissions to custody rather than the duration of terms of imprisonment (e.g. Graham, 1990; Kommer, 2003). In jurisdictions that employ formal sentencing guidelines, the sentencing matrix or grid should prevent judges from using the sanction for offenders other than those for whom a term of custody is appropriate. Any alternative to this formula is likely to result in widening of the net, as experience in several countries shows that judges will impose a community custody in some cases that formerly would have been sentenced to a term of probation or a fine.[2]

The reactions of offenders (and their families and partners) in the Canadian research were highly determined by two factors: the likelihood that the offender would have been sent to jail and the duration of the order. Offenders and families who perceived themselves to have been spared the pains of imprisonment were far more positive about the sanction than those for whom imprisonment was a possibility rather than a probability. This is further reason for having a statutory framework that requires a court first to impose a term of custody. Widening of the net is usually discussed within the context of avoiding drawing more offenders into the penal net, but it is equally important to ensure that community custody offenders adopt a positive attitude towards serving a sentence of imprisonment at home. The importance of offenders' attitudes is apparent from research on compliance with court-imposed conditions. Bonta, Wallace-Capretta and Rooney (1999) found that offenders who held a positive view of the legitimacy of the sanction were less likely to violate conditions and more likely to complete the order successfully.

Require a thorough inquiry into the suitability of the offender and his or her residence

Confining a person to their home is not an appropriate sanction for all offenders. A thorough case planning exercise should precede the imposition of a term of community custody. This inquiry should investigate the suitability of the offender for such a sanction, as well as provide an accurate description of the conditions in which the sentence will be served. The opinions of co-residents also need to be canvassed and their views communicated to the sentencing court.

Clearly, judges must be mindful of the impact on other people living in the offender's residence. Courts must have a clear idea of the nature of the residence to which the offender will be confined for the period of the order. Before imposing a community custody order courts should commission a report to assess the suitability of the offender for such a disposition. Such an inquiry will address the impact on third parties among many other issues, but it will also provide information on the environment in which the offender will be confined, as well as the offender's life situation (see Box 8.1). This is also necessary to help the court craft the duration and conditions of the order. Only some jurisdictions require such inquiries to be undertaken before the offender is committed to the virtual prison.

Box 8.1. *The case of Kimberly Rogers.*

A tragic case in Ontario Canada illustrates the importance of considering the offender's home environment. Kimberly Rogers, forty, was eight months pregnant when she killed herself in August 2002. She was serving a six-month community custody order which restricted her to her small flat except for three hours a week to attend medical appointments and religious events. She had been convicted of illegally collecting welfare payments. Testimony at the inquest into her death revealed that she had suffered from chronic depression, panic attacks, insomnia and intermittent physical pain following surgery a couple of years before her conviction. Rogers expressed the opinion shortly before her death that the sentence was too restrictive, although she had not applied for a variance in her restrictions. In August 2002, Ontario experienced a near record heat wave, and temperatures inside the woman's apartment must have been unbearable. A witness at the Inquest testified that Rogers had 'stuck her head inside the freezer to get relief from the heat' (Committee to Remember Kimberly Rogers, 2003).

We shall never know whether the restrictions created by the community custody order played a role in this tragedy. Nevertheless, it illustrates well the importance of considering carefully the nature of the offender's residence, as well as the suitability of the offender for the sanction. It seems unlikely that this tragedy would have occurred if the woman had been in a residential setting. The mental and physical health of the offender must be carefully considered before community custody is imposed. One of the Coroner's Inquest recommendations was that when an offender is sentenced to house arrest, the government should ensure that adequate housing is available.

Labelling the sanction

Requiring judges first to impose a term of imprisonment before making a community custody order therefore makes this sanction a form of imprisonment, and it should be labelled as such. The sanction will gain credibility if the name reflects its nature: community custody. A label of this kind is likely to promote public acceptance to a greater extent than 'conditional sentence of imprisonment', or the like. Calling the sentence an 'intermediate punishment' lumps it together with other such sanctions (including intensive supervision probation) and thus diminishes its stature. As noted, calling the sanction a sentence of imprisonment can strain the credulity of a public that is already sceptical of the sentencing process. Members of the public are likely initially to be resistant to the concept of community imprisonment, and their resistance is going to increase in direct function to the seriousness of the crime. However, the experience in Finland and Canada suggests that the public will become accustomed to viewing this sentence as form of custody, the same way that people now accept periodic or intermittent custody as a kind of imprisonment.

Provide judges with the discretion to make a community custody longer than the term of custody which it replaces

In the early years of the community custody regime in Canada, the jurisprudence favoured the position that a community custody must be exactly the same length as a term of custody that it replaced. Thus a court might impose a six-month term of custody, and then decide whether the *six* months could be spent in the community. Since, in most cases, six months' community imprisonment does not carry the penal equivalent of six months in actual custody, two offenders with comparable profiles who are sentenced one to community imprisonment the other to custody are usually going to be serving sentences of varying onerousness. This violates the principle of parity in sentencing. 'Yoking' the community custody to the term of custody can thus undermine proportionality in sentencing. If a fit sentence is three months' custody, and this is replaced with three months in the community, a less severe sanction (in almost all cases), the sentence may have become less proportional.

Obliging judges to respect a 'one-to-one' correspondence between the community custody and the term of custody that it replaces is therefore a mistake. The Canadian Supreme Court recognized as much in its guideline judgment (*R. v. Proulx*), wherein it noted that a community custody could be longer for the very reason that it cannot match the penal value of custody. As a result of this decision, judges became free to impose, for example, a twelve-month community custody in the place of six months' 'real time'. In addition to promoting the principles of sentencing, this move also makes judges more likely to employ community custody as a sanction. If the court can impose, say, up to twelve months' community punishment instead of six months' jail time, the former sanction becomes a more plausible alternative than the latter. The public will also be more supportive of a sanction which replaces custody if the replacement is longer than the term of imprisonment that would have been imposed. The only danger with this approach is that judges may protract the length of a community custody order to such a degree that compliance with conditions will be extremely difficult, and the impact on co-residents will also be too hard to bear.

Limit the ambit of the community custody regime

Considerable thought must be devoted to the ambit of the sanction. The controversy over community custody in Canada has raged around its use for a relatively small number[3] of serious offences that had attracted sentences of community custody in excess of eighteen months. Setting the ceiling at two years (less one day) allows judges to impose a community custody in very serious cases, assuming that the other statutory pre-requisites have been met. However, the use of community custody in such cases often provokes considerable criticism in the media and this undermines the entire concept of community custody in the eyes of the public.

As the statistics on the lengths of community custody in Canada discussed earlier (in chapter 6) reveal, adopting a lower limit would eliminate the more serious cases from consideration of the sanction, but without any marked loss of effectiveness with respect to reducing the number of admissions to custody. The challenge is to find the right balance: a statutory platform with a low 'ceiling' (say three months) will prove ineffective in terms of reducing the volume of admissions to custody. If the upper limit is set too high, the sanction will be used for cases of such seriousness that they will attract widespread community opposition, and the entire regime will be threatened. Had the Canadian Parliament set the limit of the community custody at twelve months, the net volume of admissions to prison would have been only slightly reduced, and the controversy that has dogged the sanction since its creation would probably have been avoided.

It might be objected that adopting a lower maximum limit would deny judges the discretion to impose a community-based sanction on offenders convicted of a crime such as manslaughter committed under exceptional circumstances. However, for these kinds of rare cases, most jurisdictions make other sentencing options available to sentencers. For example, in Canada, judges can impose a suspended sentence accompanied by up to three years of probation for grave personal injury cases to reflect offences committed in circumstances of extreme mitigation. How should the limit be determined? Sentence length statistics provide a useful guide. Jurisdictions in which the public are unlikely to countenance a community custody sentence even for crimes of intermediate seriousness may need to begin with a more modest upper limit, perhaps the median sentence length of all custodial sentences in the particular jurisdiction. Establishing this as an upper limit would still leave the sanction with considerable power to reduce the number of admissions to custody.

There is another, possibly even more important reason to constrain the length of the order to something well below two years. As documented in chapter 5, terms of community custody create significant hardships for sponsors – partners, parents, and above all the children of home detention offenders. These peoples' lives are restricted in many ways by the sanction. As well, it is clear that they assume considerable responsibility for encouraging the detainee to respect the conditions and thereby avoid a breach hearing carrying the possibility of incarceration. These responsibilities create strains upon family units, and personal relationships.

Pressures such as these may be tolerable for several months, but the burden on sponsors raises questions about the length of home detention that can reasonably be imposed. It is one thing to ask sponsors to assist an offender, and be constrained in their daily lives for two or three months, but is it reasonable for the justice system to expect this degree of co-operation over much longer periods, such as two years less a day? Confronted with a relatively brief (say up to three months) period of living with an offender subject to house arrest, most people appear to accept these limitations as a reasonable price for sparing their family member or spouse from being admitted to prison. But facing years of living together under restrictive conditions is a far more daunting prospect.[4] In addition, the likelihood of continued compliance is inversely related to the length of time that the offender is required to respect these conditions. In Canada, the community custody sentence of a conditional term of imprisonment can be up to two years less one day, which is a long period in which to be subject to house arrest or a restrictive curfew.

There are two solutions to this problem. One involves restricting the length of the sentence to something shorter[5] (such as one year; this limit has been adopted in England and Wales for the suspended sentence of imprisonment).[6] The second option is to encourage or require, through statutory conditions, judges to conduct periodic reviews of the order. If an offender sentenced to an eighteen-month community custody sentence completes six months with total compliance, perhaps the court should consider relaxing the conditions, by increasing the time allowed out of the home, or changing the limits of the curfew. Continued compliance with the revised conditions might lead to further relaxing of conditions at the twelve-month point, and so forth. Such a procedure would encourage offenders to maintain compliance, mitigate the impact of the sentence upon innocent parties such as family members, and also permit the court to better understand the conditions that are likely to cause greatest difficulty for both parties. In several jurisdictions (including Canada) judges exercise their discretion in this regard; far better however, that these periodic reviews be placed upon a statutory footing.

Allowing the upper limit to change over time

Although the ceiling should be established after a careful examination of sentence length statistics, there is no reason why the 'ceiling' should not rise over time. Public attitudes to community penalties have evolved considerably over the past few decades (see Roberts and Hough, 2002; Roberts 2002b), and acceptance of community imprisonment is likely to increase still further. As it does, legislators (or a sentencing commission) should react by raising the limit of the sentence of custody that can be served in the community, in step with the evolution of public reaction. This would be a positive example of sentencing policy evolving to reflect the evolution of community views of punishment.[7]

Indeed, the Canadian experience is again illustrative. When the community custody sentence was first introduced, it was described as a sanction applicable to the least serious property crimes, committed by first offenders. This early 'packaging' was probably strategic: introducing a community sentence for offenders convicted of manslaughter and the aggravated forms of sexual assault would have provoked a storm of public protest, and the enabling legislation would probably have been expeditiously amended during the parliamentary review process, before any judge had had the opportunity to impose the sentence.

However, over time, the range of offences for which a community custody sentence could be imposed was widened considerably. This can be illustrated by reference to crimes of sexual aggression, the offences that provoke the gravest concern to the public and victims' advocates. It is in cases like these that prosecutors, through their sentencing submissions, are likely to take the strongest stand in opposing a community custody.[8] In 1996–7, the first complete year of the community custody regime in Canada, crimes of sexual aggression accounted for less than 1 per cent of all orders imposed. The percentage of community custody sanctions imposed for sexual assault rose to 9 per cent in 1998/9, 10 per cent in 1999/00, 14 per cent in 2000/1 and 16 per cent in the most recent year for which data are available (2001/2; see Kong, Johnson, Beattie and Cardillo, 2003).

Statutorily excluded offences?
One issue that has repeatedly surfaced in the debate surrounding community custody in a number of countries concerns the propriety of excluding specific offences by statute. Many jurisdictions have created community custody regimes in which certain categories of offenders are statutorily excluded from consideration. For example, offenders convicted of a serious violent offence are not eligible to apply for home detention in New Zealand. As noted earlier, in Canada, several provinces have called upon the federal Parliament to restrict the sanction to non-violent offences.

The problem with creating a schedule of excluded offences, or reserving the sanction for non-violent offences, is that it prejudges the relative seriousness of crimes. Schedules are also subject to political interference, as parliamentarians sometimes add crimes to the schedule for reasons other than their relative seriousness. In addition, while the use of statutory exclusions may seem a simple means by which to eliminate the most serious cases from receiving a community custody sanction, it requires a careful review of the entire sentencing framework, including an examination of the other sanctions.

For example, if offenders convicted of, say, sexual assault are rendered ineligible for a community custody sanction, should they still be eligible for other, less severe punishments such as a suspended sentence accompanied by a term of probation? If no change is simultaneously made to the ambit of the suspended sentence, an anomaly is created: the court is prevented from imposing community custody but is permitted to impose a less severe sanction (probation). If all sanctions less severe than a community custody are also proscribed with respect to particular offences, these crimes effectively carry a mandatory sentence of imprisonment, with all the problems associated with such sentences (e.g. Tonry, 1996).

Special categories of offenders

An issue that has been insufficiently explored concerns the application of home confinement/community custody sanctions to particular offender populations. It may be neither necessary nor desirable to exclude specific groups by means of the statute, but clearly there are offenders for whom community custody is particularly appropriate, and others for whom it is an inappropriate sanction.

Offenders convicted of domestic violence should not be considered for a community custody sanction. If the assault were serious enough to warrant imprisonment, the term should be served in an institution or a community-based residence.[9] Having committed an offence against a co-resident, and in their common home, an offender convicted of domestic assault should not be returned there to serve his sentence. Moreover, offenders who used their residence in some way to commit the offence should not, having been sentenced to a term of custody, be allowed to return to the 'scene of the crime'. This restriction includes drug dealers using their homes to store or sell drugs, and offenders convicted of cultivating drug plants on their property. (It also includes cases such as the individual in Canada who was convicted of arson and who had requested a community custody order even though he had burned his own house down in order to obtain the insurance money.)

Wealthy offenders, and homeless offenders

Although few in numbers, wealthy offenders pose a particular challenge for community custody regimes. If an individual who lives in considerable comfort is sentenced to spend his sentence of custody at home, public and professional confidence in the sanction will be greatly harmed. Allowing a rich defendant to purge his sentence in luxury would scandalize public opinion. One solution is to make the sentence more restrictive or longer than it would otherwise be, or to impound some of the offender's property.[10] In all likelihood, these strategies are unlikely to prove sufficient. Denying the sanction to wealthy offenders is as inequitable as denying community custody to offenders who have no fixed address. The best solution involves sending the wealthy and the homeless to serve their prison sentences not in a correctional institution, but in a residential halfway house.

Recidivists

Repeat offenders should not be denied access to the sentence merely on the grounds that they have previously offended. This would result in cumulative sentencing, and violate the principle of proportionality.[11] Recidivists are less likely to be considered good candidates for home confinement on the basis of risk; they are more likely to re-offend, and most community custody regimes (including the conditional sentence of imprisonment in Canada) assign an important role to the offender's likelihood of re-offending. However, offenders who have previously received a community custody sentence, and who have violated the conditions of the sentence – particularly those who have re-offended while serving their sentences in the community – should be precluded from receiving another community custody sentence, at least for a certain period of time. Regardless of the onerousness of its conditions, community custody is a mitigated form of imprisonment, and the offender's rejection of the conditions should disentitle him to further consideration for this sanction. Non-compliance with the conditions of a previous community custody order also makes the offender a poorer risk in terms of compliance with another such order.[12]

Special needs offenders

Community custody is particularly appropriate for certain offenders. As a general rule, community custody should be imposed on offenders who need treatment that can best be delivered in the community, or who have needs that cannot be met in prison. Offenders with needs that require community-based treatment, or residency in a therapeutic environment therefore constitute a priority for community custody regimes. House arrest (with or without electronic monitoring), combined with community-based drug treatment has proven to be a potent combination which is associated with lower re-arrest rates (see Jolin and Stipak, 1992; Courtright, Berg and Mutchnik, 2000[13]).

A number of jurisdictions with high rates of Aboriginal offenders in prison have taken the position that custody is particularly inappropriate for Aboriginal offenders. In Canada for example, one of the statutory sentencing principles requires judges to consider alternatives to custody for all offenders, but 'with particular attention to the circumstances of aboriginal offenders' (section 718.2(e)). The Supreme Court has interpreted this to mean that judges should make an additional effort to keep the offender out of custody if he or she is Aboriginal (see *R.* v. *Gladue*). The consequence of this judgment is that Aboriginal offenders should be less likely to be imprisoned than non-Aboriginals convicted of crimes of comparable seriousness.

For the most serious offences, however, the court noted that differences between the groups should disappear. Community custody offers courts a way of keeping Aboriginal offenders out of prison, although, as noted in chapter 6, one of the failures of the conditional sentence of imprisonment in Canada is that it has not reduced the number of Aboriginal admissions to prison.

The proportion of female prisoners has been rising steadily in most Western nations. A number of factors account for this trend, including the application of drug laws, and a shift in the gender ratio of people coming before the court. Whatever the cause, the reality is that more and more women are being imprisoned and this has accordingly increased the impact of imprisonment on third parties, in this case the women's children. Harris (1995) notes that over three-quarters of incarcerated women and two-thirds of incarcerated men have children. The lives of these children are inevitably changed for the worse as a result of the incarceration of their parents (see Gabel and Johnston, 1995, for a review of the effects of parental incarceration).

Women are more likely to be primary caregivers, and this alone implies that they should be considered as a primary target for community custody. However, current practices do not necessarily provide such female offenders with the anticipated benefits. King and Gibbs (2003) for example, report that women serving home detention orders in New Zealand were particularly burdened by home detention. Maidment (2002) and Ansay and Benveneste (1999) also identify concerns about the impact of electronic monitoring in Canada, and community control in Florida. The assumption should not be made that being confined to one's residence has an equal impact upon men and women. To a degree, home confinement confirms and may exacerbate inequalities that existed prior to the imposition of sentence. This reality further underscores the need for a suitability inquiry, one of the goals of which is to inform judges as to the likely impact of the sentence upon the specific offender before the court.

Consider the interests of the victim

Some victims' advocates in Canada have expressed strong opposition to the concept of community custody when it is applied to serious personal injury offences and have supported political attempts to restrict the sanction to offenders convicted of non-violent offences. Individual victims may be critical of courts that impose a community custody sentence in the case involving 'their offender'. To allow victims' views to determine the legislative agenda, or whether a specific offender is committed to prison or allowed to serve the sentence at home, would distort the sentencing principles of equity and proportionality. Nevertheless, victims have an interest in the matter. To what extent, then, should victim interests be considered with respect to community custody? Clearly, there are a number of legitimate victim concerns. Reparation is very important to many crime victims, and by keeping the offender in the community (and possibly working), the community custody sentence increases the likelihood that restitution to the victim will be paid.[14] The issue of victim compensation should therefore be central in the statutory framework of the sanction, and judges should be alert to order compensation where they are not compelled to do so by statute.

If the victim of the offence is a co-resident, the court will have to consider carefully security issues. But what of the case in which the victim simply lives in the offender's neighbourhood? Victims of violence in Canada have expressed dismay that the offender appears to come and go as before, through the streets of the community to which they both belong (Roberts and Roach, 2004). This negative impression is exacerbated by the fact that many of the conditions imposed on community custody offenders are invisible to external observers, leaving the impression that little has changed in the offender's life. If the offender had been in custody prior to trial, sentencing may appear to victims to have liberated, rather than punished the individual. Having been detained in custody prior to conviction, he is now 'at liberty' as a result of the sentence of the court. The presence of the victim in relatively close proximity to the offender's residence underlines still further the importance of house arrest as a condition of the order.

To introduce some form of victim input beyond the impact statement currently used in most common law jurisdictions would undermine the nature of the adversarial process. It would also undermine equity in sentencing, if the approbation of the victim was required before an offender convicted of a serious violent crime can be sentenced to a term of community custody. Nevertheless, a much greater effort could be made to help victims understand their role in the sentencing process, and why a particular sentence such as community custody is imposed for such a crime. Courts should consider the location in which the offender will serve his sentence. If the victim lives very close, consideration should be given to ordering the sentence to be served in some other community location. At the very least, an additional effort should be made to explain the nature and purpose of community custody to victims of violence in which the offender is ordered to serve a sentence of community custody.

Take seriously the impact of the sentence on co-residents

The imposition of a term of community custody should be preceded by a thorough inquiry into the suitability of the offender's residence, and the likely impact of the sentence on other people residing at the address. The Assessment Report used in New South Wales offers a good example of such an inquiry. The consent of co-residents should be obtained before a community custody order is imposed, and they should have the ability to withdraw this consent at any point during the administration of the order. As well, co-inhabitants such as spouses and parents of offenders living at home should be given the opportunity to provide some input into the conditions attached to the order. Family members of offenders should not determine the penal value of the sanction (through the nature of conditions imposed), but their familiarity with the offender means that they may be able to offer the court valuable suggestions as to the kinds of conditions likely to promote rehabilitation. Family members in jurisdictions that ignore the interests of co-residents tend to have a much less positive view of the sanction, seeing it as something imposed upon them, rather than a sentence in which they may participate.

In the event that the offender's co-resident(s) do not consent to his serving a community custody order at their common residence, the offender should serve the sentence at a halfway house, or some location other than a prison. Otherwise the wishes of the co-residents will become determinative of the whether the offender is sent to prison.

Importance of conditions imposed on offenders serving community custody sentences

In order to make a community-based sanction like community custody acceptable to the public and crime victims, the court must ensure that significant conditions are imposed which have a real impact on the offender's life. In this way the sentence is not simply a 'warning' to the offender to henceforth remain law-abiding. If this can be accomplished, the public will often support the imposition of a community custody over a term of imprisonment, even for a personal injury offence. Of course, if news media stories do not accurately describe the community custody to members of the public, then the most well-crafted community custody will still attract public disapproval.

There is a more general lesson for other community-based sanctions, such as probation. The public clearly accept the principle that offenders can be adequately punished while remaining in the community. However, public support is highly dependent upon the presence of conditions that have an impact on the offender's lifestyle. If community sanctions are ever to achieve general acceptance as a legitimate alternative to prison (see Doob, 1990, for discussion) these penalties will have to have impose significant restrictions on offenders. This is particularly true for community custody, which, unlike a term of probation, is supposed to carry the same 'penal value' as a term of custody. A community custody sentence can be a viable penal alternative in the mind of the public. But it has to be appropriately constructed and adequately explained to the community.

The conditions must also be enforceable. Some conditions imposed on offenders in Canada have been unenforceable, at least without the co-operation of 'whistle-blowers'. For example, offenders have been ordered to abstain from watching television, or from using a mobile phone. In one case an offender was ordered to retire to his bedroom in the event that visitors arrived at his family where he was living and serving his community custody sentence. Conditions of this are impossible to enforce, invite non-compliance, and bring the notion of community custody into disrepute, in the eyes of the public and criminal justice professionals and possibly offenders themselves.

Penal content of community custody orders

The nature of restrictions also requires careful consideration. Indeed, the ethics of community custody need to be explored to a far greater degree than has been the case to date. Over a decade ago, Andrew von Hirsch (1990) published an article dealing with the ethics of community sanctions in which he distinguished between acceptable and unacceptable elements of such dispositions. Conditions that humiliate or shame the offender (such as requiring the offender to parade outside a store carrying a sign reading 'I am a thief') are unacceptable, and will be viewed by most people in this way. The conditions of community custody – whether defined by statute or crafted by judges – need to conform to exacting ethical standards.

The conditions of community custody need therefore to be clearly specified. And, although courts should be able to craft specific conditions to reflect the needs of the offender, certain conditions should be common to all offenders serving this sentence. Foremost among these is a curfew. Offenders serving sentences at home who do not have a curfew may nevertheless be subject to numerous restrictions and privations. Some intensive supervision programs in the USA are very intrusive, but they are not *custodial*. In order to change conceptions of imprisonment, the community version must first assume some of the essential characteristics of custody. Restricting the offender's movements is the most obvious of these. The ability to freely circulate without having to consider the time is one of our most prized liberties. If offenders continue to exercise this liberty, society will continue to see a clear conceptual distinction between two sentences: imprisonment and 'community-based alternatives'.

When courts send offenders to prison, the conditions imposed apply to all prisoners, and although most judges probably have insufficient knowledge of life inside, at least they know that treatment will not differ that much for prisoners within the same security classification. Although there is a tendency for judges to become more engaged in sentence administration, this is still largely a matter for correctional authorities. The daily lives of community custody prisoners, however, are far more influenced by judicial decision-making. Beyond the limited number of statutory conditions, most jurisdictions allow judges considerable discretion to devise conditions appropriate to the needs of individual offenders. While necessary to maximize the effectiveness of the sanction, such a policy also carries important dangers. It is possible that some judges will craft conditions that are demeaning or humiliating, or indeed more aversive than those conditions associated with the prison. Von Hirsch and Narayan (1993) offer the following definition of acceptable penal content: 'Acceptable penal content, then, is the idea that a sanction should be devised so that its intended penal deprivations can be administered in a manner that is *clearly* consistent with the offender's dignity, that is, manifestly not objectionable' (p. 84, emphasis in original).

The use of electronic monitoring needs to be given careful consideration. Although technological advances have meant that the portable transmitters are fairly unobtrusive, it is by no means clear that they should be used in all cases. All too often, the justice system creates an invidious choice between being tagged and going to prison. In May 2002, a twelve-year old girl became the youngest person in Britain to be tagged, as a result of the introduction of tagging for twelve to sixteen-year olds.[15] The girl's solicitor was quoted as welcoming the court's decision to tag the girl, as being 'preferable to the alternatives, which would have included locking her up' (*Guardian*, 20 May 2002). Preferable to imprisonment it may have been, but should the justice system create such a choice? This would appear to be a failure to offer the court something other than these two alternatives, rather than a positive argument in favour of tagging.

Nature of statutory conditions

A judge in Canada with considerable experience in sentencing published a paper about community custody entitled 'Conditions, conditions,

conditions' (Renaud, 1999). The title captures the importance of the conditions imposed on the offender, for these define the sanction the way that duration largely defines the severity of a term of institutional custody. If the sanction carries the name of imprisonment (as it does in Canada), it needs to carry at least some of the properties of incarceration. This means the imposition of significant restrictions on a person's liberty. An offender free to come and go as he or she pleases, to enjoy the fruits of liberty enjoyed by the rest of society will not be regarded by the public (or judges) as serving a sentence of imprisonment. Most jurisdictions permit judges to impose rigorous restrictions, but left to judicial discretion, they are not always invoked. The experience in Canada is illustrative of this point: house arrest is imposed in only approximately half the cases as a condition of the community custody sanction.

House arrest should be a presumptive condition

Offenders sent to prison are confined to an institution, and even have their sleep patterns regulated by institutional lighting timetables. Any sanction which attempts to divert cases bound for custody must attempt to create an analogous environment for the community custody. A community custody sentence must therefore carry house arrest, or a curfew as a presumptive condition. The Canadian Supreme Court recognized this in its guideline judgment with respect to community custody (see *R. v. Proulx*). The Court noted that 'Conditions such as house arrest or strict curfew should be the norm, not the exception' (p. 20). Thus an offender serving a sentence at home will be presumed to have a strict curfew, or to be under house arrest. If the imposition of such a condition is clearly inappropriate in light of the offender's circumstances, the court would have the discretion to waive the condition, or to modify it in some way. There will be cases in which house arrest is inappropriate, and judges should have the freedom to depart from the presumption. But a sentence of community custody which permits the offender to come and go as he or she pleases is not a term of custody, but some form of enhanced probation. Such a sentence will undermine the whole community custody regime, and several adverse effects will ensue.

First, the public will not regard the sentence as the equivalent of custody. Second, this will eventually create pressure on judges to avoid imposing the sanction for more serious cases, in apprehension of the negative response from the public, the news media and possibly crime victims. Third, offenders will probably regard the sentence as little more than an enhanced form of probation. And finally, it will become even harder to respect the principle of parity in sentencing. Two equally culpable offenders sentenced to, respectively, terms of institutional and community custody will be serving very different sentences if one is free to leave his residence at any time. Indeed, house arrest, or a curfew, is essential to maintaining the integrity of the community custody regime; it is far more than simply a tool which can enhance the penalty for certain cases, as some commentators have suggested.

Ensure that conditions do not become so punitive that compliance is too difficult

Judges may be tempted to pile on the conditions of a community custody order, by taking advantage of 'basket clause' provisions that permit the imposition of any conditions deemed necessary to ensure some specific sentencing objective, such as preventing re-offending. One reason why they may want to do this is to ensure some degree of equivalence between institutional and community custody. The temptation should be resisted because it will inevitably result in more breaches, and undermine or ultimately defeat the intention of reducing admissions to prison, as many offenders will be sentenced to custody for breach. This tendency is particularly worrying with respect to the community custody regime in Canada, as judges often protract the length of the community custody order, again, to achieve the penal equivalence of a term of institutional confinement. This places offenders who breach their orders early at risk of a significantly longer term of imprisonment than would have been the case had they been sent to prison from the outset.

The relationship between the number of conditions and the likelihood of breach has been demonstrated in a number of jurisdictions, with different sanctions. It also emerges from the recent experience with community custody in Canada. As noted in chapter 6, the success rate of community custody orders in Manitoba declined steadily over the period 1997 to 2001. One reason for the increase in breaches can be seen in Table 8.1. The number of conditions imposed on offenders increased steadily over this same period. For example, the use of house arrest jumped from 5 per cent to 47 per cent of cases.[16] This was clearly related to the failure rate, as can be seen in the reasons for failure of orders. The percentage of orders cancelled as a result of breach of conditions (rather than allegations of fresh offending) rose from 9 per cent to 22 per cent of all orders (Roberts, 2002a).

The conditions imposed on community custody offenders should be clearly directed towards a sentencing objective. Offenders on whom the conditions are imposed should understand *why* they have to comply with these conditions. Interviews with community custody offenders suggest that in

Table 8.1. *Conditions imposed on community custody offenders, Manitoba, 1997–8 and 2000–1.*

Condition	% 1997/8	% 2000/1
Abstain from drugs/alcohol	63	79 (+16)
Weapons restriction	15	22 (+7)
Community service	43	32 (−11)
Alcohol/drug rehabilitation	30	37 (+7)
Other treatment program	35	55 (+20)
Association restriction	30	43 (+13)
House arrest	5	47 (+42)
Curfew	66	43 (−23)
Maintain employment	7	7
Maintain residence	25	48 (+23)
Restitution	10	8 (−2)
Education	10	13 (+3)
Other (average number)	0 (0)	100 (1.6)

Source: Roberts (2002a).
Note: column totals exceed 100% due to imposition of multiple conditions.

many cases these individuals saw their conditions as a punishment for the offence, rather than as a means to change aspects of their lifestyle. Finally, the principle of restraint should be considered with respect to the number and nature of conditions imposed. The statutory conditions applicable to all offenders define the sanction, and distinguish it from probation. The remaining conditions that reflect the specific needs of individual offenders should be imposed with restraint; any restriction on the offender's liberty should be justified in terms of the objectives of sentencing.

Ensure that the threat of imprisonment following breach is credible
As noted in chapter 1, the concept of an imminent threat is central to community custody. In order to avoid imprisonment, offenders sentenced to custody at home must know that violation of their conditions without reasonable excuse will result in committal to custody. If there is one finding that emerges clearly from the complex and at times contradictory results of research into deterrence, it is that offenders will only be deterred if the threat facing them is real. In reviewing this literature, Nagin (1998) notes that 'Credibility is assuredly critical. If a sanction threat is not credible it will

not be effective' (p. 34). Lax enforcement will have many adverse effects on the regime. It will ultimately result in higher breach rates, and this will impede judicial 'uptake' of the sanction. As well it will undermine public and professional confidence in the sentence. Research with crime victims in cases resulting in community custody in Canada revealed deep scepticism regarding the enforcement of the sanction. Most victims claimed to know of violations that had resulted in no official action by the courts (Roberts and Roach, 2004). Many intermediate sanctions suffer from the problem that they are not rigorously enforced (e.g. Langan, 1998), and this is one of the reasons that they have assumed only a limited proportion of the custodial caseload.

Without preventing judges from exercising some discretion with respect to offenders who breach conditions, the enabling legislation should create a credible threat for offenders serving terms of custody in the community. Since a community custody is effectively defined by the conditions it imposes on offenders, it is vital to assure compliance. Rather than allowing courts a wide range of response – including doing nothing – a better approach would be to create a statutory presumption in favour of incarceration for the time remaining on the order.

Determining the legal threshold for establishing a breach of the order

An offender deemed to have violated his conditions without reasonable excuse should be presumed to be committed to custody for some period of time. As well, the threshold should be a balance of probabilities; requiring the state to prove a breach to the higher standard of a reasonable doubt creates an almost insuperable hurdle for prosecutors.[17] Some commentators would argue that if the offender is at risk of imprisonment in the event that a breach is established (as is the case in Canada as well as most other jurisdictions including England and Wales), the higher threshold should be required. This perspective on response to breach treats the breach hearing as though it were a criminal proceeding in which an accused, presumed innocent, is at risk of conviction and possibly incarceration. Yet there is surely an important distinction between an accused facing trial, and an offender facing a hearing in which a court will determine, if a breach is found, the manner in which an existing court order will be discharged.

Adopting the lower 'balance of probabilities' threshold seems more reasonable, for although the consequences may be comparable for the two (accused persons, and offenders in breach hearings), not all of the constitutional protections afforded accused persons apply to an offender discharging a sentence of custody. Ensuring a rigorous response to breach will maximize the deterrent value of the sanction, create a clearer distinction between a community custody and probation, and undermine arguments that community custody represents a 'soft' response to offending.

Responding to breach is far from straightforward and requires the thoughtful exercise of judicial discretion. The response should reflect some consideration of the nature of the breach. The most obvious consideration is the seriousness of the breach. Late arrival home in breach of a curfew should not provoke committal to custody; more serious breaches such as violation of an order restricting the offender from approaching the victim's residence should result in committal to custody. The timing of the breach is also important. A breach occurring after nine months of a twelve-month order should receive a different response from the court than one which occurs very early in the life of the order.

Provide judges and community custody supervisors with guidance regarding breaches

The response to breaches of community custody orders should be consistent as well as firm. Several jurisdictions allow both probation officers who supervise offenders and judges much discretion regarding the response to allegations of breaches. For the sake of effectiveness as well as equity, guidelines should be created. For example, Corrections procedures manuals in Florida provide examples of behaviours constituting major and minor violations.[18]

Encourage appellate review to promote consistency in sentencing

In Canada, the leading judgment regarding community custody provided guidance for trial judges with respect to the imposition of the sanction. However, it also undermined the entire appellate process by articulating the principle of deference to the trial bench. Appellate courts are strongly discouraged from interfering with a sentence unless there has been an error in law, or the sentence imposed by the trial judge was 'manifestly unfit'. This direction from the Supreme Court carries a number of dangers.

The direction permits considerable variability to develop in the application of the sanction across the country (Roberts, 2002a). Second, it may have a chilling effect on the appellate process. Prosecutors and defence counsel may be less likely to appeal sentencing decisions because of the high standard of review. The appellate courts have traditionally played a muted role in sentencing in Canada (see Young, 1988; Trotter, 1999); as a result of the position taken by the Supreme Court in Proulx and other decisions (see Manson, 2001) their influence has been diminished still further. In a jurisdiction without a body such as the Sentencing Advisory Panel (found in England and Wales) or a Sentencing Guidelines Commission, the appellate courts represent the only source of guidance for judges. These courts should be encouraged to shape the response of the trial court with respect to the sanction.

Provide adequate resources for supervision of community custody offenders

Writing about the home detention scheme in the Australian Northern Territory, Challinger (1994) notes that 'Fundamental to the success of the home detention program is the perception on the part of courts, police, offenders, and the community at large that home detainees will be subject to strict surveillance under a system that cannot be circumvented' (pp. 274–5). Community custody should not be introduced unless and until correctional services personnel are given additional resources to devote more time to supervision and surveillance. Offenders ordered to serve community sentences of imprisonment are going to represent a higher risk to re-offend (than probation offenders) since they have been convicted of more serious crimes and probably have more extensive criminal histories. They are going to need more assistance to avoid relapse, and supervision will need to be more intensive as they face more conditions.

The experience in Canada underlines the importance of devoting adequate resources to the supervision of offenders serving such sentences. The constitutional division of powers assigns the administration of justice to provincial authorities in Canada. Although the federal government created the new sanction, no new resources were provided for probation officers who supervise offenders serving community custody sentences in the community. These offenders represent a higher risk than probationers, and accordingly require more assistance and monitoring. In addition, community custody orders carry more conditions than probation orders, a trend accelerated by the Supreme Court judgment relating to conditional sentencing (*R. v. Proulx*).

Ensuring that curfews, non-association orders and other conditions are respected consumes additional time and attention from community custody supervisors. A common complaint from these professionals in Canada at least has been that they do not have adequate time to supervise these offenders. In addition, some judges have refused to impose a community custody sentence because they have lacked confidence that the conditions of the order will be adequately enforced. The lack of supervisory resources has therefore threatened the very existence of the conditional sentencing regime. The result was that many probation officers became demoralized as a result of the additional responsibilities created by this new category of client. Offenders were aware that unless they had been classified as high risk by supervisory authorities, monitoring of their behaviour would be minimal.

Probation officers who supervise community custody offenders in Canada often have caseloads in excess of 100 individuals. This is far too many; the Florida limit of twenty-five is much more appropriate. In addition, it can only undermine the distinctiveness of the sanction if it is supervised by probation officers. The needs of community custody offenders are quite different from probationers, and this reality should be recognized by the use of dedicated officers. The use of specialized probation officers with reduced caseloads would also encourage offenders to see the sanction as sanction clearly apart from probation.

Create statutory reviews of the order and offer incentives for compliance with conditions

As a result of the more extensive opportunities open to them, the lives of offenders serving community custody sentences are likely to change and evolve more rapidly than those of prisoners in custody. During the course of the sentence, community custody offenders may complete compensation requirements, graduate from treatment regimes, and make progress towards rehabilitation in a number of ways. The community custody order may need revisiting in light of these developments. For example, an offender with absolute house arrest as a condition of an eighteen-month community custody order may have the house confinement condition relaxed, to a less restrictive curfew perhaps. Or the nature of the authorized absences may change; young adults may be allowed to leave their residences if accompanied by a family member. If periodic reviews were held, perhaps every three months, the offender would have the right to make representations as to ways in which the order may be amended. As well, such reviews would permit family members to bring to the court's attention particular conditions which may be causing undue hardship or which may have proved to be counterproductive.

Offenders serving time in prison in most countries benefit from the possibility of parole, or 'good time' remission schemes. These 'early' release mechanisms encourage prisoners to take positive steps towards rehabilitation, and contribute to the running of the institution by providing a reward for good behaviour. Community custody offenders should also be offered some analogical incentive for protracted compliance, particularly with respect to long sentences. It is noteworthy that a survey of electronic monitoring programs in the USA found that the majority supported some form of 'good time' credit for electronically monitored offenders (Payne and Gainey, 2000).

A community custody sentence can empower offenders to exercise some control over their lives, and the sentence that they are serving. This carries benefits for offenders as well as their families. Offenders need some degree of control in order to return to a law-abiding lifestyle. Maruna (2001) describes one of the essential characteristics of what he refers to as the 'redemption' script in the lives of offenders. By this he refers to the offender's sense of control over their life. In his study of desistance, Maruna found that offenders who 'had a plan and were optimistic that they could make it work' (p. 147) were more likely to desist from further offending. In contrast, offenders who continued to re-offend had little sense of self-control or plan for the future.

Through continued compliance the offender should be able to earn his or her way to less stringent conditions, thereby exercising even more control over his lifestyle. But since these changes affect the penal content or severity of the sanction, they should be determined by judges, not community custody supervisors. In addition, limits need to be placed on the extent to which community custody conditions can be relaxed following a judicial review. If all conditions save reporting are eventually dropped, external observers may reasonably question whether the offender is still serving a sentence of custody at all.

Educate the public about the benefits of a community custody of imprisonment

Another important lesson concerns the importance of ensuring that the public understand the nature and purpose of the sanction. A systematic attempt should be made to educate the public about the disposition. Research in many jurisdictions shows that knowledge of the sentencing process is poor. Most people subscribe to the view that sentencing is too lenient, and that judges are out of touch with what ordinary people think (see Hough and Roberts, 2002). As noted in the last chapter, findings from a poll in Canada found that when provided with a simple, three-option forced choice question about the community custody sentence, most respondents confused the sanction with probation or parole. A community custody sentence, whether it is called a community custody sentence or something else such as 'custody minus', or a suspended term of imprisonment has the danger of contributing to public cynicism with respect to the courts. It is important therefore to convince the public that this sentencing option is not a 'let off', for this perception went some considerable way towards undermining the suspended term of imprisonment (see Bottoms, 1981). This initiative would have to include an aggressive media strategy.

As Brownlee notes, 'if penal policy is to advance in a sensible and consistent fashion those charged with its formation must be prepared, at times, to take on the task of leading and educating public opinion' (pp. 3; 193–4; see also Bishop, 1988, p. 7). This is abundantly clear for the issue of community custody; public support is essential if community custody is to make inroads into the caseload of offenders sentenced to prison. Generally speaking, this element of implementation strategy has been overlooked, although jurisdictions are now paying more attention to responding to public opinion (see Home Office, 2001). The American Correctional Association guidelines for electronic monitoring schemes include creation of a public information programme to address community concerns and promote community support (see Whitfield, 1997; Appendix I), and the need is even greater for a sanction of which electronic monitoring is simply a condition.

No jurisdiction has come to grips with the issue of public opinion and sentencing policy. Nor has any government to date devoted significant resources to understanding the nature of public opinion or educating the public about the nature and limits of the sentencing process. Scholars, too, have neglected the issue; only a few publications have explored the complex and sensitive relationship between public opinion and penal policy (see Davies, 1993). Such negligence is at best going to limit the utility of community custody as a sanction; at worst it is a recipe for disaster. Proceeding with sentencing reform without attempting to engage the views of the public invites the worst kind of newspaper headlines, which can only undermine public confidence in the sentencing process.

How then might community custody be explained to the public? First, the concept needs to make sense; the criminal justice system needs to have good 'product' to sell to the community in the place of prison. Second, it might at first need to be implemented conservatively. A few high-profile cases can rapidly undermine the legitimacy of the entire regime.

Public education initiatives also need exploring. Other social policy issues result in significant attempts to educate the community. When the SARS outbreak occurred in Toronto in 2003, the government launched an aggressive (and expensive) information campaign to explain to the community the ways in which the disease could be (and could not be) contracted. Lives were at stake (along with a billion dollar tourist industry); nevertheless, it is not beyond the realm of possibility to conceive a similar, but less expensive, educational initiative to explain to the public exactly what community custody does (and does not) entail for the offender and the community.

The one element of the prison that cannot be adequately recreated in the community is the notion of secure detention. The public are aware of this, which is why they tend to be sceptical of the sanction as a way to control crime (see chapter 7). Part of the public opposition to community custody springs from the fact that most people over-estimate both the probability and seriousness of re-offending. The public feels that the risk that offenders pose cannot be adequately contained at home, even if the offender is subject to electronic monitoring. But few offenders committed to prison for relatively short periods of incarceration (the prime candidates for community custody) constitute a serious risk to the community, and this needs to be conveyed to the public.

Educate offenders about the purpose and potential of the sanction

Many criminal justice innovations have been undermined by what is referred to as the 'banalization' of the justice system; reforms are assimilated by criminal justice professionals and lose their power to improve the lives of offenders and victims.[19] This has undoubtedly happened to a degree with home confinement. The sanction has become a court-ordered disposition like any other: probation with more restrictive conditions, or a 'softer' version of custody. Research with offenders serving community custody sentences in Canada suggested that some were unclear about the nature of the sanction that they were serving (Roberts et al., 2003). Clearly pleased at not having to go to prison, these individuals appear to have devoted little further thought to the sanction that they were serving. The active rather than passive character of home confinement was lost on these individuals. If offenders in other jurisdictions share this reaction, the sanction will fail to fulfil its potential.

Conclusion

Stable – or worse, rising – prison populations continue to defy policy-makers and Parliamentarians in most common law jurisdictions, including England and Wales. If properly implemented, community custody holds considerable promise but carries equally significant dangers. The challenge to legislators is to construct a community custody sanction that is successful in reducing admissions to custody but without placing further strains on public faith in sentencing.

There are two opposing perspectives on community imprisonment. Critics of the more punitive elements of community custody may condemn the attempt to convert a restorative sanction into a punitive one, through the use of tight conditions, curfews, electronic monitoring and house arrest: Once her castle, an offender's home has become her prison. A more optimistic perspective would argue that reconciliation, restoration and rehabilitation can only flourish while the offender remains a part of the community against which he or she has offended.

But the sentence can also be seen as a bridge between the traditional retributive model of sentencing, with its emphasis on proportionality, and restorative justice that affirms the importance of reparation and reconciliation. If community custody is constructed with conditions that ensure that the sentence conforms to parity requirements of proportional sentencing, then the requirements of desert-based sentencing would be satisfied. At the same time, the presence of reparative conditions and the presence of the offender in the community to fulfil these conditions reflect the goals of restorative justice (see Braithwaite, 1999; Van Ness and Strong, 2002). In order to serve as an effective bridge, the sanction must be firmly planted on both sides of the divide. A community custody which is excessively punitive will undermine the restorative component; on the other hand, an order with no hard treatment, and designed purely to promote rehabilitation or restoration will be unpalatable to retributive justice advocates, and is likely to prove unacceptable to the community, particularly when imposed for serious personal injury cases.

The evolution of community custody

In this book I have argued that community custody represents another step in the evolution of imprisonment, and indeed, the concept of legal punishment.[20] To the extent that this true, we can expect the sanction itself to evolve. This evolution will take the form of expanding the range of offences and offenders to which it applies. Jurisdictions in which community views will not countenance this form of custody for serious violent crimes will in all probability become more accepting of the sanction. As community acceptance increases, the opposition of victims may well also diminish. The nature of conditions imposed will also change, as knowledge accumulates about the kinds of restrictions and demands on the offender that are most likely to promote the goals of the sanction.

Detention in a private residence may well encourage society to see a greater role for the community in the administration of legal punishments. Rather than expel individuals to a secure facility outside society, society may see greater merit in allowing offenders to discharge their debt while remaining part of the community to which they belong. Ultimately, community custody will become the norm rather than the exceptional form of imprisonment. Even offenders who have committed offences serious enough to justify a significant deprivation of liberty will be able to serve their sentences in the community, retaining their (restricted) autonomy and preserving a level of dignity that is impossible within the walls of a prison.

Notes

1 INTRODUCTION TO THE CONCEPT OF COMMUNITY CUSTODY

1. There is empirical support for this assertion. For example, Sigler and Lamb (1996) asked a sample of the public and criminal justice professionals to rate the extent to which ten different dispositions 'punish' offenders. There was concordance with respect to imprisonment: both groups rated prison as the most punitive. The two samples differed however in their perceptions of some of the other sanctions.
2. Harland (1998) writes that 'The challenge, therefore, is not simply to meet a need for more sanctioning options, but to develop options that will have clear relevance and credibility in the eyes of the practitioners and policymakers on whose understanding and support their long-term survival depends' (p. 71).
3. As will be seen during the course of this volume, the image is not always apposite; in many jurisdictions the threat against the offender for non-compliance with the requirements of the order is neither severe nor imminent.
4. Most jurisdictions with a community custody sanction also have a suspended sentence.
5. *R. v. Sangster* (1973).
6. For example, suspended sentences are sometimes imposed for manslaughter, where the offender has been subject to extraordinary abuse resulting in the commission of the crime.
7. I refer here to house arrest as a political sanction. There is some evidence that house arrest was occasionally used as a penal sentence. Parisi (1980) cites the case of offenders in the seventeenth century who were permitted to 'be abroad from Eight of the clock in the morning till Six of the clock at night' (p. 387). There is therefore some historical precedent for house arrest as a legal sanction.
8. These examples derive from Canada, where second-degree murder carries a mandatory life sentence, but with the possibility of release on parole after at least ten years. Almost all offenders convicted of this offence are released from prison after having served ten years, but remain on licence for the rest of their lives. Most other offenders may apply for day parole after having served one-sixth of the sentence in prison.

9. This is the typical result from polls that ask whether respondents are opposed to or in favour of parole for violent offenders. Given more time to make a decision, and more information, Canadians at least generally prefer a correctional system that includes discretionary release on parole to 'flat time' sentencing (no parole) systems (see Roberts, Nuffield and Hann, 2000). Although this research was conducted in a single jurisdiction, it is likely that the public in other countries would respond to the issue in a similar way.

10. The parole analogy is apt; in the early days of the conditional sentencing regime in Canada, the sanction was referred to as 'judicial parole'.

11. Recent administrations of the British Crime Survey (BCS) have revealed that judges attract the lowest ratings of any criminal justice profession, and that this negative rating is due in large measure to the perception that sentencing practices are excessively lenient (see Mattinson and Mirrlees-Black, 2000).

12. Victim impact forms used in some Canadian provinces employ language such as 'You [i.e. the victim] may also write down anything else you think the judge should know' (Roberts, 2003c).

13. New Zealand introduced weekend custody as a sanction in the 1960s, and Canada in 1972.

14. According to section 718 of the *Criminal Code*, restorative objectives of sentencing, including reparation and promoting 'a sense of responsibility in offenders, and acknowledgement of the harm done to victims and to the community' are no less important than the more traditional goals of deterrence, denunciation and incapacitation (see discussion in Roach, 1999).

15. In his seminal book *Crime, Shame and Reintegration*, Braithwaite does not discuss community custody directly, but the sanction is clearly consistent with the concepts outlined in that work. For example he notes that 'It follows that, if we must resort to incarceration, maximum effort must be made to integrate the person within the community – work release, study release, easy access for family visits – is recommended' (1989, p. 180).

16. The most popular options were 'better parenting', 'more police on the beat' and 'better discipline in schools', all of which were supported by approximately half the sample (multiple responses were permitted; see Rethinking Crime and Punishment, 2002).

17. Landreville (1987; 1999) for example, warns of the dangers that electronic monitoring will expand the reach of the criminal justice system. See discussion of such predictions in Cusson (1998).

2 THE WAY WE PUNISH NOW

1. In Canada, subsections 718.2(d) and (e) of the *Criminal Code* state that: 'an offender should not be deprived of liberty, if less restrictive sanctions may be appropriate in the circumstances; and (e) all available sanctions other than imprisonment that are reasonable in the circumstances should be considered for all offenders, with particular attention to the circumstances of aboriginal offenders'. Similar provisions exist in most other common law jurisdictions.

2. The National Crime Victimization Survey data show that total violent crime rates declined from fifty-one victimizations per 1,000 population in 1994 to thirty-two in 1999 (Bureau of Justice Statistics, 2000). The 1999 rate was the lowest level ever recorded.

3. Some Western nations such as France, Denmark and Finland reported declines in their prison populations over the decade. However, of the thirty-nine nations included in the survey conducted by the Home Office (see Barclay and Tavares, 2003), thirty-four reported increases.

4. Data from the USA reflect felony sentencing which is more likely to involve custody.

5. Freiberg (2002) examined sentencing patterns for a specific offence (burglary). Even in a small number of jurisdictions (five Australian states plus New Zealand, Canada, England and Wales, and Scotland) the variability was striking: imprisonment rates varied from 16 per cent in Western Australia to 61 per cent in Canada.

6. This is important because one explanation for an increasing or stable proportionate use of custody could be an increased reliance on diversion. The cases most likely to be diverted from court are the less serious cases. If a jurisdiction experienced an increased use of diversion, the 'mix' of offences being sentenced would change, and resemble a more serious caseload than prior to the introduction of diversion programs. Such a transformation in the profile of offender being sentenced could explain changes in the probability of a custodial sentence, or the length of sentence. Simply put, the less serious cases are dropping out, and the cases proceeding to sentencing are the more serious ones that are also more likely to result in a term of custody.

7. The decline in the crime rate in New Zealand was not as striking as in some other jurisdictions such as Canada, nevertheless a decline was recorded from the peak in 1992 (132 per 1,000 population to 111 per 1,000 population in 2000 (see Statistics New Zealand, 2002)).

8. For example, 11 per cent of non-trafficking offences were imprisoned. Incarceration rates were much higher in the superior courts as the following examples reveal: 43 per cent of cases of receiving or handling proceeds of crime, 79 per cent of motor vehicle cases, and 63 per cent of fraud were incarcerated (New South Wales Bureau of Crime Statistics and Research, 2002).

9. Quoted in the *Guardian*, 22 November 2002.

10. Section 79 (2) of the Powers of Criminal Courts (Sentencing) Act 2000 states that: 'Subject to subsection (3) below, the court shall not pass a custodial sentence on the offender unless it is of the opinion –

   (a) that the offence, or combination of the offence and one or more offences associated with it, was so serious that only such a sentence can be justified for the offence; or

   (b) where the offence is a violent or sexual offence, that only such a sentence would be adequate to protect the public from serious harm from him.'

11. As Hough et al. (2003) note, crime statistics are not capable of sustaining or refuting this perception of sentencers.

12. The first three are statutory sentencing objectives in Canada, while proportionality has been codified as the 'fundamental principle' of sentencing in that jurisdiction.
13. This survey was conducted in the early days of the community custody regime in Canada (in 1999). The next year the Supreme Court issued a guideline judgment (*R. v. Proulx*) that encouraged judges to make the sanction tougher (by introducing 'presumptions' in favour of the use of house arrest, and committal to custody in the event of a breach of conditions). It is quite possible that if the survey were repeated in 2004, judges would see the conditional sentence as a more effective deterrent.
14. The sample included defence lawyers, prosecutors and probation and parole officers.
15. Bishop (1988) reached a similar conclusion in his survey regarding the use of alternatives in Europe. He concluded that 'non-custodial alternatives are insufficiently used . . . and when they are used, are often substituted for other non-custodial sanctions rather than imprisonment' (p. 5).

3 CONCEPTUALIZING COMMUNITY CUSTODY

1. Richard II (v. 5. 1). Shakespeare's words illustrate the originally sharp distinction between custody and community, which the subject of this book attempts to explore. The deposed king's ruminations on prison and society are spoken while he reposes in a castle, not a dungeon; Richard was effectively under house arrest.
2. A jailer had charge of the prison, and scrupulously recorded the number of prisoners each month to the government.
3. Although the issue has not been explored in the last few years, earlier public opinion research has demonstrated that many members of the public subscribe to a number of negative stereotypes of prisoners, or ex-prisoners. In 1967, respondents to a survey in the USA were asked whether they would feel uneasy at the prospect of personal contact with someone who had served time. Even if the personal contact was as a result of this person being the respondent's insurance agent, 60 per cent of the sample said that they would feel uneasy. Almost half indicated they would be uneasy working in an organization with someone who had served time in prison (Joint Commission on Correctional Manpower and Training, 1968).
4. For example, a survey conducted in 1999 found that three-quarters of the public in Canada over-estimated the percentage of parolees who would commit offences while on parole (Roberts, Nuffield, and Hann, 2000).
5. Hamlet's celebrated description 'Denmark's a prison' also captures this sense that imprisonment connotes restriction of movement rather than penal confinement.
6. Cited in Christiansen (1981).
7. Webster's defines incarceration as 'a confining or state of being confined'. The verb to imprison is defined as either 'to put in prison' or 'to limit, restrain or confine as if by imprisoning'.
8. The *OED* offers the following quotation which captures this well: 'Imprison thy tongue, lest it imprison thee' (*Oxford English Dictionary*, 1933/61, p. 113).

9. The use of house arrest as an exercise of state power goes back much further; medieval monarchs would confine nobles to their residence, or order them to reside in a monastery as a way of removing them from society without resorting to imprisonment.

10. The amalgamation of prison and community has been accelerated by the perception that prison life is easy, and by a desire for tough community penalties. Reform proposals advanced in 2003 by the Liberal Democrats would result in people convicted of burglary, shoplifting or minor drug crimes being forced to work in the community rather than being sentenced to 'the cushy option of prison'. One liberal democrat said that 'prison is a very easy life in many ways for lots of people . . . it's actually a cushy number' and advocated a tough community-based alternative (quoted in the *Guardian*, 23 September 2003).

11. See Ball et al., 1988, pp. 137–44, for an earlier discussion of the advantages of home confinement.

12. 'Doing nothing time' might be a better phrase to describe the monotony of prison life.

13. This view may seem dismissive of the attempts by many prisoners to ameliorate their lives by actively participating in prison programs and devising programs of their own. This is not the intention; several of my own students have been prisoners undertaking and completing their studies, even within the constraints of a penal institution. The point is rather that the prison complicates these attempts, while the community facilitates them.

14. For a discussion of the attempts to promote positive prison environments, see West (1997).

15. In Canada, in addition to the possibility of release on parole, federal prisoners can benefit from release at the two-thirds point of the term of imprisonment. This is a statutory entitlement; the prisoner will leave the institution to spend the last third of the sentence in the community, unless correctional authorities deem him to be a threat.

16. A report published in December 2003 by the Home Office is a good example of this correctional managerialism. It is entitled 'Managing offenders, reducing crime'.

17. It will be recalled that Sykes was describing life within a maximum security prison, where prisoners' lives are subject to more restrictive conditions. Nevertheless, as anyone who has worked or served time in institutions at lower levels of security will attest, many restrictions still apply to a prisoner's daily life.

18. The exception to this observation arises when the offender serving a term of home confinement lives in a very small community. When there are only a few hundred people in the village, it seems unlikely that an offender could be subject to house arrest without the other residents becoming aware of the fact. In fact, the whole community may know of the sentence imposed on one of its members. Ironically, then, in this exceptional context, house arrest may be stigmatizing in a way that prison is not. An offender sent to prison may serve a sentence of imprisonment without anyone outside his or her immediate family ever knowing.

19. This judgment was issued before the Supreme Court of Canada handed down a guideline decision regarding the way in which a community custody sentence

should be constructed. That guideline judgment prescribed a number of ways in which the sanction should be tougher, and in this way responded to the criticisms made by the Alberta Court of Appeal (see Roberts and Healy, 2001).

20. Clear makes the point well: 'To be blunt, how can any program in the community compare in the symbolics of punitiveness to the moment in court when the judge says "I sentence you to ten years in the state prison"' (1997, p. 127).

21. Under some conditions offenders may prefer to go to prison; for example, if the community custody sentence is much longer than the custodial term for which it is a substitute, or if the offender lives in a small village where everyone will know that he is serving a sentence at home (see discussion in chapter 5).

22. The Canadian conditional sentence of imprisonment is a community custody sanction that carries this restriction.

23. In Canada, house arrest or a curfew can be imposed on offenders sentenced to a conditional sentence of imprisonment. However, even after the Supreme Court encouraged lower courts to use these restrictions when imposing such a sentence, only approximately half the conditional sentence orders carry such restrictions (see Roberts, 2002a).

24. Introduced in Canada in 1996, the community custody option was not available to sentencers in youth court. When the new Youth Criminal Justice Act was proclaimed in 2003, it created a community custody as one of the new sanctions available in youth court. However, the government appears to have thought twice about the label: at the youth court level the sanction carries the murkier name of a 'deferred custody and supervision order' (see Roberts and Bala, 2003). The adoption of this term may have been provoked by the negative publicity associated with the community custody sentence available in adult court.

25. In Canada, a fairly relaxed minimum security federal correctional institution is repeatedly referred to as 'Club Fed'.

26. The sentencing reforms introduced by the Criminal Justice Act 2003 in England and Wales include creation of a part-time custodial sentence.

27. The only public opinion survey of which I am aware revealed that American respondents were significantly more likely to see weekend jail sentences as effective than ineffective (University of Arkansas, 1998).

28. A notable exception is the work of Ball and Lilly (e.g. 1986). In the time since that article was published, however, the penal landscape has changed considerably, most noticeably with respect to the rise of restorative justice. Although elements of this paradigm are discussed by Ball and Lilly (see 1986, pp. 21–2), restorative considerations now permeate sentencing policy and practice in many countries. As well, community custody is now applied to a much wider range of offenders than almost twenty years ago when, as Ball and Lilly (1985) noted, the sanction applied to 'certain types of offenders' (p. 95).

29. The Comprehensive Crime Control Act identifies four purposes of sentencing: punishment; deterrence; incapacitation and rehabilitation (18 USCS 3553(a)(2)).

30. A survey of electronic monitoring supervisors reported by Payne and Gainey (2000) found that they attributed many purposes to home confinement, including punishment, rehabilitation, incapacitation and retribution.

31. These are self-report findings from the offenders themselves.

32. In a small community, the sight of the offender sitting in a pub – when people know he should be shopping or at home – will also have a negative impact on the public image of home confinement as a sanction. Some offenders interviewed in Canada highlighted the impact of community custody when the offender lived in a small community. One individual explained that the sentence was hard to serve because 'the community watches you'. She lived in a small community and apparently felt a lot of stigma and shame within that community. These feelings accompanied her wherever she went while on a court-authorized absence from home, and had proved to be a source of considerable discomfort and difficulty for her.

33. For example, several of these young adults expressed guilt at the fact that family gatherings had to be curtailed, or cancelled as a result of a home confinement or curfew restriction (see chapter 5 of this volume).

34. In Canada, this principle has been identified as fundamental in sentencing; in New Zealand the importance of proportionality in sentencing is established through an inter-related set of principles (see Roberts, 2003b).

35. Wasik observes that 'it would be unacceptable, within a desert sentencing frame-work, to have a sentence labelled "box 13", which offered no immediate sanction on the outside but contained a wide range of penal consequences which might or might not flow in the event of the commission of the next offense. Sometimes conditional sentences give very little indication of the likely outcome on breach, and afford sentencers considerable discretion. Such a sentencing option could not be ranked in desert terms because the sanction it would represent would be unknown' (1994, p. 55). Wasik is describing a classic 'conditional sentence', but the observation holds for many elements of some community custody regimes.

36. See von Hirsch (1993), pp. 72–7 for discussion of the difference between these two communicative theories of sentencing. In essence, the von Hirsch model consists of an appeal to the offender which may or may not elicit a response. Duff, however, is more concerned to create the conditions that spawn change within and by the offender, penitence being a key transformation.

37. For example, in a recent chapter, Braithwaite writes that 'I am not attracted to any conception of proportionality in restorative programmes' (2002, p. 152).

38. Thus Duff argues that: 'what we should aspire to create is a system which seeks neither restoration rather than retribution, nor retribution without restoration, but restoration through retribution' (p. 98).

39. Daly (2003) reports that 60 per cent of the offenders in the South Australia Juvenile Justice project (SAJJ) accepted responsibility and expressed remorse for the offence.

40. Restorative programs do exist in some prison systems, notably Belgium and Italy. For example, a restorative correctional project has been active in six Belgian prisons since 1998 (see Robert and Peters, 2003). However, such initiatives are relatively rare, involve small numbers of victims and offenders, and exist despite, rather than as a result of the prison environment.

41. In some American states, victims are allowed to make direct representations to the sentencing court. Research into victim impact statements in Canada found that a significant proportion of statements submitted contained sentence recommendations (Roberts and Edgar, 2003).

42. Research published by the Home Office Sentencing Review found that half the offenders committed to prison in England and Wales had been employed at the time of sentencing (Home Office, 2001).
43. The Court of Appeal was following the principle of appellate deference laid down by the Supreme Court several years earlier. According to this principle, appellate courts should not interfere with a trial court sentence unless the disposition was manifestly unfit, or there had been an error in law. The issue of the role of appellate courts will be explored at greater length in chapter 8.
44. Quoted in Globe and Mail, 27 November, p. A18.
45. Cited in Toronto Star, 21 June 2002, p. B5.
46. The dimensions proposed by Harland include: retributive severity, crime reduction, recidivism reduction, reparation, economic cost and public satisfaction (see Harland, figure 2).

4 REPRESENTATIVE MODELS OF COMMUNITY CUSTODY

1. In many respects, community custody is a more appropriate sanction for young offenders, for whom home confinement may be particularly beneficial. However, exploring community custody as it applies to juvenile offenders who usually have separate statutory sentencing regimes, is beyond the scope of the present volume.
2. The options included creating a schedule of offences for which the sanction would be unavailable, and lowering the ceiling from two years less one day.
3. In one case in Canada, a conditional sentence offender was summoned to a breach hearing for returning home fifteen minutes after his curfew, with no reasonable excuse. In another, the offender was deemed by a police officer to have violated his home confinement condition by sitting on the front steps of his house. Such cases should not have been brought to court and were dismissed once they were before a judge.
4. This last principle is a curious version of the principle of restraint with respect to the use of custody. In other jurisdictions such as New Zealand and Canada, judges are exhorted to avoid imposing custody because of the adverse effects of incarceration on offenders. In Florida, judges are enjoined to be parsimonious regarding sentences of imprisonment because of the fiscal consequences for the state.
5. For example, if the offender's age prevents him from obtaining employment, if the offender is a student, or if the offender has diligently attempted, but been unable to find employment.
6. In Canada, a provision allows most life prisoners to apply for 'early parole' (i.e. before their parole eligibility date). This controversial provision was amended to create a structure in which applicants have to receive the approbation of a judge, then a jury, and finally the National Parole Board before they can obtain early parole. This multiple-stage procedure has helped to preserve the provision in the face of repeated calls for its repeal (see Roberts, 2002c).
7. Home detention is also possible for offenders serving sentences in excess of two years who may serve three months under the scheme prior to their first parole

date. This is a form of conditional release and is therefore not included in this book which focuses on sentencing rather than correctional programs.

8. Spier (2002) Table 4.3; calculation excludes cases sentenced to life imprisonment, preventive detention and corrective training.

9. The statute defines relevant as in the case of a family residence, every person eighteen or over who 'ordinarily lives [in the residence]'.

10. Total custodial sentences includes 7,864 custodial sentences and 18,502 periodic detention orders (Spier, 2002).

11. These included the most serious driving offences, including dangerous driving causing death.

12. The amendment came into force six months after the original legislation was proclaimed.

13. It is noteworthy that a court is not obliged to order periodic reviews; for many less serious offenders, there may be little need for a review which will consume valuable court time.

5 COMING HOME TO PRISON: OFFENDER PERCEPTIONS AND EXPERIENCES

1. People also 'discount' the sentence, assuming that all prisoners get released on parole, and at their first application. In Canada, a significant proportion of penitentiary prisoners do not even apply for federal parole, and of those who do, less than half are granted release, and not often after the first application. In 2001/2, 43 per cent of federal full parole applications were granted (Carriere, 2003).

2. An alternate myth is that community custody, with its myriad conditions, constant surveillance and imminent threat of imprisonment, is as harsh, or even harsher than life in prison. This view is equally implausible as a description of community custody, regardless of the specific regime under consideration. The constraints of even the most rigorous community custody sentence (the Community Control sentence in Florida) cannot match the privations, restrictions on liberty, and aversive nature of life in prison.

3. This underlines the need to ensure that community custody carries meaningful conditions, designed to promote rehabilitation or restoration and also to distinguish the sanction from a very different disposition such as probation.

4. For example, they were not allowed to watch tv, use a computer, or use the telephone more than once a day, considerable deprivations for university students.

5. One judge I know sometimes offers offenders a choice of sanction: x months in prison, or y months in the community as part of a community custody order (where y is usually greater than x). Apparently, in a significant minority of cases, the offender chooses prison. This reaction supports the argument that prison is not necessarily always the worst alternative.

6. A number of publications also cite individual stories of offenders who having been placed on electronic monitoring then asked to be sent to prison instead (e.g. Nellis, 1991).

7. Unless otherwise indicated, all offender quotes in this chapter come from focus groups and interviews with community custody offenders and their co-residents conducted in Canada (see Roberts, Maloney and Vallis, 2003).

8. The Home Detention Curfew offenders were most aware of the advantages of community custody; imprisonment had been more than a possibility in their case, as they were released from custody to the HDC program.

9. This is a good illustration of the conflict that can arise between the need for the community custody order to be punitive and restorative; punishment often interferes with rehabilitation.

10. House arrest with a curfew was rated as being much less difficult to comply with, but the curfew specified was 10 pm, which is less onerous.

11. In Canada, although the federal government has exclusive jurisdiction over the *Criminal Code* (and was therefore responsible for creating the community custody sanction in 1996), the provinces are responsible for the administration of the criminal justice system. This includes supervising offenders serving community custody orders across the country. Whether community custody offenders are subject to electronic monitoring is a decision taken by provincial correctional authorities.

12. This raises the issue of the professional activities in which the offender is engaged. Individuals with stimulating jobs will find community custody far less aversive than offenders who are either underemployed or unemployed, and therefore confined to home for long stretches of time. Women may well be disadvantaged in this respect, being less likely to be employed and more likely to be primary caregivers for children. King and Gibbs (2003) report that women on home detention were more likely to be employed domestically, men more likely to be in a formal workplace. A number of female offenders in Canada have been placed on community custody for welfare fraud; unable to work, their time will weigh more heavily on their hands.

13. One detainee had her request for an out-of-hours excursion denied 'on the basis that she had not organized herself well enough in advance' (Gibbs and King, 2001, p. 78).

14. According to s. 742.3(2)(f), the optional conditions of this sanction in Canada should secure 'the good conduct of the offender' and prevent 'a repetition by the offender of the same offence or the commission of other offences'.

15. Ethical problems abound with respect to the role of sponsors. Is it ethical to create pressure upon these individuals to report violations of conditions occurring at home? If they report to the authorities, the offender will probably be arrested. If they decide not to report such incidents, sponsors may feel complicit in the offender's failure to comply with his conditions.

16. These reactions differ from those of family members in the research by Blomberg et al. (1993), who had a less positive view of the home confinement program in Florida. However, this seems due to the fact the offenders in the Florida research 'believed they would have been placed on probation' (p. 192) had they not been placed on the community control program; this perception must have coloured their attitudes to the experience and will have been communicated to their families as well.

6 THE EFFECT OF COMMUNITY CUSTODY ON PRISON ADMISSIONS

1. 'This type of control could be imposed on offenders who would have received a term of probation.'

2. *R.* v. *Brady* (1998).
3. In 1950, the rates of prisoners per 100,000 were as follows: Finland, 187; Sweden, 35; Denmark, 88; Norway, 51 (Lappi-Seppala, 2003).
4. Some of the analysis that follows derives from Roberts and Gabor (2004).
5. Conditional sentence statistics are as yet unavailable from the remaining provinces and territories.
6. Data were not available for certain provinces and territories.
7. This suggests an hypothesis that has not been explored in the literature, namely the possibility that community custody can breathe some additional life into other alternatives to custody by creating renewed judicial interest in alternative sanctions.
8. Since rates of probation have increased, not decreased since the time that community custody was introduced, it seems more likely that these offenders would previously have been sentenced to a fine. And this is borne out by the sentencing statistics. In the last year before the inception of the community custody regime, a fine was imposed in 41 per cent of convictions across Canada (Roberts and Grimes, 2000). In 2000–1, four years after the introduction of the community custody sanction, only 33 per cent of convictions resulted in a fine (Thomas, 2002).
9. For example, an offender might be sentenced to nine months of community custody instead of four months of institutional imprisonment. If he breaches the conditions of the order after three months, he faces the possibility at least of serving six months in prison, longer than the period to which he might initially have been sentenced.
10. These statistics mirror those of sentences of institutional custody, of which the vast majority are under six months in Canada.
11. One statutory sentencing principle in Canada directs judges to make an especial effort to avoid incarcerating Aboriginals. In light of this, it might have been anticipated that the volume of Aboriginal admissions to custody would decline at an even faster rate. However, for reasons that remain unclear, this has not happened (see Roberts and Melchers, 2003).
12. The Supreme Court judgment may have contributed to protecting the sentence by making it harder for opponents to pressure the government to amend the framework.
13. See description in Roberts and Bala (2003).

7 PUBLIC ATTITUDES TO COMMUNITY CUSTODY

1. This can be demonstrated in a number of ways, one of which involves making comparisons between attributions of public attitudes (by policy-makers or criminal justice professionals) and the actual attitudes. A number of studies have shown that policy-makers believe that the public is more punitive than is the case (e.g. Elrod and Brown, 1996).
2. The public become even more punitive when asked about the sentencing of sex offenders. A Canadian survey found that 85 per cent of respondents believed that sentences were too lenient for sex crimes, and approximately half favoured mandatory castration for paedophiles (Le Soleil, 2002).

3. Mirrlees-Black (2001) analysed data from the 2000 British Crime Survey and found a significant association between attitudes to the courts and confidence in the justice system.

4. Timothy Flanagan writes that: *'The key to understanding the lack of support for community corrections is, in my view, the long-term, widespread perception that probation represents leniency in the criminal justice system'* (1996, p. 6, emphasis in original).

5. To a degree, the public view of alternative sanctions simply reflects a lack of imagination about their impact, and hence relative severity; we find it hard to imagine the effect of a sanction with which we have so little familiarity. This is particularly true when the sanction can be so variable with respect to the number and nature of conditions attached.

6. This was demonstrated over twenty years ago now, in an experiment in which people were asked to read either a newspaper account of a sentencing hearing, or a summary of court documents. Those who read the media version of the sentence held far more negative views of the sentence, the judge and the offender (see Doob and Roberts, 1983; 1988). One of the most reliable findings in the public opinion literature is that the public have very different views when they are given more information about the offence or the offender than the minimal amount usually provided in a newspaper article (see Covell and Howe, 1996; Hough and Roberts, 2004b).

7. The news media represent prison life as being relatively easy as well, a fact noted seventy years ago by Smith (1934) who wrote about the two public perspectives on prison, one of which sees prisons as places of torture. The other, more popular view 'also excited by a sensational newspaper article, is that prisons are luxurious establishments, in which worthless offenders are "petted" and "pampered"' (p. 4).

8. This misrepresentation would have been less likely had the sanction been restricted to a smaller number of cases, and had the government made curfews and house arrest statutory (rather than optional) conditions. Once again, then, the nature of the statutory framework is critical to the eventual success of the sanction.

9. *Globe and Mail*, 25 February 2004, p. A13. Many of the community custody offenders interviewed in Canada (see Roberts, Maloney and Vallis, 2003) were aware of the nature of stories in the press about community custody sentences. Offenders said that they were quite upset with the opinions being expressed in the media, and felt the stories misrepresented the reality of life on a community custody.

10. As noted in chapter 5, it is surprising that a significant number of offenders sentenced to a community custody of imprisonment in Canada were subject to 'absolute' curfews, despite the presence of young children in the household.

11. A second crime scenario was used on the two latter surveys. Respondents were asked to sentence an offender convicted of assaulting his wife, who required medical attention for her injuries. The offender had no previous convictions. In 2000, 62 per cent of the sample favoured community custody, 38 per cent prison. When the question was repeated two years later, the percentages were almost the same: 61 per cent community custody, 39 per cent prison (Sanders and Roberts, 2004).

12. This view is not restricted to members of the public. Surveys of criminal justice professionals also find that while support for home confinement sanctions is

strong, it declines when respondents are asked about serious crimes, particularly violent offences. Thus Johnson, Haugen, Maness and Ross (1989) conducted a survey of probation officers in Tennessee and found that while over half supported home confinement for serious property offenders, less than one-quarter were in favour of this disposition if the offence involved violence. Research in Canada approached the issue from another direction. Judges were asked to identify the offences for which a community custody order was appropriate. Of those who had an opinion on the issue, few judges identified crimes of violence, while over two-thirds of the sample identified property offenders as being the appropriate target for community custody (Roberts et al., 2000).

13. For example, Hough and Park (2002) provide comparisons between attitudes held before the weekend began and responses to the same questions fully ten months later. They found significantly less public support for harsher sentencing after the weekend sessions (see Hough and Park, 2002, Table 9.2).

14. Respondents were also asked about reparation and punishment, with the same pattern of results.

15. In Canada, the median length of time served in prison in 1998 was 24 days (Reed and Roberts, 1999). Hough et al. (2003) note that the average sentence of immediate custody in magistrates' courts in England and Wales was under three months.

8 MAKING COMMUNITY CUSTODY SENTENCES WORK

1. In *R. v. Proulx*, the Supreme Court identified this as a problem with the statutory framework in Canada: 'There has been some confusion among members of the judiciary and the public alike about the difference between a conditional sentence [the community custody sanction] and a suspended sentence with probation. The confusion is understandable, as the statutory provisions regarding conditions to be attached to conditional sentences (s. 742.3) and probation orders (s. 732.1) are very similar' (para 23). The similarities go beyond simply these provisions, and include the supervision of the two categories of offenders.

2. Even in Canada, where the community custody regime has resulted in a reduction in admissions to custody, there has been a small degree of 'widening of the net' – see chapter 6.

3. For example, in Saskatchewan, over the period 1997–8, non-murder homicide and attempted murder cases accounted for only two of over 6,000 community custody sentences imposed. Even a more common serious offence such as sexual assault accounts for only approximately two per cent of community custody orders each year.

4. Co-residents, or sponsors as they are referred to in certain jurisdictions, may not appreciate the hardships that they will be facing when they agree to a lengthy community custody sanction being served in their residence.

5. The criminal justice professionals with the most knowledge of the impact of community custody – probation officers who supervise these offenders – clearly see difficulties with community custody orders that run over a year. Rackmill (1994) reports the findings from a survey of probation officers many of whom believed that a six-month maximum limit on home incarceration was appropriate; similar sentiments have been expressed by probation officers in Canada.

6. This issue has to be considered in conjunction with another proposal advanced here, namely that a 'two for one' rule be adopted regarding the length of community custody and the term of custody that it replaces. If the former are always twice as long as the latter, a twelve-month limit means that only prison sentences up to six months can be replaced by a term of community custody.

7. In contrast to the more numerous examples where punitive legislation has been precipitated by public opinion, or what politicians perceive to be public opinion.

8. In Canada, unlike England and Wales and some other jurisdictions, prosecutors play a very active role in sentencing, making submissions to the court in every case.

9. Requiring offenders convicted of domestic assault to serve their sentences in prison would be tantamount to having a statutory exclusion; as well, in many cases, incarcerating the offender creates additional hardships for his partner and dependants. Committing them to serve their terms custody in a halfway house allows them to continue working and supporting their families.

10. Impounding property belonging to the offender will in all probability make life worse for co-residents.

11. Under a proportional sentencing model, offenders convicted for the first or second time are accorded some mitigation, but penalties should not rise monotonically in severity to reflect the seriousness of the offence. This is referred to as the principle of the progressive loss of mitigation.

12. In Canada, a record of previous non-compliance with court orders, particularly a community custody order, is a powerful factor in determining whether the offender should be sentenced to community rather than institutional custody.

13. Courtright et al. (2000) report that regular attendance at treatment combined with continued employment were significantly related to a successful outcome.

14. Judges in Canada are clearly alive to the issue of restitution to the victim, in part as a result of the amendments to the Criminal Code introduced in 1996. See for example, the judgment in *R. v. Visanji, Lall and Akbar* and discussion in Bacchus (1999).

15. See *Guardian*, 20 May 2002.

16. Table 8.1 reveals that the use of curfews declined significantly, but this is an artifact of the increase in house arrest; if the offender is confined to his residence for twenty-four hours a day (except for authorized absences), it is unnecessary to add a curfew condition to the community custody order.

17. The legal limen under the Canadian legislation is a balance of probabilities.

18. An example of a major violation is committing a new offence or failing a drug test; examples of minor violations include submitting a written report a day late or missing an office appointment by a few hours (see Florida Corrections Commission, 2003).

19. It has been argued that the victim impact statement is an example of a criminal justice reform that has been 'assimilated' by criminal justice professionals (see Young, 2001).

20. Lilly and Ball (1987) provide a similarly evolutionary analysis when they talk of the phases of punitive policy development in Western nations.

References

Abrahamson, A. (1991). Home Unpleasant During House Arrest, Judge Learns. *Corrections Today*, 53: 76.

Ahmed, E., Harris, N., Braithwaite, J., and Braithwaite, V. (2001). *Shame Management Through Reintegration*. Cambridge: Cambridge University Press.

Albrecht, H-J. and Kalmthout, A. (eds.) (2002). *Community Sanctions and Measures in Europe and North America*. Freiburg: Edition iuscrim.

Ancel, M. (1971). *Suspended Sentence*. London: Heinemann.

Ansay, S. J. and Benveneste, D. (1999). Equal application or unequal treatment: practical outcomes for women on community control in Florida. *Women and Criminal Justice*, 10: 121–35.

Aungles, A. (1994). *The Prison and the Home*. Sydney, Australia: Institute of Criminology Monograph No. 5.

Bacchus, S. (1999). The Role of Victims in the Sentencing Process. In J. V. Roberts and D. Cole (eds.) *Making Sense of Sentencing*. Toronto: University of Toronto Press.

Bagaric, M. (2002). Home Truths About Home Detention. *Journal of Criminal Law*, 66: 425–43.

Baird, S. and Wagner, D. (1990). Measuring Diversion: The Florida Community Control Program. *Crime and Delinquency*, 36: 112–25.

Ball, R., Huff, C., and Lilly, J. (1988). *House Arrest and Correctional Policy. Doing Time at Home*. Newbury Park: Sage.

Ball, R. and Lilly, J. (1985). Home Incarceration: An International Alternative to Institutional Incarceration. *International Journal of Comparative and Applied Criminal Justice*, 9: 85–97.

(1986). A Theoretical Examination of Home Incarceration. *Federal Probation*, 50: 17–24.

(1988). Home Incarceration with Electronic Monitoring. In J. Scott and T. Hirschi (eds.) *Controversial Issues in Crime and Justice*. Newbury Park: Sage.

Barclay, G. and Tavares, C. (2002). *International Comparisons of Criminal Justice Statistics 2000*. London: Home Office, Research, Development and Statistics.

(2003). *International Comparisons of Criminal Justice Statistics 2001*. London: Home Office, Research, Development and Statistics.

Baumer, T. L. and Maxfield, M. G. (1993). A Comparative Analysis of Three Electronically Monitored Home Detention Programs. *Justice Quarterly*, 10: 121–42.

Baumer, T. L. and Mendelsohn (1992). Electronically Monitored Home Confinement: Does it Work? In J. Byrne, A. Lurigio, and J. Petersilia (eds.) *Smart Sentencing. The Emergence of Intermediate Sanctions*. Newbury Park: Sage Publications.

Beattie, J. (1986). *Crime and the Courts in England, 1660–1800*. Princeton: Princeton University Press.

Beck, J. L. and Klein-Saffran, J. (1991). Home Confinement. The Use of New Technology in the Federal Bureau of Prisons. *Federal Prisons Journal*, 2: 23–7.

Beck, J. L., Klein-Saffran, J., and Wooten, H. (1990). Home Confinement and the Use of Electronic Monitoring with Federal Parolees. *Federal Probation*, 54: 22–33.

Bellamy, J. (1973). *Crime and Public Order in England in the Late Middle Ages*. London: Routledge and Kegan Paul.

Bishop, N. (1988). *Non-Custodial Alternatives in Europe*. Helsinki: Helsinki Institute for Crime Prevention and Control Affiliated with the United Nations.

Blomberg, T. G., Bales, W., and Reed, K. (1993). Intermediate Punishment: Redistributing or Extending Social Control? *Crime, Law and Social Change*, 19: 187–201.

Bondeson, U. (2002). *Alternatives to Imprisonment. Intentions and Reality*. New Brunswick: Transaction Publishers.

Bonta, J., Wallace-Capretta, S., and Rooney, J. (1999). *Electronic Monitoring in Canada*. Ottawa: Solicitor General Canada.

Bottoms, A. (1981). The Suspended Sentence in England, 1967–1978. *British Journal of Criminology*, 21: 1–26.

(2001). Compliance and Community Penalties. In Bottoms, A., Gelsthorpe, L., and Rex, S. (eds.) (2001). *Community Penalties. Change and Challenges*. Cullompton: Willan Publishing.

Bottoms, A., Gelsthorpe, L., and Rex, S. (eds.) (2002) *Community Penalties. Change and Challenges*. Cullompton: Willan Publishing.

Braithwaite, J. (1989). *Crime, Shame and Reintegration*. Melbourne: Cambridge University Press.

(1999). Restorative Justice: Assessing Optimistic and Pessimistic Accounts. In M. Tonry (ed.) *Crime and Justice. A Review of Research*. Chicago: University of Chicago Press.

(2002). In Search of Restorative Jurisprudence. In R. Walgrave (ed.) *Restorative Justice and the Law*. Cullompton: Willan Publishing.

Brodeur, J. P., Roberts, J. V., Mohr, R., and Markham, K. (1988). *Views of Sentencing: A Survey of Judges in Canada*. Ottawa: Research Reports of the Canadian Sentencing Commission, Department of Justice Canada.

Brookbank, C. and Kingsley, B. (1999). Adult Criminal Court Statistics, 1997–98. *Juristat*, 18, 14.

Brown, M. P. and Elrod, P. (1995). Electronic House Arrest: An Examination of Citizen Attitudes. *Crime and Delinquency*, 41: 332–46.

Brown, M. P. and Elrod, P. (1999). Citizens' Perceptions of a 'Good' Electronic House Arrest Program. *Corrections Management Quarterly*, 3: 37–42.

Brown, D. and Wilkie, M. (2002). *Prisoners as Citizens. Human Rights in Australian Prisons*. Sydney: The Federation Press.

Brown, M. and Young, W. (2000). Recent Trends in Sentencing and Penal Policy in New Zealand. *International Criminal Justice Review*, 10: 1–31.

Brownlee, I. (1988). *Community Punishment. A Critical Introduction.* London: Longman.

Bureau of Justice Statistics (2000). *National Crime Victimization Survey Violent Crime Trends.* Available at www.ojp.usdoj.gov/bjs.

Canadian Sentencing Commission (1987). *Sentencing Reform: A Canadian Approach.* Ottawa: Supply and Services Canada.

Carlisle, R. (1988). Electronic Monitoring as an Alternative Sentencing Tool – or My Week on an Electronic Ball and Chain. *Georgia State Bar Journal*, 24: 131–5.

Carcach, C. and Grant, A. (1999). Imprisonment in Australia: Trends in Prison Populations and Imprisonment Rates 1982–1998. *Trends and Issues*, No. 130. Canberra: Australian Institute of Criminology.

Carriere, D. (2003) Adult Correctional Services in Canada, 2001/2. *Juristat*: 23, no. 11.

Cavadino, M. and Dignan, J. (2002). *The Penal System. An Introduction.* 3rd edn. London: Sage Publications.

Challinger, D. (1994). An Australian Case Study: The Northern Territory Home Detention Scheme. In U. Zvekic (ed.) *Alternatives to Imprisonment in Comparative Perspective.* Chicago: Nelson-Hall Publishers.

Chicknavorian, E. (1990). House Arrest: A Viable Alternative to the Current Prison System. *New England Journal on Criminal and Civil Commitment*, 16: 53–66.

Christiansen, K. (1981). *The American Experience of Imprisonment, 1607–1776.* PhD Dissertation, State University of New York at Albany.

Church, A. and Dunstan, S. (1997). *Home Detention: The Evaluation of the Home Detention Pilot Programme 1995–1997.* Wellington: New Zealand Ministry of Justice. Available at www.justice.govt.nz/pubs/reports/1997/homedetention/Default.htm.

Clark, C. (2002). *The Use of Home Detention Since the Introduction of the Sentencing and Parole Acts on June 30 2002.* Wellington: New Zealand Ministry of Justice, Research and Evaluation Unit.

Clear, T. (1997). Evaluating Intensive Probation: The American Experience. In G. Mair (ed.) *Evaluating the Effectiveness of Community Penalties.* Aldershot: Avebury.

Committee to Remember Kimberly Rogers (2003). *Justice with Dignity.* Available at http://dawn.thot.net/Kimberly_Rogers.

Connelly, L. (2001). Electronic Monitoring in the United States. *Canadian Criminal Law Review*, 6: 326–35.

Courtright, K., Berg, B., and Mutchnik, R. (2000). Rehabilitation in the New Machine? Exploring Drug and Alcohol Use and Variables Related to Success Among DUI Offenders Under Electronic Monitoring – Some Preliminary Outcome Results. *International Journal of Offender Therapy and Comparative Criminology*, 44: 293–311.

Covell, K. and Howe, B. (1996). Public Attitudes and Juvenile Justice in Canada. *The International Journal of Children's Rights*, 4: 345–55.

Crouch, B. (1993). Is Incarceration Really Worse? Analysis of Offenders' Preferences for Prison over Probation. *Justice Quarterly*, 10: 67–88.

Cullen, F., Fisher, B., and Applegate, B. (2000). Public Opinion about Punishment and Corrections. In M. Tonry (ed.) *Crime and Justice: A Review of Research*, vol. 27. Chicago: University of Chicago Press.

Cullen, F., Wright, J., and Applegate, B. (1996). Control in the Community? The Limits of Reform? In A. Harland (ed.) *Choosing Correctional Options that Work.* Thousand Oaks: Sage.

Cusson, M. (1998) Peines intermédiares, surveillance electronique et abolitionisme. *Revue internationale de criminologie et de police technique et scientifique,* 1: 34–45.

Daly, K. (2003). Mind the Gap: Restorative Justice in Theory and Practice. In A. von Hirsch, J. V. Roberts, A. E. Bottoms, K. Roach, and M. Schiff, M. (eds.) *Restorative and Criminal Justice. Competing or Reconcilable Paradigms?* Oxford: Hart Publishing.

Daubney, D. and Parry, G. (1999). An Overview of Bill C-41. (The Sentencing Reform Act). In J. V. Roberts and D. Cole (eds.) *Making Sense of Sentencing.* Toronto: University of Toronto Press.

Davies, M. (1993). *Punishing Criminals. Developing Community-Based Intermediate Sanctions.* Westport, Conn.: Greenwood Press.

Davies, M., Takala, J.-P. and J. Tyver (1996). *Penological Esperanto and Sentencing Parochialism. A Comparative Study of the Search for Non-Prison Punishments.* Aldershot: Dartmouth.

Department of Justice Canada. (1994). Minister of Justice Introduces Sentencing Reform Bill. *News Release,* 13 June 1994.

Dictionnaire historique de la langue francaise. Tome 3. Paris: Dictionnaires Le Robert.

Dignan, J. (1984). The Sword of Damocles and the Clang of the Prison Gates: Prospects on the Inception of the Partly Suspended Sentence. *The Howard Journal of Criminal Justice,* 23: 183–200.

Doble, J. (1987). *Crime and Punishment: The Public's View.* New York: Public Agenda Foundation.

Doble Research Associates (1995a). *Crime and Corrections: The Views of the People of Oklahoma.* Englewood Cliffs, NJ: Doble Research Associates.

(1995b). *Crime and Corrections: The Views of the People of North Carolina.* Englewood Cliffs, NJ: Doble Research Associates.

(1998). *Crime and Corrections: The Views of the People of New Hampshire.* Englewood Cliffs, NJ: Doble Research Associates.

Dodgson, K. and Mortimer, E. (2000). *Home Detention Curfew: The First Year of Operation.* London: Home Office Research Development and Statistics Directorate. Research Findings No. 110.

Dodgson, K., Goodwin, P., Howard, P., Llewellyn-Thomas, S., Mortimer, E., Russell, N. and Weiner, M. (2001). *Electronic Monitoring of Released Prisoners: An Evaluation of the Home Detention Curfew Scheme.* HORS 222. London: Home Office, Research, Development and Statistics Directorate.

Doherty, D. (1995). Impressions of the Impact of the Electronic Monitoring Program on the Family. In K. Schulz (ed.) *Electronic Monitoring and Corrections: The Policy, the Operation, the Research.* Burnaby, BC: Simon Fraser University.

Doob, A. N. (1990). Community Sanctions and Imprisonment: Hoping for a Miracle but not Bothering Even to Pray for it. *Canadian Journal of Criminology,* 32: 415–28.

(2001). *Youth Court Judges' Views of the Youth Justice System: The Results of a Survey.* Toronto: Centre of Criminology, University of Toronto.

Doob, A. N. and Marinos, V. (1995). Reconceptualizing Punishment: Understanding the Limitations on the Use of Intermediate Punishments. *University of Chicago Roundtable,* 2: 413–33.

Doob, A. N. and Roberts, J. V. (1983). *Sentencing: An Analysis of the Public's View.* Ottawa: Department of Justice Canada.

(1988). Public Punitiveness and Public Knowledge of the Facts: Some Canadian Surveys. In N. Walker and M. Hough (eds.) *Public Attitudes to Sentencing. Surveys from Five Countries.* Aldershot: Gower.

Doob, A. N., Sprott, J. B., Marinos, V. and Varma, K. (1998). *An Exploration of Ontario Residents' Views of Crime and the Criminal Justice System.* Toronto: Centre of Criminology, University of Toronto.

Doob, A. N. and Webster, C. (2004). Sentence Severity and Crime: Accepting the Null Hypothesis. In M. Tonry (ed.) *Crime and Justice. A Review of Research,* 30: 143–95.

Dowds, L. (1995). *The Long-Eyed View of Law and Order: A Decade of British Social Attitudes Survey Results.* London: Home Office.

Duff, R. A. (2001). *Punishment, Communication, and Community.* Oxford: Oxford University Press.

(2002). Restorative Punishment and Punitive Restoration. In L. Walgrave (ed.) *Restorative Justice and the Law.* Cullompton: Willan Publishing.

Duguid, S. (2000). *Can Prisons Work? The Prisoner as Object and Subject in Modern Corrections.* Toronto: University of Toronto Press.

Elrod, P. and Brown, M. P. (1996). Predicting Public Support for Electronic House Arrest. *American Behavioral Scientist,* 39: 461–73.

English, K., Crouch, J. and Pullen, S. (1989). *Attitudes toward Crime: A Survey of Colorado Citizens and Criminal Justice Officials.* Denver, Colorado: Department of Public Safety, Division of Criminal Justice.

Fattah, E. (1982). Public Opposition to Prison Alternatives and Community Corrections: A Strategy for Action. *Canadian Journal of Criminology,* 24: 371–85.

Faugeron, C. (1996). The Changing Functions of Imprisonment. In R. Mathews and P. Francis (eds.) *Prisons 2000. An International Perspective on the Current State and Failure of Imprisonment.* London: MacMillan Press.

Flanagan, T. (1996). Community Corrections in the Public Mind. *Federal Probation,* 60: 3–9.

Florida Department of Corrections (1997). *Corrections in Florida: What the Public Thinks. Results of a March 1997 Survey of Floridians.* Miami: Florida Department of Corrections.

Florida Corrections Commission (2003). *A Review of the Community Control Program and Electronic Monitoring within the Florida Department of Corrections.* Miami: Florida Corrections Commission.

Flynn, L. (1986). House Arrest. *Corrections Today,* July issue.

Freiberg, A. (2002). What's it Worth? A Cross-Jurisdictional Comparison of Sentence Severity. In C. Tata and N. Hutton (eds.) *Sentencing and Society. International Perspectives.* Aldershot: Ashgate.

Frost, S. and Stephenson, G. (1989). A Simulation Study of Electronic Tagging as a Sentencing Option. *The Howard Journal of Criminal Justice,* 28: 91–104.

Gabel, K. and Johnston, D. (eds.) (1995). *Children of Incarcerated Parents.* New York: Lexington Books.

Gainey, R. R. and Payne, B. (2003). Changing Attitudes Toward House Arrest With Electronic Monitoring: The Impact of a Single Presentation? *International Journal of Offender Therapy and Comparative Criminology,* 47: 196–209.

(2000). Understanding the Experience of House Arrest with Electronic Monitoring: An Analysis of Quantitative and Qualitative Data. *International Journal of Offender Therapy and Comparative Criminology*, 44: 84–96.

Galaway, B. (1984). A Survey of Public Acceptance of Restitution as an Alternative To Imprisonment for Property Offenders. *Australia and New Zealand Journal of Criminology*, 17: 108–16.

Gallup (2000). *The Gallup Monthly*, no. 420. Princeton: The Gallup Poll.

Gandy, J. and Galaway, B. (1980). Restitution as a Sanction for Offenders: A Public's View. In J. Hudson and B. Galaway (eds.) *Victims, Offenders, and Alternative Sanctions*. Toronto: Lexington Books.

Garland, D. (2001a). *The Culture of Control. Crime and Social Order in Contemporary Society*. Chicago: University of Chicago Press.

(2001b). *Mass Imprisonment. Social Causes and Consequences*. London: Sage.

Gibbs, A. and King, D. (2001). *The Electronic Ball and Chain? The Development, Operation and Impact of Home Detention in New Zealand*. Dunedin, New Zealand: University of Otago, Department of Community and Family Studies.

(2003a). Home Detention with Electronic Monitoring: The New Zealand Experience. *Criminal Justice*, 3: 199–211.

(2003b). The Electronic Ball and Chain? The Operation and Impact of Home Detention with Electronic Monitoring in New Zealand. *Australian and New Zealand Journal of Criminology*, 36: 1–17.

Gottfredson, S. and Taylor, R. (1984). Public Policy and Prison Populations: Measuring Opinions about Reform. *Judicature*, 68: 190–201.

Graham, J. (1990). Decarceration in the Federal Republic of Germany. *British Journal of Criminology*, 30: 150–70.

Harkins, J. R. (1990). House Arrest in Oregon: A Look at What Goes on Inside the Home. *Corrections Today*, 52: 146–52.

Harris, J. (1995). Foreword. In K. Gabel and D. Johnston (eds.) *Children of Incarcerated Parents*. New York: Lexington Books.

(1968). Changing Public Attitudes Toward Crime and Corrections. *Federal Probation*, 32: 9–16.

Haverkamp, R. (2003). *Implementing Electronic Monitoring. A Comparative, Empirical Study on Attitudes towards the Measure in Germany and Sweden*. Available at www.iuscrim.mpg.de/forsch/krim/haverkamp.

Hayes, B. (2002). Making a Case for House arrest. *Halifax Herald*, Friday December 6, 2002.

Heggie, K. (1999). Review of the NSW Home Detention Scheme. *Research Publication*, no. 41. Sydney, NSW: NSW Department of Corrective Services.

Hendrick, D., Martin, M., and Greenberg, P. (2003). *Conditional Sentencing Data in Canada: A Statistical Profile 1997–2001*. Ottawa: Ministry of Industry.

Hobbes, T. (1651/1957 (reprint)). *Leviathan or the Matter, Forme and Power of a Commonwealth Ecclesiastical and Civil*. Oxford: Basil Blackwell.

Hollis, V. and Cross, I. (2003). *Prison Population Brief. England and Wales: April 2003*. London: Home Office.

Holman, B. and Brown, R. (2004) Beyond Bricks, Bars, and Barbed Wire: The Genesis and Proliferation of Alternatives to Incarceration in the United States. In C. Sumner (ed.) *The Blackwell Companion to Criminology*. Oxford: Blackwell Publishing.

Holman, J. and Quinn, J. (1992). Dysphoria and Electronically Monitored Home Confinement. *Deviant Behavior: An Interdisciplinary Journal*, 13: 21–32.

Home Office (1999). *Prison Statistics. England and Wales. 1998*. Cm 4430. Norwich: The Stationery Office.

——— (2001). *Making Punishments Work. Report of a review of the sentencing framework for England and Wales*. London: Home Office.

——— (2002). *Criminal Statistics England and Wales. 1998*. Cm 5696. Norwich: The Stationery Office.

——— (2003). *Managing Offenders, Reducing Crime*. London: Home Office.

Hough, M. and Park, A. (2002). How Malleable are Attitudes to Crime and Punishment? Findings from a British Deliberative Poll. In J. V. Roberts and M. Hough (eds.) *Changing Attitudes to Punishment. Public Opinion, Crime, and Justice*. Cullompton: Willan Publishing.

Hough, M. and Roberts, J. V. (1998). *Attitudes to Punishment: Findings from the British Crime Survey*. Home Office Research Study 179. London: Home Office.

——— (1999) Sentencing Trends in Britain Public Knowledge and Public Opinion. *Punishment and Society. The International Journal of Penology*, 1: 7–22.

——— (2002). Public Knowledge and Public Opinion of Sentencing: Findings from Five Jurisdictions. In N. Hutton and C. Tata (eds.) *Sentencing and Society: International Perspectives*. Aldershot: Ashgate Publishing Company.

——— (2004a). *Public Confidence in Justice: Findings from Around the World*. ICPR Research Paper No 1. London: Kings College.

——— (2004b). *Youth Crime and Youth Justice: An Analysis of Public Opinion in Great Britain*. ICPR Research Paper No 3. London: Kings College.

Hough, M., Jacobson, J., and Millie, A. (2003). The Decision to Imprison. *Sentencing and the Prison Population*. London: The Prison Reform Trust.

Howard, J. (1929). *The State of the Prisons*. New York: J. M. Dent and Sons.

Hume, D. (1834). *The History of England*, vol. 2. London: A. Valfy.

Johnson, B., Haugen, L., Maness, J. and Ross, P. (1989). Attitudes Toward Electronic Monitoring of Offenders: A Survey of Probation Officers and Prosecutors. *Journal of Contemporary Criminal Justice*, 5: 153–64.

Johnson, S. (1979/reprint edition). *A Dictionary of the English Language*. New York: Arno Press.

Johnstone, G. (2002). *Restorative Justice. Ideas, Values, Debates*. Cullompton: Willan Publishing.

Joint Commission on Correctional Manpower and Training (1968). *The Public Looks at Corrections*. Washington: DC: Joint Commission on Correctional Manpower and Training.

Jolin, A. and Stipak, B. (1992). Drug Treatment and Electronically Monitored Home Confinement: An Evaluation of a Community-Based Sentencing Option. *Crime and Delinquency*, 38: 158–70.

Keay, N. (2000). Home Detention – An Alternative to Prison. *Current Issues in Criminal Justice*, 12: 98–105.

Kemp, B. (1981). *The Impact of Enforced Separation on Prisoners' Wives*. Research Bulletin No. 4. New South Wales Department of Corrective Services.

King, D. and Gibbs, A. (2003). Is Home Detention in New Zealand Disadvantaging Women and Children? *Probation Journal*, 50: 115–26.

Kirkpatrick, J. (ed.) (1880). *MacKenzie's Studies in Roman Law*, 5th edn. Edinburgh: Blackwood.

Kommer, M. (2003). Punitiveness in Europe Revisited. *Criminology in Europe*, 3: 1–12.

Kong, R., Johnson, H., Beattie, S., and Cardillo, A. (2003). Sexual Offences in Canada. *Juristat*, 23, no. 6.

Kuhn, A. (2003). Prison Population Trends in Western Europe. *Criminology in Europe*, 2: 1–16.

Kury, H., Obergfell-Fuchs, J., Smartt, U. and Wurger, M. (2002). Attitudes to Punishment: How Reliable are International Crime Victim Surveys? *International Journal of Comparative Criminology*, 2: 133–50.

Landreville, P. (1987). Surveiller et prévenir: L'assignation à domicile sous surveillance electronique. *Déviance et Société*, 11: 251–69.

(1999). La Surveillance electronique des délinquants: une marche en expansion. *Déviance et Société*, 23: 105–21.

Langan, P. (1998). Between Prison and Probation: Intermediate Sanctions. In J. Petersilia (ed.) *Community Corrections. Probation, Parole, and Intermediate Sanctions.* New York: Oxford University Press.

Lappi-Seppala, T. (2001). Sentencing and Punishment in Finland: The Decline of the Repressive Ideal. In M. Tonry and R. Frase (eds.) *Sentencing and Sanctions in Western Countries.* New York: Oxford University Press.

(2002). *Prisoner Rates: Global Trends and Local Exceptions.* Helsinki: National Research Institute of Legal Policy.

(2003). *Non-Custodial Sanctions in Finland.* Helsinki: National Research Institute of Legal Policy.

Law Reform Commission of New South Wales (1996). *Sentencing.* (Report 79) chapter 7: Home Detention. Available at www.agd.nsw.gov.au/lrc.nsf.

Le Soleil (2002). Sondage pancanadien: La justice n'est pas assez dure pour les crimes sexuels. 9 April 2002, page A3.

Leibrich, J. (1994). What Do Offenders Say About Supervision and Going Straight? *Federal Probation*, 58: 41–6.

Lilly, J. R. (1990). Tagging Reviewed. *Howard Journal of Criminal Justice*, 29: 229–45.

Lilly, J. and Ball, R. (1987). A Brief History of House Arrest and Electronic Monitoring. *Northern Kentucky Law Review*, 13: 343–74.

Lilly, J., Ball, R., Curry, G. and Smith, R. (1992) The Pride, Inc., Program: An Evaluation of Five Years of Electronic Monitoring. *Federal Probation*, 56: 42–53.

Logan, R. (2001). Crime Statistics in Canada, 2000. *Juristat*, 21, no. 8.

Mande, M. and English, K. (1989). *The Effect of Public Opinion on Correctional Policy: A Comparison of Opinions and Practice.* Denver: Colorado Department of Public Safety.

Maidment, M. R. (2002). Toward a 'Woman-Centred' Approach to Community-Based Corrections: A Gendered Analysis of Electronic Monitoring (EM) in Eastern Canada. *Women and Criminal Justice*, 13: 47–68.

Mainprize, S. (1995). Social, Psychological, and Familial Impacts of Home Confinement and Electronic Monitoring: Exploratory Research Findings From B. C.'s Pilot Project. In K. Schulz (ed.) *Electronic Monitoring and Corrections: The Policy, the Operation, the Research.* Burnaby, B.C.: Simon Fraser University.

Mair, G. (2001). A Decade of Electronic Monitoring in England and Wales. *Canadian Criminal Law Review*, 6: 317–26.

— (2002). Technology and the future of community penalties. In A. Bottoms, L. Gelsthorpe and S. Rex (eds.) *Community Penalties. Change and Challenges.* Cullompton: Willan Publishing.

Mair, G. and Nee, C. (1990). *Electronic Monitoring: The Trials and Their Results.* Home Office Research Study No. 120. London: HMSO

Mair, G. and Mortimer, E. (1996). *Curfew Orders with Electronic Monitoring: An Evaluation of the First Twelve Months of the Trials in Greater Manchester, Norfolk, and Berkshire, 1995–1996.* London: Home Office.

Mande, M. and Butler, P. (1982). *Crime in Colorado. A Survey of Citizens.* Boulder: Division of Criminal Justice.

Manson, A. (2001). *The Law of Sentencing.* Toronto: Irwin Law.

Marinos, V. and Doob, A. N. (1999). Understanding Public Attitudes Toward Conditional Sentences of Imprisonment. *Criminal Reports*, 21: 31–41.

Martinovic, M. (2002). *The Punitiveness of Electronically Monitored Community Based Programs.* Paper presented at the Probation and Community Corrections Conference, Perth, September 2002.

Maruna, S. (2001). *Making Good. How Ex-Convicts Reform and Rebuild Their Lives.* Washington, DC: American Psychological Association.

Mathieson, T. (2000). *Prison on Trial* (2nd edn) Winchester: Waterside Press.

Mattinson, J. (2002). Results from the 2000 BCS. Personal Communication with author.

Mattinson, J, and Mirrlees-Black, C. (2000). *Attitudes to Crime and Criminal Justice: Findings from the 1998 British Crime Survey.* HORS 200. London: Home Office, Research, Development and Statistics Directorate.

Mayhew, P. and van Kesteren, J. (2002). Cross-National Attitudes to Punishment. In J. V. Roberts and M. Hough (eds.) *Changing Attitudes to Punishment. Public Opinion, Crime, and Justice.* Cullompton: Willan Publishing.

McGarrell, E. F. and Sandys, M. (1996). The Misperception of Public Opinion toward Capital Punishment: Examining the Spuriousness Explanation of Death Penalty Support. *American Behavioral Scientist*, 39: 500–13.

McMahon, M. (1990). 'Net-Widening'. Vagaries in the Use of a Concept. *British Journal of Criminology*, 30: 121–49.

Mirrlees-Black, C. (2001). *Confidence in the Criminal Justice System: Findings from the 2000 British Crime Survey.* Research Findings No. 137. London: Home Office, Research, Development and Statistics Directorate.

Mitchell, K. (1999). Home Detention. *New Zealand Law Journal,*. October: 363–6.

Moore, M. (1997). The Strategic Management of Intermediate Sanctions. *Corrections Management Quarterly*, 1: 44–52.

MORI Social Research Institute (2000). *Crime and Punishment Survey.* London: MORI House.

— (2003). *Criminal Justice System Confidence Survey.* Topline Results. London: MORI House.

Morris, A. (2004). Youth Justice in New Zealand. In M. Tonry and A. Doob (ed.) *Youth Crime and Youth Justice. Comparative and Cross-National Perspectives.* Chicago. University of Chicago Press.

Morris, N. and Tonry, M. (1990). *Between Prison and Probation. Intermediate Punishments in a Rational Sentencing System.* New York: Oxford University Press.

Muncie, J. (1990). 'A Prisoner in my Own Home': The Politics and Practice of Electronic Monitoring. *Probation Journal,* 37: 72–7.

Nagin, D. (1998). Criminal Deterrence Research at the Outset of the Twenty-First Century. In M. Tonry (ed.) *Crime and Justice. A Review of Research.* Chicago: University of Chicago Press.

Nellis, M. (1991). The Electronic Monitoring of Offenders in England and Wales. *British Journal of Criminology,* 31: 165–85.

(2002). Community Penalties in Historical Perspective. In A. Bottoms, L. Gelsthorpe and S. Rex. (eds.) *Community Penalties. Change and Challenges.* Cullompton: Willan Publishing.

New South Wales Bureau of Crime Statistics and Research (2002). *Local Courts Statistics.* Available at www.lawlink.nsw.gov.au.

Newburn, T. (2003). *Crime and Criminal Justice Policy* (2nd edn) Harlow: Pearson Education.

Northern Territory of Australia (1996). *Prisons* (Correctional Services) (Home Detention Orders) Regulations. Available at www.nt.gov.au/justice.

Observer (2003). *Crime Uncovered. A Nation under the Cosh? The Truth about Crime in Britain in 2003.* The Observer Magazine, 27 April.

O'Malley, P. (2004) Penal Policies and Contemporary Politics. In C. Sumner (ed.) *The Blackwell Companion to Criminology.* Oxford: Blackwell Publishing.

Oxford English Dictionary (1933/61). Vol. v. Oxford: The Clarendon Press.

Parisi, N. (1980). Part-Time Imprisonment: The Legal and Practical Issues of Periodic Confinement. *Judicature,* 63: 385–95.

Payne, B. and Gainey, R. (1998). A Qualitative Assessment of the Pains Experienced on Electronic Monitoring. *International Journal of Offender Therapy and Comparative Criminology,* 42: 149–63.

(2000). Electronic Monitoring: Philosophical, Systemic, and Political Issues. *Journal of Offender Rehabilitation,* 31: 93–111.

(2002). The Influence of Demographic Factors on the Experience of House Arrest. *Federal Probation,* 66: 64–71.

Petersilia, J. (1990). When Probation Becomes More Dreaded Than Prison. *Federal Probation,* 54: 23–7.

Petersilia, J. and Piper Deschenes, E. (1994). Perceptions of Punishment: Inmates and Staff Rank the Severity of Prison Versus Intermediate Sanctions. *The Prison Journal,* 74: 306–28.

(1998). What Punishes? Inmates Rank the Severity of Prison Versus Intermediate Sanctions. In J. Petersilia (ed.) *Community Corrections. Probation, Parole, and Intermediate Sanctions.* New York: Oxford University Press.

Petersilia, J. and Turner, S. (1998). Prison versus Probation in California: Implications for Crime and Offender Recidivism. In J. Petersilia (ed.) *Community Corrections. Probation, Parole, and Intermediate Sanctions.* New York: Oxford University Press.

Pranis, K. and Umbreit, M. (1992). *Public Opinion Research Challenges Widespread Public Demand for Harsh Punishment.* Minneapolis: Citizens' Council.

Pratt, J. (1992). Punishment and the Lessons from History. *Australia and New Zealand Journal of Criminology*, 25: 97–114.

(2000). Emotive and Ostentatious Punishment. Its Decline and Resurgence in Modern Society. *Punishment and Society*, 2: 417–41.

Quinn, J. and Holman, J. (1991). Intrafamilial Conflict Among Felons Under Community Supervision: An Examination of the Co-Habitants of Electronically Monitored Offenders. *Journal of Offender Rehabilitation*, 16: 177–92.

R. v. Brady 121 *Canadian Criminal Cases* (3d) 504.

R. v. Gladue (1999). 1. SCR 688.

R. v. Jurisic (1998). 101 *Australian Criminal Reports* 259.

R. v. Knoblauch (2000). 149 *Canadian Criminal Cases* (3d) 1.

R. v. Proulx (2000). 30 *Criminal Reports* (5th) 1, 140 CCC (3d) 449 (SCC).

R. v. Sangster (1973). 21 CRNS 339 (Quebec Court of Appeal).

Rackmill, S. J. (1994). An Analysis of Home Confinement as a Sanction. *Federal Probation*, 58: 45–52.

Reed, M. and Roberts, J. V. (1999). Adult Correctional Services in Canada, 1997–98. *Juristat*, 19, no. 4.

Reitz, K. (2001). The Dissasembly and Reassembly of US Sentencing Practices. In M. Tonry and R. Frase (eds.) *Sentencing and Sanctions in Western Nations*. New York: Oxford University Press.

Renaud, G. (1999) *Conditions, Conditions, Conditions*. Available at Alan Gold Newsletter, Quicklaw, June 17.

Renzema, M. (1992). Home Confinement Programs: Development, Implementation, and Impact. In J. Byrne, A. Lurigio, and J. Petersilia (eds.) *Smart Sentencing. The Emergence of Intermediate Sanctions*. Newbury Park: Sage Publications.

Rethinking Crime and Punishment (2002). *What Does the Public Think about Prison?* Available at www.rethinking.org.uk.

Roach, K. (1999). *Due Process and Victims' Rights*. Toronto: University of Toronto Press.

(2000). Changing Punishment at the Turn of the Century: Restorative Justice on the Rise. *Canadian Journal of Criminology*, 42: 249–80.

Robert, L. and Peters, T. (2003). How Restorative Justice is able to Transcend the Prison Walls: A Discussion of the 'Restorative Detention' Project. In E. Weitekamp and H.-J. Kerner (eds.) *Restorative Justice in Context. International Practice and Directions*. Cullompton: Willan Publishing.

Roberts, J. and Smith, M. (2003). Custody Plus, Custody Minus. In M. Tonry (ed.) *Confronting Crime. Crime Control Policy under New Labour*. Cullompton: Willan Publishing.

Roberts, J. V. (1992). Public Opinion, Crime, and Criminal Justice. In M. Tonry (ed.) *Crime and Justice. A Review of Research*, vol. 16. Chicago: University of Chicago Press.

(1997). Conditional Sentencing: Sword of Damocles or Pandora's Box? *Canadian Criminal Law Review*, 2: 183–206.

(1999a). The Hunt for the Paper Tiger: Conditional Sentencing after the judgment in *R. v. Brady*. *Criminal Law Quarterly*, 42: 38–66.

(1999b). Sentencing Patterns and Sentencing Disparity. In J. V. Roberts and D. Cole (eds.) *Making Sense of Sentencing*. Toronto: University of Toronto Press.

(2001). Unearthing the Sphinx: The Evolution of Conditional Sentencing. *Canadian Bar Review*, 80: 1019–38.

(2002a). The Evolution of Conditional Sentencing in Canada. *Criminal Reports*, 3 (6th Series): 268–82.

(2002b). Public Attitudes to Community-Based Sanctions. In J. V. Roberts and M. Hough (eds.) *Changing Attitudes to Punishment. Public Opinion, Crime, and Justice*. Cullompton: Willan Publishing.

(2002c). Determining Parole Eligibility Dates for Life Prisoners: Lessons from Jury Hearings in Canada. *Punishment and Society. The International Journal of Penology*, 4: 103–14.

(2003a). Evaluating the Pluses and Minuses of Custody: Sentencing Reform in England and Wales. *Howard Journal of Criminal Justice*, 42: 229–47.

(2003b). Sentencing Reform in New Zealand: An Analysis of the Sentencing Act 2002. *Australia and New Zealand Journal of Criminology*, 36: 249–71.

(2003c). Victim Impact Statements and the Sentencing Process: Recent Developments and Findings. *Criminal Law Quarterly*, 47: 365–96.

Roberts, J. V., Antonowicz, D. and Sanders, T. (2000). Conditional Sentences of Imprisonment: An Empirical Analysis of Conditions. *Criminal Reports*, 30: 113–25.

Roberts, J. V. and Bala, N. (2003). Understanding Sentencing under the *Youth Criminal Justice Act. Alberta Law Review*, 41: 395–423.

Roberts, J. V. and Cole, D. (eds.) (1999). *Making Sense of Sentencing*. Toronto: University of Toronto Press.

Roberts, J. V., Doob, A. N. and Marinos, V. (2000). *Judicial Attitudes to Conditional Terms of Imprisonment: Results of a National Survey*. Ottawa: Department of Justice.

Roberts, J. V. and Edgar, A. (2003). Victim Impact Statements: Findings from a survey of the judiciary in Canada. *International Journal of Victimology*, 1, no. 4 (online journal).

Roberts, J. V. and Gabor, T. (2004). Living in the Shadow of Prison: Lessons from the Canadian Experience in Decarceration, *British Journal of Criminology*, 39: 92–112.

Roberts, J. V. and Grimes, C. (2000). Adult Criminal Court Statistics, 1998/99. *Juristat*, 20, no. 1.

Roberts, J. V. and Healy, P. (2001) The Future of Conditional Sentencing. *Criminal Law Quarterly*, 44: 309–41.

Roberts, J. V. and Hough, M. (2001). Public Opinion, Sentencing and Parole: International Trends. In R. Roesch, R. Corrado and R. Dempster (eds.) *Psychology in the Courts: International Advances in Knowledge*. Amsterdam: Harwood Academic.

(eds.) (2002). *Changing Attitudes to Punishment. Public Opinion, Crime, and Justice*. Cullompton: Willan Publishing.

(forthcoming). *Understanding Public Attitudes to Criminal Justice*. Maidenhead: Open University Press.

Roberts, J. V., Maloney, L. and Vallis, R. (2003). *Coming Home to Prison. A Study of Offender Experiences of Conditional Sentencing*. Ottawa: Department of Justice Canada.

Roberts, J. V. and Melchers, R. (2003). The Incarceration of Aboriginal Offenders: An Analysis of Trends, 1978–2001. *Canadian Journal of Criminology and Criminal Justice*, 45: 211–42.

Roberts, J. V., Nuffield, J. and Hann, R. (2000). Parole and the Public: Attitudinal and Behavioural Responses. *Empirical and Applied Criminal Justice Research*, 1: 1–29.

Roberts, J. V. and Reed, M. (1999). Adult Correctional Services in Canada. In *A Statistical Overview of the Canadian Criminal Justice System*. Toronto: Thompson Educational Publishing.

Roberts, J. V. and Roach, K. (2003). Restorative Justice in Canada: From Sentencing Circles to Sentencing Principles. In A. von Hirsch, J. V. Roberts, A. E. Bottoms, K. Roach and M. Schiff. (eds.) *Restorative and Criminal Justice*. Oxford: Hart Publishing.

(2004) *Community-Based Sentencing: The Perspectives of Crime Victims*. Ottawa: Department of Justice, Canada.

Roberts, J. V. and Stalans, L. S. (1997). *Public Opinion, Crime, and Criminal Justice*. Boulder, Colorado: Westview Press.

(2004). Restorative Justice and the Sentencing Process: Exploring the Views of the Public. *Social Justice Research*, in press.

Roberts, J. V., Stalans, L. S., Indermaur, D. and Hough, M. (2003). *Penal Populism and Public Opinion*. New York: Oxford University Press.

Roberts, J. V. and Verdun-Jones, S. (2002). Directing Traffic at the Crossroads of Criminal Justice and Mental Health: Implications of the Supreme Court Judgment in *R. v. Knoblauch*. *Alberta Law Review*, 39: 788–809.

Roberts, J. V. and von Hirsch, A. (1998) Conditional Sentencing and the Fundamental Principle of Proportionality in Sentencing. *Criminal Reports*, 10: 222–31.

Robinson, P. (2003). Adult Criminal Court Statistics, 2001/2. *Juristat*, 23, no. 2.

Rogers, R. and Jolin, A. (1989). Electronic Monitoring: A Review of the Empirical Literature. *Journal of Contemporary Criminal Justice*, 5: 141–52.

Rubin, B. (1990) Offender attitudes toward home arrest. *Journal of Offender Monitoring*, 3: 8, 10–11.

Sanders, T. and Roberts, J. V. (2000). Public Attitudes toward Conditional Sentencing: Results of a National Survey. *Canadian Journal of Behavioural Science*, 32: 199–207.

(2004). Exploring public attitudes to conditional sentencing. In J. Winterdyk, L. Coates and S. Brodie (eds.) *Qualitative and Quantitative Research Methods*. Toronto: Pearson.

Scher, S. J. and Darley, J. M. (1997). How Effective are the things People Say to Apologize? Effects of the Realization of the Apology Speech Act. *Journal of Psycholinguistic Research*, 26: 127–40.

Sebba, L. (1996). *Third Parties. Victims in the Criminal Justice System*. Columbus, Ohio: Ohio State University Press.

Secretary of State (2002a). *Criminal Statistics for England and Wales 2001*. Cm 5696. London: Secretary of State.

(2002b). *Justice for All*. London: The Stationery Office.

Selke, W. (1993). *Prisons in Crisis*. Bloomington: Indiana University Press.

Sherman, L. (1992). *Policing Domestic Violence*. New York: Free Press.

Sigler, R. and Lamb, D. (1996). Community-Based Alternatives to Prison: How the Public and Court Personnel View Them. *Federal Probation*, 59: 3–9.

Smith, M. (1934/reprint 1970). *Prisons and a Changing Civilisation.* London: John Lane and The Bodley Head Ltd.

Smykla, J. and Selke, W. (1982). The Impact of Home Detention: A Less Restrictive Alternative to the Detention of Juveniles. *Juvenile and Family Court Journal,* May: 3–9.

Somer, R. (1976). *The End of Imprisonment.* New York: Oxford University Press.

Sourcebook of Criminal Justice Statistics (2003). *Attitudes towards Severity of Courts.* Table 2.54. Available at www.albany.edu/sourcebook.

Spelman, W. (1995). The Severity of Intermediate Sanctions. *Journal of Research in Crime and Delinquency,* 32: 107–35.

Spier, P. (2002). *Conviction and Sentencing of Offenders in New Zealand: 1992 to 2001.* Wellington: New Zealand Ministry of Justice.

Stando-Kawecka, B. (2002). Community Sanctions in Polish Penal Law. In H.-J. Albrecht and A. van Kalmthout (eds.) *Community Sanctions and Measures in Europe and North America.* Freiberg: Edition iuscrim.

Stanley, S. and Baginsky, M. (1984). *Alternatives to Prison. An Examination of Non-Custodial Sentencing of Offenders.* London: Peter Owen Publishers.

Stanz, R. and Tewksbury, R. (2000). Predictors of Success and Recidivism in a Home Incarceration Program. *The Prison Journal,* 80: 326–44.

Statistics New Zealand (2002). *Overall Offence Rate.* Available at www.stats.govt.nz.

Stern, V. (1998). *A Sin Against the Future. Imprisonment in the World.* London: Penguin Books.

Stinchcomb, J. (2002). Prisons of the Mind: Lessons Learned from Home Confinement. *Journal of Criminal Justice Education,* 13: 463–78.

Sugg, D., Moore, L., and Howard, P. (2001). *Electronic Monitoring and Offending Behaviour – Reconviction Results for the Second Year of Trials of Curfew Orders.* Home Office Findings 141. London: Home Office, Research, Development and Statistics Directorate.

Sykes, G. (1958). *The Society of Captives. A Study of a Maximum Security Prison.* Princeton: Princeton University Press.

Thomas, M. (2002). Adult Criminal Court Statistics, 2000/1. *Juristat,* 22, no. 2.

Thompson, B. (1996). *Trends in Custodial Sentences in NSW: 1990–1995.* Research Bulletin. New South Wales: Department of Corrective Services.

Tonry, M. (1996). *Sentencing Matters.* New York: Oxford University Press.

(1998). Intermediate Sanctions in Sentencing Guidelines. In M. Tonry (ed.) *Crime and Justice. A Review of Research.* Chicago: University of Chicago Press.

(2002). Community Penalties in the United States. In H.-J. Albrecht and A. van Kalmthout (eds.) *Community Sanctions and Measures in Europe and North America.* Freiberg: Edition iuscrim.

Tufts, J. and Roberts, J. V. (2002). Sentencing Juvenile Offenders: Comparing Public Preferences and Judicial Practice. *Criminal Justice Policy Review,* 13: 46–64.

Turner, J. (1993). *Sentencing in Adult Criminal Provincial Courts: A Study of Six Canadian Jurisdictions, 1991 and 1992.* Ottawa: Statistics Canada.

Turner, M. (1964). *A Pretty Sort of Prison.* London: Pall Mall Press.

Turner, M., Cullen, F., Sundt, J. and Applegate, B. (1997). Public Tolerance for Community-Based Sanctions. *The Prison Journal,* 77: 6–26.

US Department of Justice (2003). *Felony Sentences in State Courts, 2000.* Washington, DC: US Department of Justice, Bureau of Justice Statistics.

——— (2004). Prison Statistics. Summary Findings. Washington, DC: US Department of Justice, Bureau of Justice Statistics. Available at: www.ojp.usdoj.gov/bjs/prisons.htm

University of Arkansas (1998). *Arkansas Crime Poll.* Little Rock: University of Arkansas, Department of Criminal Justice.

van Ness, D. and Strong, K. (2002). *Restoring Justice* (2nd edn) Cincinnati, OH: Anderson Publishing Co.

van Zyl Smit, D. (1994). Degrees of Freedom. *Criminal Justice Ethics*, 13: 31–8.

van Kalmthout, A. (2002). From Community Service to Community Sanctions: Comparative Perspectives. In H.-J. Albrecht and A. van Kalmthout (eds.) *Community Sanctions and Measures in Europe and North America.* Freiberg: Edition iuscrim.

Vass, A. (1990). *Alternatives to Prison: Punishment, Custody and the Community.* London: Sage Publications.

Vollum, S. and Hale, C. (2002). Electronic Monitoring: A Research Review. *Corrections Compendium*, 27: 1–4; 23–7.

von Hirsch, A. (1990). The Ethics of Community-Based Sanctions. *Crime and Delinquency*, 36: 162–73.

——— (1993). *Censure and Sanctions.* Oxford: Clarendon Press.

von Hirsch, A., Bottoms, A., Burney, E., and Wikstrom, P.-O. (1999). *Criminal Deterrence and Sentence Severity. An Analysis of Recent Research.* Oxford: Hart Publishing.

von Hirsch, A. and Narayan, U. (1993). Degradingness and Intrusiveness. Ch. 8 in von Hirsch, A. (1993). *Censure and Sanctions.* Oxford: Clarendon Press.

von Hirsch, A., Roberts, J. V., Bottoms, A., Roach, K. and Schiff, M. (eds.) (2003). *Restorative and Criminal Justice. Competing or Reconcilable Paradigms?* Oxford: Hart Publishing.

Walters, I. (2002). *Evaluation of the National Roll-Out of Curfew Orders.* Home Office Online Report 15/02. London: Home Office: Research, Development and Statistics Directorate.

Weitekamp, E. and Kerner, H.-J. (2003). *Restorative Justice in Context. International Practice and Directions.* Cullompton: Willan Publishing.

Walgrave, L. (2002). *Restorative Justice and the Law.* Cullompton: Willan Publishing.

Walmsley, R. (2002). World Prison Population List (3rd edn). *Research Findings.* No. 166. London: Home Office, Research, Development and Statistics Directorate.

Wasik, M. (1994). Sentencing Guidelines: The Problem of Conditional Sentences. *Criminal Justice Ethics*, 13: 50–7.

Webster's Third New International Dictionary of the English Language (unabridged). Springfield, Mass.: Merriam-Webster.

West, T. (1997). *Prisons of Promise.* Winchester: Waterside Press.

Whitfield, D. (1997). *Tackling the Tag. The Electronic Monitoring of Offenders.* Winchester: Waterside Press.

——— (2001). *The Magic Bracelet. Technology and Offender Supervision.* Winchester: Waterside Press.

Willis, A. (1986). Alternatives to Imprisonment: An Elusive Paradise? In J. Pointing (ed.) *Alternatives to Custody.* Oxford: Basil Blackwell.

Wright, M. (1982). *Making Good. Prisons, Punishment and Beyond.* London: Burnett Books Limited.

Young, A. (1988). *The Role of An Appellate Court in Developing Sentencing Guidelines.* Research Reports of the Canadian Sentencing Commission. Ottawa: Department of Justice, Canada.

(2001). *The Role of the Victim in the Criminal Process. A Literature Review, 1989–1999.* Ottawa: Department of Justice, Canada.

Young, A. and Hoyle, C. (2003). Restorative Justice and Punishment. In S. McConville (ed.) The *Uses of Punishment.* Cullompton: Willan Publishing.

Young, A. and Roberts, J. V. (2001). *Research on the Role of the Victim in the Criminal Process in Canada.* Ottawa: Department of Justice Canada.

Zamble, E. and Kalm, K. (1990). General and Specific Measures of Public Attitudes toward Sentencing. *Canadian Journal of Behavioural Science,* 22: 327–37.

Zamble, E. and Porporino, F. (1988). *Coping, Behavior and Adaptation in Prison Inmates.* New York: Springer.

Zvekic, U. (ed.) (1994). *Alternatives to Imprisonment in Comparative Perspective.* Chicago: Nelson-Hall Publishers.

Index